Case Studies
in Organizational Communication

THE GUILFORD COMMUNICATION SERIES

Case Studies in Organizational Communication

Edited by

BEVERLY DAVENPORT SYPHER

THE GUILFORD PRESS
New York   London

© 1990 The Guilford Press
A Division of Guilford Publications, Inc.
72 Spring Street, New York, NY 10012

Printed in the United States of America

This book is printed on acid-free paper.

Last digit is print number: 9 8 7 6 5 4 3

Library of Congress Cataloging-in-Publication Data

Case studies in organizational communication / edited by Beverly
Davenport Sypher
    p. cm.
    Includes bibliographical references.
    ISBN 0-89862-309-X   ISBN 0-89862-287-5 (pbk.)
    1. Communication in organizations.
    HD30.3.C37 1990
    302.3'5—dc20   89-25917
                                                CIP

Contents

Part III. Issues of Power and Ethics

Part IV. Managerial Communication

Part V. Communication and Organizational Change

Part VI. Communication and New Technology

Foreword

In the 20 years since the first textbooks focusing on organizational communication appeared, the study of organizations has changed greatly. While members of organizations have always had to make difficult judgments using diverse, incomplete, and at times contradictory information, our theory and teaching has often been simplified, abstract, and forgetful of the daily context of decision making. With the development of contingency theories, counterrational models, and cultural studies, theories have redirected our attention to the complex situational and human dimensions of corporate life. With our renewed sensitivity we have abandoned our quick textbook answers and had to reconsider the relation between "book learning" and the understanding of organizations.

The organizations that have been the object of study have also changed. The instability of the corporate environment owing to mergers and takeovers, the international market organization, the rapidity of new product development, and changing consumer needs and demands, creates constant internal restructuring and greater demand for coordination through communication. New internal issues have arisen with the implementation of new communication technologies, with the coexistence of professional men and women, and with new employee needs arising from dual-career families.

Educational programs must meet the new challenges. The concept that some instructors and students have of training for a specified job no longer matches what it will take to succeed over time in modern organizations. Whether one is studying organizations or working within them, the ability to conceptualize a situation quickly and make a sound, if usually imperfect, judgment is essential. To accomplish this a person must be both smart and wise. Learning how to conceptualize and make judgments is quite different from learning behavioral skills or abstract knowledge. Both universities and organizations have been slow to fully recognize this.

Leading conceptions of the learning process have often hampered rather than helped the development of useful programs and instruction. For example, both teachers and students sometimes contrast deductive learning with inductive learning, leading to a false tension between learning through theory and learning through experience. In the popular myth, the former happens largely in the classroom and the latter outside of it. Part of this misconception has resulted because certain instructors have treated knowledge as the end of education, rather than emphasizing it as a means. And, unfortunately, many students are more than anxious to throw away their notes at the end of the semester so that they can start their "real" education out in the work world. In some cases, such a separation is institutionalized through offering textbook-centered theory courses supplemented by a theory-less internship. When students and instructors unwittingly conspire to keep the two worlds apart, the theory becomes abstract and finally unusable, and no general principles are constructed out of the work experience. Theory that does not help answer a real problem is forgotten and experience alone rarely teaches.

Life is too short for those studying organizations to learn from experience alone the insights and sensitivities necessary to understand complex modern organizations adequately. Book knowledge alone often appears to be merely a restatement, in a new vocabulary, of what is already known. This need not be the case. A good theoretical concept is not just to be remembered, it is to enable the perception of what is difficult to see, the distinction of things that seem the same, or the pulling together of what seems different. For a theoretical concept to work in this way there must be a potential experience toward which it is directed.

The use of case studies is one of the best ways to overcome the misleading separation of theory and practice, and to provide skills in conception and judgment. Business schools have used case-study-based education for years. While its payoff has been primarily in professional development, the academic enterprise can be served as well. A well-designed case serves both the need for theoretical and experiential learning. From the standpoint of theory, the case simplifies the organizational dynamics sufficiently to allow key theoretical elements and processes to stand out, yet retains enough complexity that the situation cannot be understood or well explained in the absence of theoretical insight. In this sense the theory is not just applied, it is practical. The case can also give better experience than experience itself. A well-designed case, like a good short story or even a 2-hour movie, can put us in touch with a world that would take years to experience fully on our own. The characterization of events, like the facial caricature, enables ways of seeing phenomena that only the best trained or most experienced eye could see in actual situations in actual time frames.

Many of us have used case studies for years but have had to modify management cases or borrow from a variety of other literatures. Thus this volume certainly fulfills a critical need. The cases are developed by important theorists in organizational communication studies, each of whom has had significant experience working with organizations. The breadth of topics and issues considered is impressive. The various cases open for examination the difficult and sensitive issues regarding ethics, career choices, race relations, and sexual harassment as well as standard topics such as power, organizational change, superior–subordinate interaction, and the implementation of new communication technologies. I believe the cases to be engaging and challenging. Rather than spending class time talking about what we know regarding these topics, the time can be better spent talking about organizations through what we know.

The cases included in this volume are more than examples of standard organization conceptions; they present important complexities in organizational life. None of them admit to quick solution, simple identification of villains, or easy consensus on what is happening. They demand that students use each other's insights, consider alternative theoretical conceptions, and carefully analyze what is going on, what the options are, and which judgments are to be preferred. I believe that they can add significantly to our insight into organizational processes.

STANLEY DEETZ
Rutgers University

Introduction

BEVERLY DAVENPORT SYPHER
University of Kansas

This volume presents various accounts of how communication contributes to organizational life. The case studies in this book address a broad array of issues faced in today's workplace, including ethics, racial tension, sexual harassment, employee health, electronic mail, and automation. Retail, manufacturing, public service, and newspaper organizations provide the contexts for the case-study research presented here. Some of the cases focus on how communication can hinder organizational functioning, while others highlight the creative and positive uses of various communication practices. In keeping with the goals of case studies in general, these examples offer answers to the "why" and "how" questions of organizational communication. They are intended to demonstrate how organizational members initiated, enhanced, or inhibited effective communication, and to focus on the antecedent and subsequent behaviors related to specific communicative performances.

The book is organized around several topics that reveal the central focus of the chapters in each section. It is important to keep in mind, however, that the headings of the various parts are not mutually exclusive. For example, the managerial communication case study in Part IV about Holiday Inn (Chapter 13) could have been grouped with the cases in Part III, which focus on power and ethics, because it is essentially a case about empowerment. The IBM case (Chapter 17) presented in Part V focuses on change, but the change is a result of a massive infusion of advanced manufacturing technology. Thus the IBM case could have been grouped with those in Part VI, which focus on new technology. There is never just one issue that sufficiently captures organizational phenomena. This grouping reflects a set of core issues around which the cases can be organized. It is not a mutually exclusive grouping just as organizational behaviors are not isolated events with only one motive and a single consequence.

1

PREVIEW OF CHAPTERS

This introduction will outline the cases in the book, describe case studies in general, offer some guidelines for writing case studies, and discuss how those presented in this volume can be used. Part I of the volume includes two cases that focus on the individual within the organization. Chapter 1 details two job screening interviews, and Chapter 2 follows the lives of two employees as they go through the various socialization stages of their new jobs. Part II takes a more macro view of organizational life. Martin and Siehl focus on the relationship between corporate culture and subcultures in Chapter 3, about General Motors, and in Chapter 4 Trujillo examines how corporate philosophy is communicated in the Texas Rangers organization. Brown's chapter concludes the section and demonstrates how NASA's culture affected the decision to launch the Challenger.

In Part III the chapters deal with some of the most sensitive issues facing contemporary American workers, and not surprisingly, the names of the relevant organizations and real characters have been changed. While most of the organizations written about in this volume were quite willing to let us read about their successes, few agreed to be named when their situations were deemed problematic. Prather's ethical dilemma (Chapter 6), Bingham's sexual harassment situation (Chapter 7), and Allen and Seibert's boundary-spanning case (Chapter 8) are real examples of real problems employees have faced. Ray's case about stress and the employee's role in a communication network (Chapter 9) uses composite characters to explain a pattern of similar incidents she observed in her research on social support in educational settings.

There are a number of issues covered in Part IV that focus on superior–subordinate or managerial communication. In Chapter 10, Seibold details decision making and group issues in a family-owned business. Issues of power and control are equally relevant in this case. DeWine and James (Chapter 11) focus on poor managerial communication in a manufacturing plant, while the Downs chapter, which follows, entails a superior–subordinate communication problem set in a city manager's office. The last chapter in this section focuses on the relatively new concept of self-management. Zorn's case study of Holiday Inn points out the attitudinal and organizational benefits of giving employees opportunities to manage themselves.

Part V focuses on the role of communication in implementing change. Fairhurst's chapter on the Pearson company could just as well be included in Part I because of its focus on culture. Here managers were trying to change a culture using language inconsistent with the philosophy they sought to adopt. The Putnam chapter, concerning JLS Office Supplies, focuses on a group's effort to withstand change, and the Prather chapter details the coming of Toyota to Kentucky through the eyes of trade-union representatives who were responsible for negotiating worker contracts. The latter case focuses on how culture as a background variable affected Japanese–American union negotiations. IBM's communication efforts during the automation of its Lexington plant are described by Sypher, Sypher, Housel, and Booth in the final chapter in Part V.

The last section focuses on new communication technologies that have been implemented at Atlantic Richfield, Xerox, and TRW Corporation. Ruchinskas, Svenning, and Steinfield outline ARCOvision, Atlantic Richfield's implementation of teleconferencing, and the Steinfield chapter focuses on the introduction of electronic mail at Xerox. The final chapter by Davidson and Housel examines TRW's process of decision making regarding the design of integrated information systems.

Each of the cases is based on real events, and are to be studied with an eye toward understanding not just what happened but how and why communication made the situation possible. Key terms and study questions at the end of each case will help direct attention to the salient issues. In addition, each of the authors suggest relevant readings for his/her topics.

DEFINING CASE STUDIES

Lawrence (1953) described a case study as "a chunk of reality. . . . It is the anchor on academic flights of speculation" (p. 215). Schramm added that the case-study approach "organizes the details of life in search of patterns and insights" (n.d., p. 1). Yin (1984) argues more specifically that "A case study is an empirical inquiry that: investigates a contemporary phenomenon within its real-life context; when the boundaries between phenomenon and context are not clearly evident; and in which multiple sources of evidence are used" (p. 23). In anthropology, case studies are by definition an observation-based method of examining some delimited class of social events (Pelto & Pelto, 1978). In business, the focus of case studies has been on administrative decisions or problems (Leenders & Erskine, 1973).

In any event, cases should make visible the qualitative features of organizational life. They should capture reality, and, in our discipline, they should illuminate communication's role in its development and change. In effect, good case studies should make us aware of the numerous considerations governing organizational communication; never is there just one factor to be considered.

There is a strong sentiment across disciplines that case studies should not involve any experimental controls or manipulation. Phenomena should be examined in their natural setting as they naturally occur (Benbasat, Goldstein, & Mead, 1987; Pelto & Pelto, 1978; Williams, Rice, & Rogers, 1988; Yin, 1984). The purpose of a case study is to describe real-life events in such a way as to enhance our understanding and to bolster our insight in ways that other methods could or normally would not do. This does not mean that quantification is somehow antithetical to case-study research; at times it can be crucial to truly understanding phenomena. Neither does this mean that case-study research is unplanned. It is, however, more flexible. The traditional reporting style associated with quantification does not lend itself to the description necessary for good case studies. Case studies can bring to life the nuances of work life and talk that usually have no place in traditional quantitative explanations.

Case studies present situations as they have developed over time and include an explanation of why, while more traditional social-science methods too often only report what exists, albeit sometimes cross-situationally, at one point in time. Moreover, traditional findings about organizational communication are often treated out of context. Case studies are context dependent. Mishler (1986) argues that dismissing context is an identity-stripping process (Goffman, 1961). It disrupts our abilities to make coherent sense out of findings. As idiographic research, case studies attempt to understand a phenomenon in its context. To clinical psychologist Mishler, this requires more attention to how respondents "name" their world. Case studies in organizational communication should include the same; they should pay particular attention to the language choices of the organizational members they describe. Focusing on naturally occurring language and messages should be a key element in organizational communication case studies. Natural settings provide the opportunity to capture these data, but secondary sources such as books, documents, archival data, public opinion, and the like can make for meaningful and significant case studies (see Chapters 3 and 5).

In a data-collecting effort dependent only on quantification, questions about the process of how and why things came to be are often relegated to subsequent rather than present issues. More importantly, such practices often replace the thick, descriptive reports necessary for good case writing. All of this suggests that case studies are by their very nature longitudinal and imbued with a sense of real life. They should examine situations as they have developed over time, looking at the series of events leading to and resulting from critical events. Pettigrew (1979) argues that longitudinal studies focus attention on the process by which things came to be rather than on what is. This focus is one of the greatest advantages of a case study. Good ones should describe a "chunk of reality" by using multiple sources of evidence to explain a series of real-life events.

WRITING CASE STUDIES

Traditionally, case studies have been thought of as a weaker or less reliable research method, but the real weakness of case studies seems to be too little research on what constitutes a good case. The criteria summarized in the previous section focus on the content of case studies; this section will describe the form or style in which case studies should be presented. It is perhaps the latter feature of case studies that causes the most frustration. Too often we have depended on intuitive criteria to evaluate the quality of a case. If one comes away from reading a case study feeling intimately involved with the situation, then the case writer has accomplished the task. Thus we need to develop guidelines for achieving identification with the issues raised in a case. Even though Kreps (1986), like others, argues that case studies may be presented orally or through videos, most case studies are written. For this reason, it is helpful in determining what a case is to focus on the stylistic elements of good case writing.

Towl (1969) argues that case studies are distinct literary forms, just as Yin (1984) contends that the case study is a distinct research method. Towl suggests that a case has elements of narration, exposition, and argumentation, and should vividly recreate the observations and experiences of the researcher. As Bantz (1983) argues, "Naturalistic research should reflect the organization's social reality. The report should be discernible to organizational members, familiarize nonmembers with subtle features of the organization, and use language and media in a skillful manner" (p. 71).

The skillful use of language can mean developing a narrative, a plot, and perhaps an argument. As narratives, case studies should have a beginning and an end. The boundaries of analysis depend on such a structure. In the plot, there should be drama and suspense. In essence, the case should be engaging. Yin (1984) argues that the reader should be enticed into reading more. It can be useful to bring personalities into the case, but it is not absolutely necessary; narratives are essentially accounts of happenings. When the focus of the narrative is individual behavior, the individual characters should be credibly developed, but there are times when the organization is the unit of analysis and aggregated perceptions and events affecting the whole are appropriate data for good case studies. Chapters 17, 18, and 19 are examples of such cases.

Many argue that it is appropriate for the case writer to take himself or herself out of the case (Leenders & Erskine, 1973; Yin, 1984) and write in the third person. Leenders and Erskine (1973), for example, note that a case "is normally written from the point of view of the decision maker involved" so students have an "opportunity to put themselves in the decision maker's or problem solver's shoes" (p. 11). This viewpoint illustrates one rather widely accepted use of case studies. Benbasat et al. (1987) also advocate removing the case writer from the situation because they more narrowly define case studies as resulting from "efforts where research questions are specified prior to the study by researchers who are observers/investigators rather than participants" (p. 371). Both of these opinions come from business researchers.

Anthropologists and sociologists such as Van Maanen (1973), in his now-classic police studies, have demonstrated the value of participant observation and the quality of case studies that can result from it. Such methods lend themselves more appropriately than other methods to first-person accounts of phenomena. The Pacanowsky (1988) case of empower-ment at W. L. Gore & Associates is one such example in the organizational communication field. However, if participation is only a function of data gathering (if one does not participate in the ongoing life of the organization), even when action research is involved, third-person reports are more appro-priate. Moreover, even in instances of participant observation, third-person accounts are likely to be perceived as more credible and more objec-tive.

In addition to narrative and plot structures, case studies should also have a clear time and expository structure. The reader must be able to determine the sequence in which events occurred. While Towl (1969) sug-gests that cases should be written in the past tense to show that the situation actually occurred, this may not always be possible or desirable if it confuses the time structure (as, for example, it could have in Chapter 4). Clarity is crucial, and in most cases, the past tense is more appropriate.

Towl's (1969) discussion of exposition and argumentation is similar to Yin's (1984) notion of completeness. A case study should not be a guessing game: It requires detailed explanations. Readers should be provided with everything they need to know. Writers must recreate the situations they have observed with attention to the details and nuances. All information needed to analyze the situation should be furnished, including details about the organization, the industry, and the background against which the observed events occurred. Yin argues that the boundaries of the case must be explicit. He feels the "the best way is to show, through either logical argument or the presentation of evidence, that as the analytic periphery is reached, the information is of decreasing relevance to the case study" (p. 141).

To reach the analytic periphery, Yin charges, the case writer must display sufficient evidence supporting and challenging the conclusions reached. Evidence should reflect the investigator's knowledge of the case. He argues that "the exemplary case study is one that judiciously and effec-tively presents the most compelling evidence, so the reader can reach an independent judgment . . ."(p. 143). Compelling evidence is often derived from multiple methods of research, which yield multiple viewpoints and perspectives to build into the case.

Another issue pertinent to case-study writing is the focus of the case. Benbasat et al. (1987) write that case-study research is particularly appropriate when "research and theory are at their early, formative stages," or for "sticky, practice-based problems where the experiences of the actors are important and the context of action is critical" (p. 369). Others argue that case studies should focus on significant or unusual events, those that have general public interest and underlying issues that are nationally important in theoretical, policy, or practical terms (Yin, 1984). However, what constitutes importance is certainly up for debate.

On the other hand, there are those who feel that case studies should describe the routine, the taken for granted, the everyday goings on of organizational members. Analyzing what and how things become ordinary or generally acceptable can make a significant contribution to our understanding of organizational communication.

There is also some question as to whether case studies should focus only on problematic situations. This issue most likely stems from the many problem-oriented business cases, especially those in the Harvard Business School tradition. Problems seem to give case studies interest, and sometimes add drama and suspense. They also heighten the readers' awareness of what can cause problems and focus analysis on problem solving. However, we risk serving only a slice of organizational life if we fail to attend to situations where communication practices contributed to a more organized, more coherent, and more successful operation. We need to know how communication contributes to both the difficulties and the successes of organizing.

The crucial issue facing the writer is what is to be learned from the case, for cases after all are "learning mechanisms." We will increase what we learn by examining all kinds of situations. Good case studies, therefore, describe situations that are sometimes of national importance and sometimes of local importance, sometimes troubled, sometimes exemplary, and sometimes a mixture of both. Good case studies should make significant contributions to our understanding of organizational communication; they do not have to focus exclusively on problematic, nationally important, or unusual events to do so.

In summary, case writing is more than an exercise in storytelling or an opinion piece (Benbasat et al., 1987). It is not merely an example or a "straight out photographic slice of life" (Towl, 1969, p. 65). The writer explains a pattern of organizational life and presents it with detail and insight. As many agree, this kind of writing calls for talent and experience. Towl (1969) writes, "case writing is an art, and a good case is a definite literary accomplishment" (p. 72). And Lawrence (1953) points out, "a case must essentially represent a good job of reporting. Case writing, indeed, is both as simple and as difficult as good reporting. A case writer must learn not only to report what he sees and no more, but also to see in the events he is observing things that to him are new and different" (p. 215).

USING CASE STUDIES

While there are many ways and reasons to do case studies, the ones presented in this volume are primarily intended as teaching tools. Some were initiated as case-study research, and some were written from experiences in more traditional types of research including survey, hypothesis testing, evaluation, and so forth. They all serve as teaching tools and as Yin (1984) points out, "for teaching purposes, a case study need not reflect a complete or accurate rendition of actual events; rather its purpose is to establish a framework for discussion and debate among students" (p. 14). While this is generally true, the criteria established early in this chapter are useful guidelines for both teaching and research purposes. As teaching tools, these cases can be used to explain theories and concepts, to teach problem-solving skills, to document the experience of practice, and to examine the role of communication in significant, contemporary issues.

Explaining Theories and Concepts

While case-study research is generally considered theory generative, case-study writing can have pedagogical value in illustrating how theories and related concepts are related to practice. The Ray case (Chapter 9) on stress and distress is a good example. She cites research that suggests that participation in an organizational communication network helps buffer stress by providing social support. However, her case depicts a school teacher who evidenced significantly less stress as an isolate than the teachers who actively communicated with one another and experienced a good deal of social support at work. (For details see Ray, 1986). Traditional research (as reviewed in Goldhaber, Yates, Porter, & Lesniak, 1978) suggests isolates are less secure, less gregarious, less motivated, and less satisfied with their jobs. Thus, the findings from this study make us question the cross-situational consistency of the social support literature and rethink the characteristics of organizational isolates.

Chapter 2, "The Tale of Two Careers" by Miller and Jablin, is another example of how case studies can help explain important concepts. Information about the assimilation process is made more relevant and understandable by the real-life examples of two new employees and their different ways of moving through each of the assimilation stages described by the authors.

The Martin and Siehl case (Chapter 3) relies on secondary sources and personal interviews to explain the "uneasy symbiosis" of a dominant culture and counterculture at G. M. In another explanatory effort (see Chapter 4), Trujillo uses first-hand accounts and observations to explain how the Texas Rangers' management communicated its philosophy. Putnam (Chapter 15) writes about a now-defunct office-supply business to explain the role of myths in perpetuating a corporate philosophy. And Fairhurst (Chapter 14) shows how corporate language reveals the values and goals of corporate leaders, despite conflicting evidence.

Solving Organizational Communication Problems

The Prather chapter, "Stalking Tiger Brown," and the Bingham chapter on sexual harassment are examples of cases written for teaching purposes. Not all viewpoints and alternative perspectives are considered, and the data-gathering techniques are not a central feature of either case (even though they both were based on interviews with the main characters), but they are accurate renditions of actual instances, and provide engaging, descriptive accounts of contemporary situations that need to be viewed critically. In this way, they furnish a framework for discussion and debate by heightening students' awareness of the possibility of such situations and by forcing them to focus on seldom talked about, sensitive issues that demand frank discussion.

A logical decision-making model based on Dewey's (1910) approach to reflective thinking is the best approach to problem-oriented case studies. Analysis should include:

1. Identifying problems. ✓
2. Determining causes. ✓
3. Setting effectiveness criteria, that is, standards by which to judge the potential success of a proposed solution.
4. Proposing alternative solutions or recommendations.
5. Evaluating solutions or recommendations using effectiveness criteria.
6. Choosing solutions or recommendations.
7. Proposing strategies for implementing and evaluating the chosen solutions.

The Downs chapter about a confrontation between a city manager and some of his staff, the Dewine and James chapter about poor managerial communication, the Ray chapter, and the Allen and Seibert chapter are all problem-solving cases. In addition to providing a framework for approaching these case studies, the problem-solving sequence also has the potential, perhaps more so than other case-study uses, to develop students' analytic abilities and to teach logical approaches to decision making that can be used across a variety of situations.

Documenting the Experience of Practice

Case studies also are well suited to capturing the knowledge of practitioners. Of special interest in this volume are cases that teach us about organizational communication practices in use. The Sypher et al. chapter about IBM's communication infrastructure gives an overview of how and why they were able to communicate quickly and effectively about the change to automation. Their communications department was organized and broad in its techniques and approaches prior to automation. Attempts to understand organizational communication have focused too little on corporate communication departments and their practices. The IBM case is a description of how IBM Lexington developed a strategy for communicating about automation, but it is also a case about the work of communication professionals, including decisions they must make, expertise they must have, and media they must produce.

The Steinfield chapter about electronic mail and the chapter by Ruchinskas et al. about teleconferencing provide us with first-hand accounts of the implementation of new technologies and users' reactions to them. The Davidson and Housel chapter points out rather clearly the necessity, and difficulty, of choosing a system to integrate TRW's various information systems. TRW has offices in multiple locations and houses some of the largest data banks in the country. In addition to presenting a contemporary case about information systems, this chapter can also be used to explain the problem-solving sequence reviewed in the previous section by discussing the format TRW followed in its design decision. Through these case studies we can capture some of the knowledge of practitioners and increase our understanding of what happens to people and organizations involved in such changes.

Explaining Significant Contemporary Issues

While exemplary cases might very well focus on time-honored issues that may or may not be of national importance (managerial communication, for instance), good case studies also need to be written about contemporary organizational communication practices that have potentially far-reaching interest in theoretical, policy, or practical matters (Yin, 1984). Prather's journalistic account, in Chapter 6, of union representatives negotiating with Toyota executives is such a case. The practical implications go beyond this case and point to the need for increased intercultural understanding in all international business communication. Brown's explanation, in Chapter 5, of

NASA's decision to launch the Challenger is similar in that it also focuses on a contemporary issue of national and international interest. This is a case about internal and external communication. The way in which crisis communication can and should be handled is equally important in this case as is how and why the decision was made to launch the Challenger.

SUMMARY

The case studies presented in this volume can be used with a text or by themselves. They provide an opportunity to apply theories and research findings, to develop problem-solving skills, to help understand communication at work and how it functions, and to focus on the role of communication in explaining significant events of national interest. While Yin (1984) and others differentiate case-study research from case studies as teaching tools, the necessary features of the content and writing style need not be so different. If case studies are only intended for teaching purposes, as some in this volume are, they need to be complete enough to be analyzed, but the methods of data collection and amounts of evidence are less important than the case's ability to stimulate discussion and debate. Case studies also need to present the points of view, either implicitly or explicitly, of the main characters, and they need to be engaging. Whether or not they are written in third person, past tense, and narrative form, they should hold the reader's interest and make coherent a complex set of events or circumstances.

For teaching purposes, cases do not need to focus only on problematic or significant contemporary issues of national and/or international importance. While such issues need our attention, the routine, everyday problems of just getting along are equally important. And while some argue that case studies as teaching tools need not be totally accurate renditions of real events, caution and discretion are advised in this regard. Case studies should not be fiction, no matter how good they are. Their purpose is to increase our knowledge about real events. The closer all case studies adhere to the suggestions reviewed in this chapter and listed below, the better they are likely to be regardless of their purpose.

In review, the following criteria are offered as guidelines for case-study development and presentation.

1. They should present a "chunk of reality," focusing on real events in their real-life context.
2. They should have some elements of narration—a beginning and an end—but need not necessarily unfold chronologically.
3. They should be longitudinal, depicting a series of events with a past as well as a present.

4. The time structure should be clear, and usually the past tense is most appropriate.
5. The writer should usually remove himself or herself from the case, focusing more on the individuals' or organization's point of view.
6. They should have some elements of argumentation, including multiple sources of evidence for support.
7. They should be engaging, with suspense and drama.
8. They should be complete with background information, explicit boundaries, and multiple viewpoints.
9. They should focus on organizational problems and successes.
10. They should examine the taken for granted, as well as the significant and unusual aspects of organizational life.

Acknowledgments. The author wishes to thank Ellen Frombach for her research assistance in the preparation of this chapter; Rosemary Booth for her help in bringing order to the many and varied tasks involved in producing this volume; and Chisholm Institute of Technology (Melbourne, Australia), University of Kentucky, and University of Kansas for their administrative support.

REFERENCES

Bantz, C. R. (1983). Naturalistic research traditions. In L. Putnam & M. Pacanowsky (Eds.), *Communication and organizations: An interpretive approach* (pp. 55–73). Beverly Hills, CA: Sage.

Benbasat, I., Goldstein, D. K., & Mead, M. (1987). The case research strategy in studies of information systems. *MIS Quarterly, 11,* 369–386.

Dewey, J. (1910). *How we think.* Boston: Heath.

Goldhaber, G., Yates, M., Porter, D., & Lesniak, R. (1978). Organizational communication: 1978 state of the art. *Human Communication Research, 5,* 76–96.

Goffman, E. (1961). *Asylums.* New York: Anchor.

Kreps, G. L. (1986). *Organizational communication theory and practice.* New York: Longman.

Lawrence, P. R. (1953). The preparation of case material. In K. Andrews (Ed.), *The case method of teaching human relations and administration* (pp. 215–224). Cambridge, MA: Harvard University Press.

Leenders, M., & Erskine, J. (1973). *Case research: The case writing process.* London, Ontario: Research and Publications Division, School of Business Administration, University of Western Ontario.

Mishler, E. G. (1986). *Research interviewing: Context and narrative.* Cambridge, MA: Harvard University Press.

Pacanowsky, M. (1988). Communication in the empowering organization. In J. Anderson (Ed.), *Communication yearbook 11* (pp. 356–390). Newbury Park, CA: Sage.

Pelto, P., & Pelto, G. (1978). *Anthropological research: The structure of inquiry*. Cambridge, England: Cambridge University Press.

Pettigrew, A. (1979). On studying organizational cultures. *Administrative Science Quarterly, 24,* 570–580.

Schramm, W. (n.d.). *Notes on case studies of instructional media projects*. Unpublished manuscript.

Ray, E. B. (1986). *Communication network roles as mediators of job stress and burnout: Case studies of two organizations*. Paper presented at the annual meeting of the Speech Communication Association, Chicago, IL.

Towl, A. (1969). *To study administration by cases*. Boston: Harvard University Press.

Van Maanen, J. (1973). Observations on the making of policemen. *Human Organization, 32,* 407–417.

Williams, F., Rice, R., & Rogers, E. (1988). *Research methods and the new media*. New York: Tice.

Yin, R. K. (1984). *Case study research: Design and method*. Newbury Park, CA: Sage.

PART I

The Individual and the Organization

CHAPTER 1

The On-Campus Job Screening Interview

FREDRIC M. JABLIN
University of Texas at Austin

VERNON D. MILLER
University of Wisconsin–Milwaukee

During the average academic year approximately 600 organizations visit the Business Placement Center at the University of the Southwest to conduct job screening interviews with graduating business students. Close to 16,000 separate (30-minute) interviews are transacted at the Placement Center during the fall and spring semesters. About 1,500 students participate in interviews at the Placement Center each year, with the average student participating in slightly over 10 interviews; however, some students interview with more than 20 companies while others interview with only one or two.

Business students planning to interview through the Placement Center must register with the office, complete a registration card, and submit 20–30 resumes. The registration card allows the Center to release student-related information that is on file to companies. Thus, on the day when a recruiter conducts interviews at the Center, he or she receives a packet containing pertinent information about Placement Center policies and procedures, transcript release forms, and a resume for each student signed up for interviews.

Students become aware of companies interviewing on campus by monitoring a bulletin board outside of the Placement Center upon which interview opportunities are posted. During peak interviewing periods (in the fall, mid-September through mid-November, and in the spring, late January through early May), interview postings are updated daily and students sign up for interviews (that usually occur 1 or 2 weeks later) each morning. If a student is not familiar with a particular company that will be interviewing on campus, he or she can consult a library of company literature (containing annual reports, brochures describing training programs, etc.) accessible in the Placement Center. Obtaining a slot for an interview with the "top" companies is not always easy (at most, recruiters can schedule 13 interviews per day). Frequently, students "camp out" at the Placement Center hours before it opens to insure a chance to sign up for interviews with the best companies. One of the companies for which there is stiff competition for interview slots is Industrial Products Titan, Inc., a subsidiary of a Fortune 100 conglomerate.

In the following pages the interviews of two students, Kathleen Calender and William Frederics, who were able to obtain interviews with the representative from Industrial Products Titan, are described.[1] Each was applying for the same position, "institutional marketing representative" (major in marketing required). Rather than selling products directly to the consumer, marketing representatives in the institutional division sell products to hospitals, nursing homes, hotels, motels, restaurants, and other "institutions." For example, one of Titan's best-selling products to health-care facilities is a line of skin-care products, including antiseptic, protein-based handsoaps and handcreams for use by doctors and nurses who must wash their hands dozens of time each day. Each marketing representative is assigned a territory of his or her own and receives compensation in the form of a base salary, commissions, and a company car.

THE SCREENING INTERVIEW OF KATHLEEN CALENDER

Kathy's watch said 11:30 A.M., the time scheduled for her interview, so she knocked on the half-opened door and in an assertive manner said, "Hello." As she pushed the door fully open she saw the representative from Industrial Products Titan sitting opposite her at the small table in the interviewing room. The room was typical of those used for employment screening interviews at the Business Placement Center. It was small, no more than a 7-foot square, and as usual there were no windows. The white walls and fluorescent lighting made the dwarfish room appear larger than its actual size and accented the map of the United States that hung on the wall to the left of the interviewer. The room was furnished in "Placement Center Style" with two hard wooden chairs and a 3 × 5 foot woodgrained Formica table.

The interviewer from Industrial Products Titan was young, maybe 25 or 26 years of age. This was no surprise to Kathleen, however, since 80% of the recruiters with whom she had interviewed were less than 30 years old. As she stepped through the doorway the interviewer looked up from the papers he was examining. Kathy could see that her resume (see Figure 1.1) was on top of the pile of documents; company brochures, annual reports, and other "glossies" were strewn across the table. When the interviewer rose to shake hands with Kathy she noticed that he was not wearing his suit jacket; Kathy wondered whether or not this would be an informal interview. As usual, she was wearing her interviewing "uniform," a conservative blue suit with a semiruffled, high-collared, off-white silk blouse, and navy-blue pumps. She wore only a modest amount of makeup, and her long brownish-blond hair was tied up in a bun. Kathy looked and felt very professional as she began her ninth screening interview at the Placement Center.[2]

MARTY (*Interviewer*): Hi, I'm Martin Jobs. (*Offers hand to shake.*)

KATHY (*Applicant*): Hi, nice to meet you. (*Shakes hands with Martin.*)

MARTY: Nice to meet you. Put your books down on the table. (*Walks over to door, shuts it, and returns to seat.*)

KATHY: Thank you. (*Sits down; sits erect with hands clasped tightly in her lap. Her chair is about 8 inches away from the table and her body is directed at the interviewer.*)

MARTY: How're you doing today? (*Speaks as he sits down.*)

KATHY: Fine.

MARTY: Do you go by Kathy or Kathleen? (*Picks up resume, crosses legs, directs body at applicant, leans back slightly.*)

KATHY: Kathy, but Kathleen's fine. Whatever really.

MARTY: O.K., you know I (*stammer*) go by Marty. Do you want to take your suit jacket off.

KATHY: Not really . . .

MARTY: Please do so cause it gets a little stuffy in here.

KATHY: I've been feeling cold all day. (*Moves hands as she speaks.*)

MARTY: O.K., fine (*pause*), um, Kathy, first of all, I'm going to have a piece of paper here (*pause*) and I might take notes, I might not; if that bothers you I'm not . . .

KATHY: No, it doesn't bother me. That's fine.

MARTY: Going to, don't want to do it (*pause*). Kathy, what I'm going to do is, uh, I'd like to start off and, ah . . . have you kind ah . . . bring me up to date on, uh, yourself and, ah (*pause*), kind of . . . I'd like to hear it from you what's on here (*points to resume*) and tell me a little bit about you . . . where you are from originally, uh, high school, what you did in high school, what you like to do (*pause*), why you chose first the University of Southeast and switched over to the University of the Southwest and (*pause*) why did you go into business, uh (*pause*), your major and some of your hobbies and things like that. (*Plays with pen while he speaks.*)

KATHY: All right. (*Nods head.*)

MARTY: Kind of bring me up to date on Kathy O.K.? (*Nods head.*)

KATHY: O.K. (*Nods head.*)

MARTY: Good. (*Nods head.*)

KATHY: So, I just begin? (*Looks directly at Marty.*)

MARTY: Just begin . . . you get the floor. (*Nods head.*)

Before beginning her response, a number of thoughts raced through Kathy's mind. She had second thoughts about taking her jacket off; she was already starting to feel warm. It was unclear why Marty was asking for a biography; all that information was listed in her resume. She did not understand why he did not ask her a question based on the information that he already had available. Moreover, she was unsure about which of Marty's questions to answer first and how much detail to provide. As she took a deep breath and prepared to speak, she asked herself "What does he *really* want to know?"

KATHY: O.K., well I went to high school in Chomedey, Alabama. I grew up there . . . pretty much. I was there since second grade and ah . . . from there I went, ah, . . . to the University of Southeast and chose the major of social work. Um, . . . originally I wanted . . .

MARTY: Social work? *(Scratches head.)* Did you . . .

KATHY: Social work. *(Twisting fingers below table, out of interviewer's vision.)*

MARTY: . . . start with . . .

KATHY: Um, like welfare, uh, working with people . . .

MARTY: I wasn't even aware they had a major. I thought . . .

KATHY: Right, yeah *(nods head)*, it's a real small school . . .

MARTY: Yeah. *(Looks down at resume.)*

KATHY: Real small school. Um, I, um, originally set out, I wanted to, you know, of course deal directly with people . . .

MARTY: Uh huh.

KATHY: That was what I wanted to do, and I thought that would be a good area . . .

MARTY: Uh, huh. *(Leans back.)*

KATHY: Then after I was in that for 2 years at the University of the Southeast and realized that's viewing people more in a negative way . . .

MARTY: Yeah.

KATHY: Um . . . It's on a negative basis instead of say positive . . .

MARTY: Um, right. *(Nods head.)*

KATHY: You know, there's a lot of problems and a lot of negative feelings *(pause)*, so I decided to change, um, . . . to do something more positive and I selected business. Um, my father being in business, and I'd always been intrigued with, you know, his line of work. And, you know, business makes the world go round.

MARTY: Sure.

KATHY: So, I decided, um, on business and um . . .

MARTY: Was that at Southeast or . . .

KATHY: No, that was before I switched, you know, I had decided . . . like midway between my um, um, . . . *(Pause.)*

MARTY: At Southeast?

KATHY: Sophomore year at Southeast. *(Nods head.)*

MARTY: Right.

KATHY: Then when I changed schools *(twists hands together)* . . . um . . .

MARTY: Uh huh.

KATHY: I *(stammer)* changed my major, you know, officially again.

MARTY: Sure.

KATHY: My family had moved from Chomedey to, um, . . . Dallas for a few years, so that's what brought me over in this area.

MARTY: Oh, I see. *(Nods head.)*

KATHY: And then I selected the University of the Southwest for its business school . . .

MARTY: Right.

KATHY: Um, outstanding record . . .

MARTY: Uh, huh.

KATHY: And, ah, um . . .

MARTY: Not because the school is bigger or anything?

KATHY: Right *(laugh)*, um, . . . and, so, um *(pause)*, I've been here at the University.

As Marty muttered, "Oh, that's good" and looked down at Kathy's resume, she reminded herself to slow down. She was speed talking! Kathy also felt unsure whether Marty understood why she had switched majors; her explanation had sounded confusing and disorganized. Since Marty was not following up her answers with probing questions, it was difficult to know how much she should talk about things. However, Kathy also realized that in contrast to some of the recruiters in her other interviews, Marty was letting her talk and was not dominating "talk time." Thus, while Marty was not probing her answers, Kathy perceived him as a good listener and someone who was easy to converse with; actually, she found him to be a really warm, friendly type of guy. Still, Kathy was uncertain if he wanted her to continue with her life story. That issue, however, was quickly resolved when Marty, pointing at Kathy's resume, asked his next question.

MARTY: Um, Kathy, could you tell me a little bit . . . bring me up to date on your work experience and, um, . . . some of the things you liked about each of your jobs, maybe some of the things you didn't like about them and, ah, . . . tell me a little bit about what you did, some of your responsibilities?"

As Kathy considered her response to Marty's question, she couldn't help but wonder why he kept asking such complicated questions! She mused to herself, "What does he want me to talk about first? I guess I'll just review my work history and wait to see what he picks up on. Should I talk about the work I did with the sorority? Other interviewers have not been particularly interested in that. I guess they don't really consider it *work* experience; yet, I probably learned more from that experience than any other job, and I did receive a nominal salary. Best to play it safe. This is a sales job I'm applying for so I'll describe my sales background. If he wants to know about the sorority, I'm sure he will ask."

KATHY: O.K., um, . . . I think, um, the most relevant, um, . . . work experience for me has been my sales experience, um, . . . I worked in, um, . . . a clothing store for men and women. Um, . . . The Clothier . . .

MARTY: Uh huh *(tilts head)*.

KATHY: That's in Chomedey and then also of course, um, . . . for a small women's clothing shop, Lavals, in Marshall, Alabama . . . and that's where I've done most of my experience and I enjoy sales, um *(pause)*, working directly with people helping them meet their needs, um, . . . a sales benefit, um, . . . for the customer, um, . . . that's what I want to begin in. I think that's relevant for me right now because that's um, . . . the position I really do want, um, . . . to begin in right now.

MARTY: Sales?

KATHY: Sales. I think it's very important, um, . . . It's a good entry level position I think for a person beginning in a company to really learn, you know, the company and then, um, . . . as a person progresses in the company they *(pause)* have that foundation and know, you know, how the customers feel, you know, directly dealt with customers and how they feel. I think it can help in the planning . . . of say, a manager, you know.

MARTY: Uh huh.

KATHY: Um, . . . and I think, again, that the sales benefit, um, . . . is very important, you know. You're dealing directly with people, meeting their needs and stuff *(voice falls off)*.

As she completed her answer, Kathy speculated about whether or not Marty understood that she didn't expect to be a manager 6 months after joining Titan. Too often in other interviews she had stressed her interest in management versus sales (the kiss of death when applying for a sales job!). She had to make sure Marty knew that she wanted to start at the bottom and work her way up—that she was *really* interested in sales. Kathy's thoughts, however, were soon interrupted by Marty's next question.

MARTY: So, that was all retail sales then?

KATHY: Right, sure was. *(Nods head.)*

MARTY: Uh, huh. Um, . . . what about the Beverly Products company?

(Points to resume.) Ah, . . . tell me a little bit about what you did there. You did office work and, um, . . . how did you like it, and, um . . .

KATHY: Right.

MARTY: . . . What you didn't like about it.

KATHY: Um . . .

MARTY: Seems to me you liked sales the best so you probably didn't like being confined in the office or wherever you were, huh?

As Marty was asking (and to some degree answering) his question, Kathy's spirits soared; she realized her interest in sales came through loud and clear! However, she was concerned that Marty assumed that she didn't like office work too. Now she would need to convey to him that she was capable of supervising an office staff. Kathy organized her thoughts on this matter and began to respond to Marty's question.

KATHY: Right, well that was, um, . . . that was, um . . . a kind of different experience, um, . . . experience also, it was, um, . . . they are a branch of a company out of New York, Techno-Fabricators. This was a summer job for me and I, um, . . . worked in the office doing typing and, um, filing and I *(pause)* . . . We were redoing the whole filing system so I was pretty much in charge of that. There were about three other temporary employees that I supervised. We were, ah, . . . a team *(moves hands for emphasis as speaking).*

MARTY: Uh huh. *(Coughs; looks down at resume.)*

KATHY: Also, they kind of let me in on the sales aspect, and it was small enough that I could see what was going on because I knew all of the customers names and the way the company was set up . . .

MARTY: Uh huh.

KATHY: And, um, . . . so I . . . I got to see, you know, how they worked everyday.

MARTY: Good, that's good. *(Pause.)* Kathy, could you tell me, ah, . . . could you . . . how would you, ah, . . . go about it you, ah, . . . had to describe yourself, ah, . . . your personality, maybe some of the assets you feel are very important to your success. How would go about describing yourself? *(Moves hands for emphasis as speaking.)*

Kathy felt disappointed as she realized Marty was not going to ask her any more questions about her work experience. It was clear that Marty was not following up with any meaningful questions about anything she said. There were many other relevant aspects of her work experience she wanted to describe to Marty. She needed to discover a way to integrate some of these other dimensions of her work experience into her answers to other questions. However, first she had to respond to another one of Marty's "tell me everything about you," multiple questions. Kathy mused over the situation, and then initiated her response to Marty's question.

KATHY: Well, I think, um, . . . a lot of . . . ah . . . some things . . . that you need to know about my . . . about me are things that I have learned through my experiences. I felt like I've been able to really learn to effectively work with people, um, . . . both like in a formal and informal basis. Um, . . . through my jobs and through working on committees and clubs and I think that, um, . . . I feel like I can work with people and work effectively with them. Uh, . . . I feel like I've, um, . . . shown leadership, um, . . . qualities through . . . (Pause.) I've had experience in being a leader especially with my Alpha Beta work.

MARTY: Uh huh. (Looks at resume.)

KATHY: I feel like I've had the chance to plan programs, to be organized, um, . . . to plan and implement programs and to carry them out, so I feel like I've, um, . . . got some feel for organization. I've had to be assertive and, um, . . . aggressive and stand out, and you know, put forth effort.

MARTY: Good . . . (Nods head.)

Immediately upon concluding her answer Kathy began to wonder if she had *really* described herself to Marty. She questioned whether or not she used enough examples. Kathy thought to herself, "I've got to remember that he doesn't seem to be probing anything I say; that means I must take initiative and make sure my answers cover all the important things about myself that I want him to know." She looked up at Marty as he began to phrase his next question.

MARTY: Um, . . . I guess right along with those lines, Kathy, what (pause) do you think are your greatest assets (raises right hand in air as speaking and moves hand back and forth), um, . . . that you offer the company and, uh, . . . some of the assets that you think will make you a success? Maybe one asset or a couple.

KATHY: I think, um, . . . a couple of things maybe, um, . . . the first one being my, um, . . . past, um, . . . experience, work experience. I've worked since 13 years old and I've just, um, you know, had the feeling for being responsible for myself. Um, . . . having some independence, um, . . . having a sense of responsibility, um, learning through my . . . learning through my jobs. I've had the best experience.

MARTY: Work experience? (Tilts head.)

KATHY: Right, exactly. I think that's one . . . the key thing that's behind me that I've had the work experience and I, you know, I know, you know, about working and, um, . . . I also feel like another quality I have through all this is that I learned to work well with people. I feel like I can get along with people very well and, um, . . . you know, accept them for what they are and um, . . . maybe if I cannot, you know, if there's something I do not like about someone else I can, um, you know, overlook that and accept them for what they are.

MARTY: That's good. *(Nods head.)*

KATHY: I feel like those two things, um, . . . will help me in my career and, um, throughout my life.

MARTY: Good, that's real good. *(Pause, coughs.)* Excuse me. *(Looks at resume.)* Kathy, what on the other hand, what are some of the things you think, ah, . . . you could improve on maybe. They might even be assets, ah, . . . but you know, sometimes we have assets that can turn into liabilities. What do you think that you can most improve on? *(Moves hands up and down as he speaks.)*

KATHY: That *(pause)* personally . . .

MARTY: Personally.

KATHY: . . . that I can improve on? *(Points at herself.)* Um, . . . let me see *(pause)*, such a deep question. Um, . . . *(Raises right hand to chin.)*

MARTY: Have to have one of those, you see. *(Laugh.)*

KATHY: *(Laugh.)* Right, for sure. *(Drops hand from face.)* Um, . . . I think maybe *(pause)* in work maybe when I, um, . . . get into a business . . . more of a business environment in my career, that I will learn to, um, . . . deal with people, all different types of people more. So, you know, they would be older people, say, and people with more experience than myself. Um, . . . I think it would give me a lot . . . I could use a lot more experience in, you know, dealing with different kinds of people, being exposed to different kinds of people . . .

MARTY: Are you talking in terms of, maybe, communication? Communicating with these people or . . . *(Moves right hand in air as he speaks.)*

KATHY: Um, I don't guess so much communication. I guess maybe dealing with them, dealing with different kinds of people, working with them, being associated with them, and carrying out projects.

MARTY: Uh huh.

KATHY: I think that, um, . . .

MARTY: Interacting . . .

KATHY: Yeah, inter . . . correct, interacting.

Kathy clenched her fists under the table and lamented to herself, "Where is my mind today? That answer was horrible and I was so inarticulate! There are lots of things I could improve on 'personally.' Why did I say I needed to improve my ability to interact with different kinds of people? If I have problems interacting with people, he must think I'll have problems in effectively managing sales meetings with new clients." Kathy also realized she was not even being consistent; earlier she had said that one of her assets was her ability to get along with people. As Marty nodded his head and responded, "Well, that's good," to Kathy's last replies. Kathy tried to calm down; she needed to think before answering questions.

MARTY: Um *(pause)*, Kathy, how do you see yourself in terms of a . . . company, be it Titan or be it Company X, or whoever you might choose to go with. *(Moves hands as he speaks.)* How do you see yourself fitting in, . . . into sales, ah, . . . the kind of sales line. Do you see yourself going from sales rep to district manager and on like that or do you see yourself maybe getting into the product end of it? Where do you see yourself fitting in with the company?

KATHY: OK, um, . . . you know it depends on how, of course, how the, um, specific company is set up . . .

MARTY: Uh huh. *(Tilts head.)*

KATHY: You know, um, . . . I would like to see myself first starting in sales and, um, . . . I can see myself kind of going two routes, going into sales management, you know . . .

MARTY: Field sales?

KATHY: Right, or I can also see myself going like the marketing route.

MARTY: Uh huh.

KATHY: Like a marketing staff position, being, um, . . . either involved with the product or products theme or say distribution . . . *(Rubs palms together.)*

MARTY: Uh huh.

KATHY: Or promotion. Um, . . . something of that sort. I'm interested in really starting in sales and seeing how that goes.

Kathy felt much better. Her answer made sense and it was clear that she understood the types of career directions one might take as one advanced in sales. As a consequence, Marty's next question was a surprise to her.

MARTY: That's good; that's good. *(Looks at resume.)* Um, . . . Kathy, what are some of your, ah, . . . career objectives? In terms of ah, . . . where you'd like to be, in terms of getting 2 years down the road, maybe 5 years down the road. What would you like to achieve along the way? *(Moves hands up and down as he speaks.)*

Kathy was puzzled. She thought she had already answered this question. What more did Marty want to know? Exactly what did he mean by "achieve along the way?" As Kathy struggled to make sense of this phrase, she began to respond to Marty's question.

KATHY: O.K., this kind of going along with what, um, . . . you know, I was saying. I do want to start with a company, ah, beginning in sales, of course a company large enough to give me some good formal training . . .

MARTY: Uh huh. *(Nods head.)*

KATHY: Because that is very important for a background. I want to be, um, . . . employed by a company with high quality, um, . . . products, that is, you know, benefitting society that I . . . products that I can stand behind and, ah, personally promote and, um, . . . a job . . . I want to be in a job that is challenging for me. That's in a challenging industry, um, . . . that I can personally . . . where I can personally grow and professionally grow also.

MARTY: Good, ah, . . . along those lines, Kathy, what are some of the things maybe *(pause)* outside the job that might, how do I say . . . help you achieve your goals? *(Moves hands up and down as he speaks.)*

KATHY: Uh huh.

MARTY: Is there any other things that, you know, outside the job that might help you achieve your goals?

KATHY: Um, . . . let me see, another toughie . . . *(Smiles, looks down.)*

MARTY: *(Laughs.)* I save them all for you actually. *(Laughs, smiles.)*

KATHY: Good, oh good! *(Laughs.)* Um, I think a lot . . . feel like I've just been able to, um *(pause)*, meet and deal with a lot of different people. I've been . . . I feel like I've been in diversified types of activities, from jobs to extracurricular activities through high school and college years and I feel like I've gained a lot of experience through that. Um, . . . dealing with people, of course you can always learn more and more about people. But I feel like I've, um, . . . been exposed to a lot of different kinds of people in different walks of life. I think that would definitely help me in my career.

MARTY: That's good . . . *(Nods head.)*

Kathy was starting to feel depressed. Despite Marty's frequent assurances that her responses were "good," she felt as if her answers were off target. His questions seemed very redundant and she didn't know what else to say about her career goals and objectives. What was Marty after that she had failed to talk about? She hoped the next question might provide a clue as to what Marty was *really* trying to find out about Kathy.

MARTY: Um, . . . Kathy, what would you like from a company . . . to offer you, let's say in terms of . . . maybe the chance for vertical mobility or, ah, . . . you know, you've mentioned training already, What are some of the things you definitely would want a company to offer to you? *(Moves hands up and down as he speaks.)*

KATHY: All right. Originally, what I said was, ah, the training. Again, um, . . . the challenge, being able to, um, . . . to succeed, of course, you know professionally and have, you know, have openings and the line of progression. Um, . . . also a company again that represents high quality products and services that is, um, you know, is growing and, um, . . . making accomplishments. So, I think those are the three main things that I am looking for right now in an employer.

MARTY: Good. *(Moves chair back 3–4 inches.)* Um, . . . Kathy, what, ah, . . . how do you see yourself in terms of, maybe a relationship with a manager? What do you like to see in a manager . . . in management? How do you view management and how should someone manage you? What are your views on that?

KATHY: Well, I feel like a manager should be formal and informal, be . . . a friend, you know, a manager should be a friend to, um, . . . the people under him. But, I think at the same time um, . . . be a person who is in charge, formal, gives instructions, you know . . .

MARTY: Uh huh.

KATHY: Someone that can relate to people, understand people and listen to them. I think that's very important. It's important to be a people-person but yet, um, . . . and be formal, you know, . . . with um, . . . the people he works with but also be informal with them.

MARTY: That's good. *(Looks at resume.)* Um, one other question, Kathy, what are some of the things about business, in terms of your school-work . . . maybe a particular class that you enjoyed a lot and why did you enjoy it? On the other turn, what are some things, you know, about school, maybe another class that you didn't like? *(Moves hands up and down as he speaks.)*

As Marty was asking his question, Kathy contemplated her response to his inquiry about desirable managerial traits. Probably she had been too vague in her answer; she might have talked more about what she wanted from a manager. Unfortunately, she was not sure what she really wanted from a manager or the management of an organization. Clearly, she needed to ponder this more; however, now was not the time to consider the matter. At the moment she needed to describe to Marty how she became interested in marketing.

KATHY: O.K., I think what really started me . . . led me to select marketing was the first class that I had. I had a very good professor. It was introductory marketing. It kind of gave me a very good view of marketing and it really was fascinating to me. And also, um, . . . this semester I'm taking a class that has interested me. It's a marketing course talking about society being conservers, you know, instead of consuming.

MARTY: Uh huh. *(Plays with pen.)*

KATHY: And we're discussing all kinds of problems . . . it's a seminar. We're discussing problems about pollution, overconsumption, and environmental health. The course has made me realize how, um, . . . many problems there are and how important this is to deal with. So, I think those two classes especially caused me to be interested in business.

MARTY: Good, good. Is there anything that turned you off about it? Um, . . . maybe some classes that turned you off about business?

KATHY: Um, . . .

MARTY: Maybe accounting. It never did much for me. *(Clasps hands together.)*

KATHY: Right, yeah. *(Laughs.)* Didn't do too much for me, but it's, you know, I think it's a good basis for everyone, you know, especially going into business you have to have it. Economics classes I did not enjoy much . . . although some days were good and some days were bad. But, again, that's good information to know.

MARTY: Well, good. What I want to do now, um, . . . I'm sure there are some questions you might have for me and I've got some things I want to give you. *(Points at brochures on table.)* Also, I want to explain a few things to you. Anytime along the way please feel free to interrupt me and ask me anything you like. *(Moves chair forward, picks up a brochure, leans across table to show it to Kathy.)*

During the next few minutes, Marty described the contents of the various company brochures he brought with him. Kathy had already looked through several of them in the Titan file in the Placement Office. However, she didn't tell Marty that she knew 50% of what he was now telling her. In addition to the material in the brochures, he spent a lot of time discussing the company's products, various markets, training, management practices, compensation system, the assigning of sales territories, locations of plant and company offices, the company's economic (profit) outlook, and a little about his own employment history with Titan. During this period of time (about 12 minutes), Kathy asked six or seven closed questions about some of the things Marty was saying, but on the whole just listened to him. Marty then asked Kathy if she had any more questions. When she responded, "I can't think of any," the interview closed as follows:

MARTY: Let me give you a few more things.

KATHY: O.K.

MARTY: Um *(pause)*, here, here is . . ., um, . . . an application.

KATHY: O.K.

MARTY: Got to have that, of course. And if you would, at your leisure *(pause)*, send it to my attention at corporate. I'll mark it off here and that will make sure it gets to me. Uh, . . . here is a benefit statement.

KATHY: O.K.

MARTY: And I'm going to . . . uh, I don't have any business cards. That's terrible . . . terrible.

KATHY: *(Laughs.)*

MARTY: I left them in the last hotel room I was in. Here . . . let me write down my business phone for you.

KATHY: O.K.

MARTY: If there's any other questions that might arise and you *(pause)*, you know, feel free to give me a call, and I'll certainly answer them for you. Um, . . . if you would fill that out *(points at application)* . . . the process takes 3 to 4 weeks, something like that.

KATHY: O.K.

MARTY: And you'll either hear from me, or one of the district managers or something like that. O.K.?

KATHY: When will it be?

MARTY: About 3 to 4 weeks. *(Pause.)* How does that sound?

KATHY: Fine.

MARTY: Good, do you have any questions, Kathy?

KATHY: No, I think that's . . . that's it.

MARTY: Good, good. Maybe you can answer a question for me.

KATHY: O.K.

MARTY: How do I get to, ah, . . . the student union to eat? I've got a meeting there.

KATHY: You just walk out front of this building, go to the left and it's about two blocks, uh, . . . on your right. *(Speaks as she stands up.)*

MARTY: Great! *(Stands, extends arm to shake hands.)*

KATHY: Thanks. *(Shakes hands with Marty.)*

MARTY: Bye.

Kathy left the interview feeling uncertain about her chances of receiving an "on-site" interview offer from Titan. Although she considered Marty's performance as an interviewer to be no better than "fair" (after all, he asked so many confusing and/or redundant questions), she felt that she had done a better than average job as an interviewee. All in all, Kathy perceived the interview as "typical" of those she had experienced at the Placement Center.

As Marty promised, 3 weeks after the interview Kathy received a letter from him. As soon as she opened the letter, she could tell from its brevity that it was a rejection letter. While she initially felt depressed about being rejected for a second interview, she soon forgot all about it. In the same batch of mail she had received an on-site interview offer from one of the other companies with which she had interviewed at the Placement Center. On Tuesday she would be flying up to Dallas for her first day-long, on-site interview.

THE SCREENING INTERVIEW OF WILLIAM P. FREDERICS

Bill was out of breath as he walked down the hall looking for room 312C. He had just run up three flights of stairs because he was afraid he was going to be late for his 1:30 P.M. interview with the representative from Industrial Products Titan. Bill was beginning to perspire and felt warm in his dark blue three-piece suit; he thought to himself, "Why can't they set the air conditioning in this building 10° cooler?" As he approached the door to room 312C, Bill stopped for a moment to compose himself; he straightened his blue and red tie, tucked his white dress shirt into his pants, and quickly combed his recently styled light brown hair. Bill took a deep breath and knocked on the partially opened door. As the force from his knock pushed the door open, Bill could see the interviewer from Titan beginning to rise from his seat to greet him. Bill immediately noticed that the interviewer was not wearing his suit jacket, and he thought to himself, "Great! This guy and I are on the same temperature wave length."

As Bill entered the room he realized that he had previously participated in interviews in this room; no other interviewing room had a full-sized map of the United States on the wall. Bill placed his books on the table as he extended his arm to shake hands with the Titan rep. As they shook hands Bill could see his resume (see Figure 1.2) on top of a stack of papers in front of the interviewer. Bill firmly grasped and shook the interviewer's hand; he remembered what his Dad always said, "You can tell more about a man's character from the firmness of his handshake than from all the things he might say about himself." Bill felt relieved as the interviewer responded with a firm handshake; he thought to himself, "Hey, 10 has always been a lucky number for me, maybe I'll 'score' in this my 10th screening interview."

MARTY: *(Standing.)* Hi, do you go by Bill, Willy, or William?
BILL: Bill.
MARTY: Bill, O.K. I go by Marty. *(Begins to sit down.)* Feel free to take off your coat . . .
BILL: Sure. *(Starts to take off suit jacket.)*
MARTY: Please do so cause it gets stuffy in here . . . How are you doing today? *(Shuffles papers in front of him after sitting.)*
BILL: Excellent. *(Hangs jacket on back of chair and sits down.)*

MARTY: Good, good. *(Pushes chair forward, leans forward across table with elbows resting at edge of table, directs body at applicant, nods head.)*

BILL: Just finished a test. *(Pushes chair forward, directs body at interviewer, leans forward with elbows resting at edge of table, one hand rests on the table and the other hand rests underneath his chin, nods head.)*

MARTY: Just finished your test? *(Looks down at resume then up at Bill.)*

BILL: Yeah, just got back from the other side of campus. *(Brings hand down from his chin so that both hands rest on the table in a moderately open position, looks directly at the interviewer.)*

MARTY: How did it go?

BILL: Real good . . . I'm sure I did real well. *(Nods head.)*

MARTY: Oh, great. *(Nods head.)* Ah, . . . it's nice and warm out there too, isn't it?

BILL: Yeah. *(Nods head.)*

MARTY: I just went outside to *(pause)* walk over to the union and, whew, I about died! *(Nods head.)* Ah, . . . Bill *(pause)*, first of all I'm going to have some paper here *(raises paper in the air)* and I don't know if I'm going to take notes. If taking notes bothers you . . .

BILL: No, it doesn't bother me. *(Places palms down flat on table.)*

MARTY: Let me know and we'll fix it. *(Pause.)* O.K., fine. *(Looks at resume.)* Um, . . . what I'd like to do is, I'd like to just start off, um *(pause)*, I've got this here *(points to resume)* and *(pause)* it kind of presents you in black and white. I want to know more about you. Tell me about you. *(Points at Bill and then drops hand.)* I see you're from Gertrudis. Tell me about high school, what you did, and, ah, . . . how you chose ending up at the University of the Southwest and a business major and maybe some of your outside activities, and things like that. *(Looks up from resume as speaks.)*

As Bill listened to Marty's first question, he thought to himself how good it felt to take his jacket off—to feel comfortable in an interview for a change! Upon realizing that Marty wanted a brief "bio," Bill pondered over his alternatives and decided to start off with his dad and how he had been an Air Force "brat." Bill figured that this approach would communicate to Marty that Bill had lived in lots of different places and knew how to adapt to new situations. As Bill looked directly at Marty and prepared to speak, he wondered whether or not Marty was the type of interviewer who asked a lot of "deep," tough questions.

BILL: O.K., I started out at *(pause)*, ah, . . . my Dad was Air Force, so I moved all around the country and, ah *(raises left hand to chin)*, . . . when I went to high school, it was like the first time I went to the same school for 2 years in a row. *(Brings left hand down.)*

MARTY: Uh huh. *(Pushes chair back 3–4 inches, crosses legs, and leans back slightly.)*

BILL: So, I lucked out and spent all 4 years of my high school in ah, Gertrudis, same high school. And while I was there, my activities were, ah, . . . student council, golf team, and key club *(pause)* and . . . so that I, you know, took part in those and then I came up to Southwest *(pause)* and how I got to that decision was *(pause)* I had a sister up at West Texas U so I was, you know, going to think about that just because, you know, peer pressure. *(Repeatedly raises hands 3–4 inches above the table then lowers them back to the table, palms down, as he speaks.)*

MARTY: Sure.

BILL: Ah, . . . I threw out West Texas U cause the weather is, you know, the dust would kill me *(laugh)* and I was thinking about going to some other schools, but through a process of elimination I just ended up here. *(Moves left hand to lap and raises and lowers right hand for emphasis as he speaks.)* I've also got a lot of friends up here, friends that graduated a year ahead of me and I came up here a lot to visit.

MARTY: Uh huh. *(Nods head.)*

BILL: I kind of enjoyed that, so, that's another factor why I came here. *(Voice falls off.)* And then, ah *(pause)*, let's see *(pause)*, well, as far as working, ah, . . . before I came up here I worked at, ah, . . . the Silverspoon Restaurant in Gertrudis.

MARTY: Uh huh.

BILL: So, um, . . . I had a lot of running around to do there, you know, *(pause)* it's busy work, restaurant work, you know.

MARTY: Sure. *(Nods head.)*

BILL: So then, ah, . . . as far as *(pause)*, ah, work when I got to college, I worked as a lifeguard every summer until last summer, and then I worked for Prairie Beer, well, not the brewery, but a distributorship. And, I went around and just delivered beer.

MARTY: *(Sits more erect.)* Driver, you . . . did driver sales? *(Pause.)* Is that what it was?

BILL: Right. *(Nods head.)*

MARTY: You took . . . you actually took orders, too? *(Series of sweeping, quick head nods.)*

BILL: Right *(pause)*, you know, everything. *(Raises and lowers left hand for emphasis.)*

MARTY: *(Smiles.)* I, I worked for a whole summer for a Quencher Beer wholesaler, so I know all about that. Um *(looks at resume)*, Bill, ah *(pause)*, could you tell me about *(pause)* wha . . . what was your decision to . . . to become a business major, and a marketing major, um, . . . narrowing that down, why . . ., why did you *(points at Bill)* choose the field of business?

"Things are going well," Bill thought to himself. Marty and I have something in common, we both delivered and sold beer while in college. As he considered Marty's reaction, Bill wondered whether or not the job at Titan might require driver sales; perhaps that explained why Marty was so interested in Bill's job at the beer distributor. Bill pondered over bringing up the job again in answering some other question. However, first he had to explain to Marty why he chose marketing as a major. Bill realized that saying he just "lucked into" the major would not do the trick.

BILL: When I first started out, as . . . I wasn't sure about marketing, you know, so I just *(pause)*, all the business classes were the same, so I figured I don't have to decide now. All I knew was I wanted to be business because I think *(pause)* that appeared to me *(pause)* something I'd like to do. *(Points at self.)*

MARTY: Uh huh. *(Nods head.)*

BILL: I thought it was best suited for me. That's why I did it. And I picked, ah, . . . marketing just through listening to other people that had jobs like, in the field of marketing, listening to them talk and . . . the fact that when I got through accounting I thought *(laughs)* I don't like this. *(Moves hands forward and backward as he speaks, then scratches head.)*

MARTY: I'll say. *(Nods head; smiles.)*

BILL: Yeah, so, ah, . . . that's how I got to be marketing.

MARTY: Do you like it so far?

BILL: Uh huh, love it. *(Opens and closes hands for emphasis.)*

Bill felt relieved that Marty didn't probe into his answer about his choice of marketing as a college major. Although he had been asked to explain his reasons for selecting his major in almost every interview, he still didn't have a "prepared" response to inquiries on this topic. As he listened for Marty's next question, Bill wondered to himself whether or not anyone ever *really* chose a career field.

MARTY: Good, that's good. *(Nods head.)* I was a marketing major so . . .

BILL: Of course, the classes have *(pause)*, you know, little effect on what you're going to do, see, you know maybe a . . . language . . .

MARTY: In the real world.

BILL: Right, right.

MARTY: Yeah, I, ah, . . . I used *(pause)*, now I can tell you from experience that really *(pause)* they don't; there are certain that you can apply and, ah . . .

BILL: Yeah.

MARTY: The principles I guess *(scratches head)*, but *(pause)* it's a totally different situation, you know, once you get out there and start in . . . I'm fresh out of it too. I'm only 3 years or so out of school. *(Rubs chin with left hand.)* So . . .

BILL: What school?

MARTY: Western State U.

BILL: Uh huh. Is that where, ah, . . . is that where they had that big NCAA investigation?

MARTY: Yeah, that's the one. *(Laughs.)* Ah, Bill *(pause)*, why don't you . . . you kind of tell me how you would describe yourself or *(clears throat)* . . . or how you think others see you and *(pause)* you know, through their eyes maybe. *(Raises left hand to chin.)*

Bill's confidence was building as he realized that he and Marty had another commonality: They agreed that most of the stuff they teach in "B" school is worthless theory. He also made mental note of the fact that Marty only graduated from college 3 years ago, yet was already in a position of responsibility at Titan. Clearly, Marty had done O.K. for himself at Titan, confirming what Bill had heard about the opportunities Titan offers its employees. As Bill organized his thoughts on how to answer Marty's question, he reminded himself to keep focused on the type of job for which he was applying—sales, and that he needed to emphasize personal qualities associated with success in that type of position.

BILL: I'd describe myself as, ah *(pause)*, ah *(pause)*, det . . ., you know, determined, and, ah *(pause)*, probably the best thing is that I would be dependable.

MARTY: Uh huh.

BILL: You know, hard working and, um *(pause)*, I think other people would see me as *(pause)*, ah, you know, relatively easy to get along with because I, would say flexible. You know, I can, you know, take, you know, roll with the punches and all that stuff. You know, I'm not *(pause)* one of these hard guys that throws his weight around all the time and, ah, . . . I can compromise. You know, I won't give in, but, you know, I can, you know, work things out. *(Moves hand up and down for emphasis as he speaks.)*

MARTY: Uh huh, what do you think your biggest asset would be in terms of, ah, . . . making you a success when you get out of school? Let's say, once you get into the working world, what do you think is the biggest asset you've got going for you that's gonna make you a success?

BILL: Well, it's either got to be *(pause)* one of the two, being dependable or hardworking.

MARTY: Good, good.

BILL: Just whatever fits in the situation.

MARTY: I guess on the other turn then, what do you think are, ah, . . . some of the things that maybe, ah, . . . you feel you should improve on? So, what are some of the things, you know, that may be a liability? It might even be an asset that might become a liability in certain situations.

BILL: *(Sits erect in chair.)* Uh, I would say nothing in specific. It's just *(pause)* I can't pick out one right now.

MARTY: Well, that's good, you know. Ah, . . . what do you think *(pause)*, Bill, are some of the things that, ah, . . . motivate you and why do they motivate you?

Bill was concerned about the odd look on Marty's face when Bill had said that he had no liabilities. He realized that such a response might indicate he didn't have a "feel" for his own strengths and weaknesses. Yet, Bill felt hesitant to criticize himself, since it might suggest that he lacked self-confidence. As he reflected on this dilemma he also thought about the things that motivated him to perform, the focus of Marty's latest question.

BILL: Ah, . . . well, I guess the thing that motivates me the most is if I like something. *(Moves chair so that it is at a slight angle away from the table, body is no longer directed at interviewer but to the side, head turned to the interviewer.)* Cause, you know, it's just like anything, if you like it . . . *(Crosses leg, leans back, relaxes body, raises left hand to chin as he speaks.)*

MARTY: You're going to do it.

BILL: You're going to do it, and you're gonna do your best at it.

MARTY: Uh huh.

BILL: It's like sports, you know, if you like it, you know, you can pick it up pretty quick and you can get going. But if, you know, you don't like it, you're not even going to try hard.

MARTY: Uh huh. That's true, if you don't like something you sure can't *(pause)*, can't do it . . .

As Bill finished speaking and reflected on Marty's subsequent remark ("That's true, if you don't like something you sure can't do it"), he knew that he had not provided a "good" response to Marty's question. He had made it sound like he wouldn't do a good job on a task that he didn't like. But that was not what he meant. Even if he didn't like parts of a job, he always tried his best. He needed to think more carefully about his answers before responding to questions. As he waited for Marty's next question, Bill took a deep breath and reminded himself that Marty was not asking tough questions; these were questions that Bill had been asked before in other interviews.

MARTY: Um, . . . Bill, can you think back, maybe in school *(looks at resume)* or . . . maybe in a work situation at *(pause)* that you had to demonstrate some leadership, ah, . . . responsibilities and how you think you fared?

BILL: Well *(looks off to side then back at interviewer),* as far as *(pause),* ah, . . . in school I can relate that to, ah, . . . the fraternity where I was like *(pause)* assistant pledge trainer. Being just . . . being in charge of, you know, 30 guys.

MARTY: Uh huh. *(Nods head.)*

BILL: You gotta get them to . . . you've got to be there at all times, tell them what to do, make sure that everything is right and . . . you should always *(pause),* you know, it's *(pause)* they don't know what's going on and you've got to keep them informed and, ah *(pause),* it's half of it, and you know . . . *(Voice falls off.)*

MARTY: How do you think it worked for you?

BILL: It's *(scratches head)* . . . you know . . . it's good experience and, ah *(pause),* everything. You know, it's kind of satisfying to me to see that . . .

MARTY: Uh huh.

BILL: Everything came out O.K. And also, ah, . . . another leadership quality would be, ah, . . . when I worked at the pool I was, you know, assistant manager there and *(pause)* I've done schedules and, you know, kept the pool, you know, we're in charge of the pool so we had to just *(pause)* keep everything fixed, the grass, keep them happy you know, just keep everything under control between us and city hall.

MARTY: Uh huh, do you think, ah, . . . maybe just these little things might . . . might, ah, . . . sometime *(pause)* help you in your career in the future?

BILL: Yeah, uh huh. *(Leans back, scratches head.)*

Bill felt better; he had offered clear-cut examples of his experiences in responding to Marty's questions. Maybe he was now on a roll. His attitude was improving and he almost was looking forward to the next question.

MARTY: Good, good. *(Pause.)* Ah, . . . what about in school, Bill? What about some of the classes that you, ah, . . . found that you either lean toward and really liked. You might not even have did well in them, but you liked them or . . . and why did you like them? And . . . what motivated you to like them?

BILL: Well, the three classes that, ah, . . . I did like the most were, ah, speech, ah *(pause),* government, and, ah *(pause, looks off to side then back at interviewer),* ah, . . . business law class. And probably the biggest motivation, the reason why I liked them, well, I thought they were all interesting.

MARTY: Uh huh.

BILL: And, you know, as topics I thought they would be useful later on. Like the, ah, . . . business law, you know, to me *(pause)* that's things that I think I needed to know . . .

MARTY: Uh huh. *(Nods head.)*

BILL: And besides needing to know those things the teacher was, in all three of those classes, was probably, you know, one of my three, three best teachers. And they just, you know, it was enjoyable to go to class whereas the other classes just . . . *(Pause.)*

MARTY: Sure.

BILL: . . . like going, well, you know, these just, you want to go because *(pause)* he's real *(pause)*, you know, instructional or real interesting.

MARTY: Uh huh.

BILL: So I liked them.

MARTY: What about some other classes you might not have liked?

BILL: Ah, . . . *(laughs)*, definitely accounting.

MARTY: Uh huh.

BILL: Because it just wasn't my thing.

MARTY: Yeah. *(Nods head.)*

BILL: Didn't like it.

MARTY: Kind of rigid *(pause)*, structured?

BILL: Right.

MARTY: Uh, . . . can you . . . can you remember of, ah, . . . think back and maybe describe, ah, . . . where you were put into a particular tough situation or problem maybe and, ah, . . . in work, or maybe in business and, ah, . . . describe the problem and maybe how you dealt with that?

BILL: *(Coughs, looks off to side.)*

Bill was stalling for time to think. He was not sure how to tackle Marty's question. There were so many "tough" situations he had experienced that he could talk about. He wondered about what Marty was *really* after. However, just as he was about to frame a response to the question, Marty further defined his inquiry.

MARTY: What you considered, ah, . . . tough problem. Maybe it might have been a research project for school or, ah, . . . maybe for the beer distributor, running somebody else's route along with yours, or something, and how you dealt with that.

Bill was thankful for the cue. He recalled how interested Marty had been earlier in Bill's job at Prairie Beer. All he had to do now was think of an applicable example to tie to the question.

BILL: Right, well, I did that but that didn't . . . that didn't seem too tough.

MARTY: Uh huh.

BILL: The only tough thing on there is *(pause)* when you go into a new store *(pause)* you're faced with a situation, ah, . . . like it's a big bar and it's you know, going full blast . . . it's a late, late night. Everyone's busy *(pause)* . . . well, a lot of times they'll try and just, you know, push you off and say just come back later and . . . First of all, since, you know, I've never been in one of these places I've got to figure out *(smiles, pauses)* who, who do I talk to? I mean there's 5,000 people running around . . . *(Moves hands up and down for emphasis as he speaks.)*

MARTY: Right.

BILL: And, ah, . . . you know, all of them are working so *(pause)* the situation there is to get, ah . . . you know, make sure you're real nice to the guy.

MARTY: Uh huh.

BILL: You're in the situation where if you tick him off, he'll definitely tell you to come back later. And you've got to, you know, just *(pause)* do everything to please the guy . . . it's his whim. So, he can even say, "You don't have to come back," you know, later.

MARTY: Good, good. *(Looks at resume than at interviewee.)* Um, . . . Bill, what about in terms of *(pause)*, ah, . . . you have your career objective down here, but in terms of, like, sales, ah, . . . where do you see yourself fitting in a sales organization? Ah, . . . What I mean is do you see yourself, ah, . . . fitting in . . . in sales management maybe or . . . maybe a type of staff position? Really, where do you see yourself?

As Bill thought about his career objectives, he patted himself on the back for his answer to the previous question. He felt the situation he described demonstrated an ability to deal with "tough" situations on a day-in, day-out basis. As he considered his career goals with respect to sales, he reminded himself not to overemphasize his desire to move into management. He kept repeating the word "flexible" in his mind as he began to respond to Marty's question.

BILL: Well, I guess I can see myself starting out like, ah, . . . you know . . . just a representative, a sales representative.

MARTY: Uh huh.

BILL: And then, ah, . . . definitely after that, ah, . . . you know, I'd do that but after a while I wouldn't want to do that. Then I'd like to go into sales management.

MARTY: What, ah, . . . what . . . which way would you, do you see yourself going, do you see yourself maybe in field management, a . . .

district manager, you know, or do you see yourself more in the line of product management or, ah, . . . national accounts management, something like that?

BILL: Ah, . . . either one. It just depends, you know, I'm not that set, you know, on what way I'll go. *(Points in one direction then the other as he speaks.)* So *(pause)* I can't tell you that.

MARTY: OK, well good. Ah, . . . Bill, what are some of the things that you, you feel that, ah *(pause)*, a company has to offer you? Um, . . . what are some of the things you're looking for in a company? That you're looking for them to give back to you if you become an employee of theirs?

BILL: Well, the first thing I would look for *(pause)*, you know, not in the company, but in the job itself.

MARTY: Job itself would be it?

BILL: Yeah. It would be, ah, . . . you know, self-satisfaction *(pause)*, you know. If I like a job, or if I'm making a million dollars a year and I hate the job, you know, it's not worth it to me.

MARTY: Sure.

BILL: So, ah, . . . that's the main thing.

MARTY: Uh huh.

BILL: Right, there, it's just, you know *(pause)*, happiness and satisfaction really. *(Voice falls off.)* And, ah *(pause)*, ah, that would be, you know, the main thing, I guess. The other benefits such as, you know, insurance or *(pause)* or I guess I mean *(pause)* it's not that quite that important to me. *(Raises left hand to chin as he speaks.)*

MARTY: Good, good . . .

Although he had not said it, Bill expected a decent salary too. He hoped that Marty had understood that. And training—Bill wanted to receive top-notch training. However, he knew there was nothing to worry about with respect to Titan; his buddies who graduated last year had told him that Titan had the best training program in the industry and paid "big bucks."

MARTY: Ah, . . . what about in terms of, ah, . . . management. How do you see ah, . . . what is the main . . . what is your idea of, ah, . . . a good manager *(pause)* to you? What's your view of a good manager and how he should manage?

BILL: Well, ah, . . . *(clears throat)*, I mean I've seen like different managers and *(pause)* they've all had their different styles. It depends on the situation and who they're working with.

MARTY: Uh huh, fair and . . .

BILL: I've seen hard-core guys that will just, you know, whip them to death and *(pause)* but they do their jobs and it gets done.

MARTY: Uh huh.

BILL: And then other ones just kind of more of a leisure style and say, you know *(pause)* will you do this for me, and *(pause)* they'll get it done. So, it depends on the situation.

MARTY: Uh huh. Are there any common things? Any traits that you *(pause)* notice that you particularly like about a manager. Maybe a good communicator or, ah, . . . you know, uses reward rather than criticism or something like that?

BILL: Ah, . . . well, as far as, ah, . . . rewards, you know, rewards would be something like, ah, . . . you know, talk . . . talking with the guy. It's like you know if you don't talk to him and it's like I must have messed up or something.

MARTY: Uh huh.

BILL: . . . and, ah, you know, a reward would be like "Hey" *(pause)* just sitting there talking to him. *(Voice falls off.)*

Bill could tell that Marty was looking for something more specific about the kind of management that he liked. "It depends" didn't seem to satisfy him. It was atypical of Marty to ask probing questions. However, once again, Marty had cued Bill about what he was after—communication. Perhaps Marty would provide some cues as to how to answer the next question as well.

MARTY: Uh huh, that's good. *(Nods head.)* Ah, . . . you have a career objective down here and *(pause)* you know, as far as I'm concerned I *(pause)*, you know, I think that's you know, someone just sits down and writes what sounds best, you know. I know I did it, and most people do it . . .

BILL: Even on a resume, it's a hassle, too. *(Laughs, raises and lowers body in chair, then leans forward.)*

MARTY: Yeah, what *(pause)*, tell me about, you know *(pause)*, kind of ink this out and you tell me what your real career objective is and, ah, . . . some of your goals and *(pause)* things like that. *(Raises hands up and down as he speaks.)*

BILL: O.K. In the, ah, . . . as far as, you know *(pause)*, exactly what I want to do . . .

MARTY: I'm talking broad sense. I'm not saying, "I want to be district manager in five years" or anything . . .

BILL: Right.

MARTY: I'm just saying, you know . . .

BILL: Goals for me would be, ah, . . . *(pause)* of course, ah, . . . you know, advancement in time, but, ah, . . . also *(clears throat)* during these stages would be like, maybe communication with the people I work with *(pause)*, ah, . . . that's, you know. a goal. And ah, . . . ah, . . . to become, to learn by my, my mistakes, to, you know, become better.

MARTY: Uh huh. O.K. We, we're limited on time, you know, and I want to make sure I cover a few things with you if I could, because I'm sure you probably have a few questions for me.

During the next 15 minutes or so Marty described the contents of the various company brochures he had brought with him to the interview. Since Bill had not read through the Titan file in the Placement Office, most of the material Marty described was new to him. As a consequence, he asked a variety of questions about some of the items Marty discussed. As in Kathy's interview, Marty also talked about the company's products, training, markets, and so forth. Marty was very consistent in what he told applicants from one interview to the next. Bill occasionally asked Marty questions during this period; in total, Bill asked about 11–12 very focused questions. After Marty finished reviewing his own employment history with Titan, he asked Bill if he had any more questions. When Bill responded, "Don't think so," Marty closed the interview in the following manner.

MARTY: Let me give you a few things here, Bill. *(Hands Bill some papers.)* That's a benefit statement that I want you to have and this is an application form. At your leisure, fill that out and, ah, . . . drop it in the mail to me. And, ah . . . the process takes about 3–4 weeks to complete and, ah, . . . if you're interested . . . certainly you know, there's no obligation to send this back to me by any means. Let me . . . I don't have any business cards and I'm *(pause)* sorry about that . . . I left them in the hotel last night. *(Laughs.)* I was in a rush to pack and get out of there this morning. Ah, . . . if you have any other questions or anything feel free to give me a call . . .
BILL: O.K.
MARTY: . . . at that number. *(Writes number on one of the brochures.)* And I'll certainly answer anything that you, you know, have.
BILL: Where are you? Are you from like a home office?
MARTY: Chicago.
BILL: Is that right?
MARTY: Based in Chicago.
BILL: O.K. Just wondering.
MARTY: Yeah. O.K. Guess that does it. *(Begins to rise from chair and extends arm to shake hands with Bill.)*
BILL: Thanks. *(Stands, shakes hands with Marty, picks up suit jacket and books, and turns to exit the room.)*
MARTY: Thank you.

Bill left the interviewing room feeling uncertain about whether or not he would receive an on-site interview offer from the Titan rep. He had learned from past experience that just because he felt good after an interview didn't mean that he would receive a second interview offer. However, Bill did feel that he had performed quite well in the interview; he had no difficulty understanding Marty's questions and had been fairly direct in answering them. Moreover, Bill felt very positive about the relationship he and Marty had developed in the interview; he had grown to like Marty. Bill perceived Marty as warm, good natured, friendly, and understanding. Marty must have also liked Bill, since 2 weeks later he sent Bill a letter inviting him to visit Titan's Chicago office for an on-site interview.

CONCLUDING THOUGHTS

In considering why Bill received a second interview offer from Titan whereas Kathy did not, it is important to realize that other factors, in addition to each individual's performance in the screening interview, likely affected Marty's decision making. For example, although the two applicants have a number of similarities in regard to their qualifications and backgrounds (see the resumes in Figures 1.1 and 1.2.), their educational and work experiences differ in several respects. Since interviewers tend to have stereotypes of the ideal applicant for a particular position, the extent to which Bill and Kathy met Marty's preconception of the "right person" for the job may have been an important determinant in their success. Hence, in analyzing the preceding interviews and in considering the discussion questions that follow, the reader should evaluate how Marty's communication behavior in each interview may have reflected his conscious or unconscious biases.

Finally, it is important to realize that the screening interview is not only a selection device, but also serves important organizational recruiting and public relations functions. In particular, since most applicants are rejected for employment after their screening interviews, their feelings about the organization that has rejected them are greatly affected by their perceptions of their interviews and interviewers. Thus, when assessing Kathy's and Bill's interviews, it is essential to consider whether Marty was effective in conducting interviews that were (1) satisfying interpersonal communication experiences for all those involved, and (2) left both his interviewees with positive feelings about Industrial Products Titan.

NOTES

1. The two interviews described in this case are based on *actual* employment screening interviews conducted at the Business Placement Center at the University of Texas at Austin. Materials presented in the case, including descriptions of nonverbal behaviors, represent segments of actual interview transcriptions and the coding of

interview videotapes. (During their interviews, applicants were unaware they were being videotaped; interviewers only knew they would be videotaped at random times during the day. The room in which the interviews were conducted contained discrete audio- and videotape monitoring equipment.) Resumes presented in Figures 1.1 and 1.2 are versions of the actual resumes the applicants submitted to their interviewers. Only such items as names, dates, locations, etc., have been changed to conceal the identities of the applicants. In addition, the interviewer's name and organizational affiliation have been changed to maintain anonymity. Information concerning applicants' thoughts during the interviews are based on information obtained in post-interview debriefings with applicants (which included responses to a variety of questionnaire items). The outcome of each interview (offer or no offer of an on-site interview) is based on whether or not the applicant actually received a second interview offer from the recruiter's organization. Detailed information about the data-collection process and the larger set of data from which the interviews described in this case were abstracted is available in Tengler and Jablin (1983).

2. Interview transcripts include all applicant and interviewer utterances, including disfluencies. Momentary pauses in speech (less than ½ second) are signified by three consecutive dots; extended pauses in speech (in excess of ½ second) are signified by the word "pause" enclosed in parentheses.

KEY ISSUES

Among the more central issues to consider when examining the communication dynamics of employment interviews are question characteristics, questioning patterns, and the manner in which the interview parties communicate their interaction involvement. Several key concepts and variables related to these issues are described below.

Question Characteristics

Closed/Open Questions: Closed questions restrict responses to fairly specific areas of inquiry; open-ended questions are broad in nature, providing the respondent with considerable control over the content and amount of information disclosed.

Neutral/Directed Questions: Neutral questions do not overtly cue the respondent about the type of response desired and/or expected by the person asking the question. In contrast, directed questions suggest a desired response, biasing the respondent's answer.

Primary/Secondary Questions: Primary questions introduce new topics of discussion in an interview while secondary (or probing) questions explore issues/topics already mentioned in response to either a previous primary or secondary question.

Single/Multiple Questions: A single question asks for a response on just one specific topic; a multiple question seeks a response on two or more distinctly different subjects.

Questioning Patterns

Confirmatory Questioning Strategy: This is a questioning approach in which an interviewer seeks via his or her questions to confirm "hunches" about an applicant based on preinterview information (such as information contained in an applicant's resume).

Funnel/Inverted Funnel Question Sequences: When an interviewer uses a funnel question sequence he or she "starts out deductively by asking open-ended questions, and then as the interview progresses gradually moves to asking more specific questions" (Tengler & Jablin, 1983, p. 247). Interviewers who use an inverted funnel question sequence begin with closed questions and then progress to more open-ended, probing questions.

Sequential Interaction Structure: This refers to the pattern or sequence of various communicative acts (for example, interviewer's and applicant's questions, answers, and statements) in an interaction episode. To assess patterns of interaction we examine the sequence of "interacts" (conversational pairs: e.g., interviewer question–applicant answer; applicant answer–interviewer statement; interviewer statement–applicant statement; and so on).

Interaction Involvement

Empathic Listening: The ability to participate verbally and nonverbally in the spirit or feeling of the interview by appearing to be interested in and concerned with the contributions of the other interview party. For example, one might show one's interest in the other party's comments by asking probing questions or seeking clarification of unclear issues.

Nonverbal Immediacy: Nonverbal behaviors such as smiling, eye contact, leaning body forward, positive head nods, direct body orientation, positive facial expressions, body movement, and posture that conveys a sense of involvement in an interaction.

DISCUSSION QUESTIONS

1. In what ways was the interaction structure of Kathy's interview distinct from that of Bill's?

2. To what degree was Marty a "reliable," consistent interviewer, that is, followed the same questioning patterns (for example, with respect to topics of inquiry) across interviews?

3. Critique the strengths and weaknesses of the types of questions that Marty asked Bill and Kathy.

4. In what ways was Kathy's nonverbal communication behavior in her interview different from Bill's in his interview.

5. How effective were Kathy and Bill in recognizing cues that Marty (consciously or unconsciously) provided about the type of applicant he was seeking?

6. To what extent did Kathy and Bill directly respond to the questions they were asked? Were Bill and Kathy effective listeners in their interviews?

7. How well prepared were Kathy and Bill for their interviews? What might have they done to be better prepared?

8. To what extent, if any, did Marty follow confirmatory questioning strategies in his interviews with Bill and Kathy?

9. What qualities were present in Bill's relationship with Marty that were not evident in Kathy's relationship with Marty?

10. To what extent did Marty show that he was an empathic listener?

SUGGESTED READINGS

Einhorn, L. J. (1981). An inner view of the job interview: An investigation of successful communication behaviors. *Communication Education, 30,* 217–228.

Jablin, F. M., & McComb, K. B. (1984). The employment screening interview: An organizational assimilation and communication perspective. In R. Bostrom (Ed.), *Communication yearbook 8* (pp. 137–153). Newbury Park, CA: Sage.

Jablin, F. M., & Miller, V. D. (in press). Interviewer and applicant questioning behavior in employment interviews. *Management Communication Quarterly.*

McComb, K. B., & Jablin, F. M. (1984). Verbal correlates of interviewer empathic listening and employment interview outcomes. *Communication Monographs, 51,* 353–371.

Ragan, S. L. (1983). A conversational analysis of alignment talk in job interviews. In R. Bostrom (Ed.), *Communication yearbook 7* (pp. 502–516). Newbury Park, CA: Sage.

Rynes, S. L., & Boudreau, J. W. (1986). College recruiting in large organizations: Practice, evaluation, and research implications. *Personnel Psychology, 39,* 729–757.

Shaw, M. R. (1983). Taken-for-granted assumptions of applicants in simulated selection interviews. *Western Journal of Speech Communication, 47,* 138–156.

Tengler, C. D., & Jablin, F. M. (1983). Effects of question type, orientation and sequencing in the employment screening interview. *Communication Monographs, 50,* 243–263.

Kathleen Calender
BBA/Marketing
May 1988

<u>PRESENT ADDRESS</u>

906 E. 11th Street, #A701
Longhorn, Texas 78745

<u>PERMANENT ADDRESS</u>

5721 Harpers Ferry Lane
Chomedey, Alabama 35312

<u>CAREER OBJECTIVE</u>:

An entry level position in the field of marketing with opportunities for advancement.

<u>EDUCATION</u>

University of Southwest at Longhorn, 1986-1988   Major: Marketing, GPA: 3.5/4.0
University of Southeast at Marshall, 1984-86   Major: Social Work, GPA: 3.67/4.0
James Madison High School, Chomedey, Alabama, 1980-1984

<u>RELEVANT EMPLOYMENT EXPERIENCE</u>:

August 1987 to present	Collegiate advisor to 155 members of recolonized chapter of Alpha Beta Sorority
June 1986 to August 1986	Clerical/Office Work, Beverly Products, Inc. Maintained filing system, prepared sales reports, performed general office duties.
June 1985 to December 1985	Salesperson, The Clothiers of Marshall, Alabama Learned to relate to and assist a wide variety of people.
October 1982 to March 1984	Salesperson, Lavals of Chomedey, Alabama Learned various areas of retailing--selling, inventory, stocking.

<u>HONORS AND ACTIVITIES</u>:

The National Dean's List, 1987
Member, American Marketing Association
Member, Student Union, Special Events Committee, 1986-1987
    Organized student campus functions and special events
Member, The University of Southwest Sailing Team
Member, Alpha Phi Beta Women's Honorary Society
Dean's List, five quarters, 1984-1986
Executive Council Member, Alpha Beta Sorority, 1985-1986
    Also Chapter Editor and Assistant Rush Chairman
Volunteer, Recording for the Blind, 1986-1987
Athletic Interests Include: tennis, sailing, jogging, and golf

<u>LOCATION PREFERENCE</u>:   Texas, Southwest, Open

REFERENCES FURNISHED UPON REQUEST

FIGURE 1.1.

William P. Frederics
BBA/Marketing
May, 1988

PRESENT ADDRESS   PERMANENT ADDRESS

6023 Canon, #321   7162 Melville Cove
Longhorn, Texas 78702   Gertrudis Texas 78920
(599) 324-6846   (997) 468-5235

CAREER OBJECTIVE:

Marketing/sales, retail buying, or advertising position with advancement opportunities.

EDUCATION:

University of Southwest at Longhorn, 1984-1988   Major: Marketing
Gertrudis College, Gertrudis, Texas   Summer of 1985
Carter High School, Gertrudis, Texas   1980-1984

EMPLOYMENT:

December 1987 &   Took orders from retailers, delivered beer, and set up displays for the Prairie Beer
    Summer 1987   Distributorship in Gertrudis

Summer 1986   Assistant manager, lifeguard, and swimming instructor at Edward Deep Pool in
        1985   Gertrudis
        1984

May 1983-   Waiter/bus help at the Silverspoon Restaurant in Gertrudis
    May 1984

ACTIVITIES:

Intrafraternity Council at The University of Southwest
Longhorn Catholic Church Young Adult Group; Coordinator
Phi Delta Epsilon Fraternity
Young Republicans at The University of the Southwest
High School-Student Council, Key Club, and Golf Team

PERCENT OF COLLEGE EARNED:

50%

PERSONAL DATA:

            Date of Birth: July 22, 1966
        Marital Status: Single
    Location Preference: Southwest, Open

References Available Upon Request

FIGURE 1.2

CHAPTER 2

A Tale of Two Careers

VERNON D. MILLER
The University of Wisconsin–Milwaukee

FREDRIC M. JABLIN
The University of Texas at Austin

INTRODUCTION

Organizational assimilation refers to those ongoing behavioral and cognitive processes by which individuals join and become integrated into organizations. In general, the assimilation process consists of both explicit and implicit attempts by organizations to influence their employees (socialization), and corresponding attempts by employees to influence their organizations (individualization). In many respects these two reciprocal processes (employee individualization and organizational socialization) characterize what is frequently referred to as organizational "role making." Organizational entry can be a precarious venture. Whereas some individuals have little difficulty adjusting and learning their new roles, others have great difficulty. Some new employees never quite "learn the ropes" and leave or are fired. However, the seeds for the ease/difficulty of entry may be sown long before a new employee's first day of work.

The first stage of organizational assimilation is vocational socialization. In this stage numerous factors (e.g., family, educational experience, part-time work, peers, media) influence individuals' expectations about the nature of work and communication in their future vocation. The second stage, anticipatory socialization, describes the degree to which individuals are prepared to occupy organizational positions, and involves the process of organizational choice (i.e., interviewing) and preparation for entry. The third stage, encounter, occurs in the initial weeks or months of an individual's employment. Encounter can be very stressful, and new employees can experience "role shock" if their expectations are incongruous with the reality of their work environment. Conversely, newcomers may

49

experience "role surprise" if their expectations are relatively accurate, and have more success at making sense of their new environment. In the final stage, metamorphosis, employees typically initiate attempts to individualize their roles to suit their needs and desires better. Employees continually attempt to modify others' (especially their supervisor's) expectations of their role's authority, rights, and privileges.

In turn, supervisors and coworkers often attempt to influence newcomers' attitudes and behaviors through the use of various socialization tactics. For instance, investiture processes involve the positive reinforcement of recruits' skills, values, and attitudes while divestiture processes attempt to strip individualistic characteristics away from them. Individuals can be involved in learning experiences common to all members of a group (collective socialization) or they can experience unique, individualistic learning (individual socialization). If a new employee knows the definite timetable attached to indoctrination periods, he or she has experienced "fixed socialization tactics." Variable tactics leave the recruit with few clues as to how long certain periods will take.

Organizational members are to some degree always adjusting their roles in keeping with their needs and the expectations of others. Organizations are constantly making incremental shifts in strategy that have profound effects upon the configuration of roles and assignments. One way to express these changes over time is embodied in the metaphor of the organizational life cycle. The life cycle portrays the properties and structural characteristics of organizations across various growth stages: birth (entrepreneurial), collectivity, formalization and control, elaboration of structure, and decline into death. Though the metaphor is imprecise (some organizations never survive beyond birth; others may never die), the categorization can be useful in explaining pressures for, as well as forces of resistance to, change. As such, the following case study portrays two new employees throughout the assimilation process in a growing and changing organization.

All-American Computer Corporation (AACC) is a publicly held computer manufacturing and sales company employing approximately 3,500 people around the world. Founded in 1952, AACC grew slowly from 12 employees and one product line to 750 employees and three product lines by 1976. From 1977 to 1985, AACC tripled its workforce, added two additional product lines, and opened manufacturing plants and sales offices in Central Europe and Southeast Asia. In late 1985, the Board of Directors hired a new CEO and authorized him to make sweeping changes to increase AACC's ability to compete in the mid-size business computer market. As part of a planned expansion, the new CEO directed the marketing and sales division to double its staff and the engineering division to increase its size by one-third. These actions led in part to the hiring of the two recruits whose cases follow.

DALE ZUZICK (Dallas, Texas)

Vocational Socialization

Growing up in a small town in Ohio, Dale Zuzick had a number of different part-time work experiences. During high school, he stocked and delivered merchandise for one of the town's grocery stores, served as a veterinarian's assistant, and worked as a lifeguard at the town pool. Dale remained fairly ambivalent, however, about his choice of a career until his freshman year at Midwestern State University. While living at home and commuting to classes, he often received career advice from others (e.g., managers, depositors) at his job as a teller and then as an assistant loan officer in one of the local banks. As most of this advice touted experience in accounting as the inside track to a successful business career, Dale chose accounting as his college major.

By the end of his sophomore year, however, Dale realized that he was not cut out to be an accountant. Working with numbers all day was too impersonal and the steady routine of an accounting job was too boring; it required a special sort of person. Dale's outgoing personality and distaste for routines just didn't fit the requirements of the accounting profession. Since a marketing major was offered in the business school, had the same prerequisite courses as accounting, and would allow him to make a career out of talking with people, he felt that a change in his course of study was in order.

Working in the purchasing department for a nearby USA Automotive plant for pay and college credit during the next two summers, Dale knew that he had made the right decision in changing majors. He liked the interaction with clients and the variation in assignments that his job offered. He felt at ease with his work—ordering small purchases and verifying the contractual details of larger purchase orders. Yet, USA's workforce was so large that his contributions seemed insignificant to the company's success. In addition, his supervisor, as well as coworkers, appeared to resort to fighting their way over other people in order to be noticed by their respective managers. He lost count of the times he observed full-time employees criticizing other workers and ingratiating themselves before their supervisor in order to get ahead. Thus, while his experiences at USA made him feel confident about his choice of career directions, he also learned that he did not enjoy working in a backstabbing organizational climate.

During his senior year, Dale interviewed at the university placement center and received job offers from IBM, Lanier, and Wrangler Jeans, which he all turned down. As he told his parents, these companies were just too large, and he was afraid of being lost in the shuffle. So, while most of his friends had jobs lined up, he faced graduating in May without a job even though he had a B+ grade average and a marketing degree from a prestigious business school. However, he was not worried. After reading an article in *Business Week* a few days before graduation about the booming job market in Dallas, Texas, he decided to move south and look for a marketing job in just the right company.

In Dallas, Dale again had difficulty finding his ideal company. After scouring the Dallas want ads, he mailed out 45 resumes, but received only 9 interviews. These screening interviews resulted in one of two outcomes: Either Dale felt a company did not meet his criteria as an employer, or he did not match the company's selection requirements. In the meantime, Dale landed a temporary job as a waiter and was pleasantly surprised by how much fun he had working with others at the restaurant. For the first time on a job, he developed close friendships with his coworkers and managers. Often they would go out on the town together after work or meet socially as a group.

As the new year began, however, Dale grew bored with taking orders and serving meals at the restaurant. He saw his dream of working in a marketing department quickly fading away. He also grew more irritated each time a new restaurant employee asked in an astonished manner, "If you've got a marketing degree, *why* are you *still* waiting tables?" By the first of March, his dormant job hunt recommenced with the mailing of resumes to prospective employers, but met with even less success than before.

Anticipatory Organizational Socialization

After working in the restaurant over a year, Dale overheard a waitress talking about a friend who wanted to hire salespersons for All-American Computer Corporation. Her description of her friend's job as a regional sales manager and what she was able to tell Dale of the job sounded fascinating. When he mentioned his interest in the job, the waitress volunteered to pick up Dale's resume and deliver it to her friend at AACC. She telephoned late the next night. Her friend would see him on Wednesday at AACC's facility for a job interview.

When Dale walked in, the interviewer greeted him. "Welcome Dale. Karen has told me a lot about you. It's good to meet you," Bill Kramer began. Dale's preinterview apprehensions lessened as their conversation centered on mutual friends. Dale estimated Bill Kramer to be in his early 40s and fairly successful judging from his clothing and manner of conducting himself. After a period of time, Bill pulled out Dale's resume and casually began asking questions about his background, interests, and previous jobs. Eventually, Bill described the sales position and gave Dale the opportunity to discuss why he thought he would be successful at AACC. This was the part of the interview that worried Dale most. He was afraid that he did not have the necessary sales experience, so he tried to give examples of his ability to adapt to customers and win their favor by meeting their needs. From there, Bill's questions mostly focused on the type of supervision Dale liked and didn't like.

After about 45 minutes, they went on a tour of the buildings and the different departments. During their walk, Dale asked Bill how he spent most of his day and discovered that Bill had been responsible for the very sales area Dale might be hired to cover. Subsequently, Dale began asking in-depth questions about AACC's products, customers' receptivity, and how salespersons were rewarded. By the end of the tour, he had met several members of the sales staff and been given brochures about AACC's products. As they approached the front door, Dale could tell the interview was ending. He figured Bill knew what it took to sell the product and that the purpose of the interview was to determine whether Dale had the personality and ability to be successful in selling the product. Dale hoped that he was coming across as having those necessary qualities, whatever they were.

When Dale left the interview he felt excited. AACC met many of his organization requirements. He was looking for a medium-sized company in which he would not have to wait years for an opportunity to advance. With AACC, he would begin as the sales representative for the entire Dallas–Fort Worth area; he would not be competing with other salespeople within a small geographical area. The next step up would be to regional manager for a large part of the nation.

Even more important, on the basis of what Bill had explained, Dale figured he could set his own work schedule (e.g., work 7 days a week if he wanted to make a lot of money or, if he wanted some extra time to himself, work only a couple of days a week) as long as he accomplished the goals that were established for his sales area. The company would provide him with life insurance, health coverage, stock sharing, and prestige. In short, he could be his own boss and still enjoy the benefits of working for someone else. There was only one problem: What did he know about selling computer systems? What did he know about selling anything? Nonetheless, he decided that he could not afford to pass up a job if one was offered. As a consequence, he was thrilled when a secretary called to schedule a Friday interview for Dale with the person in charge of sales in the United States and Canada.

This time, the atmosphere of the interview was formal and businesslike. The first 25 minutes centered on Dale's job at the restaurant, why he was suddenly eager to leave that job, and why he had not obtained a job in marketing for a year. The interviewer inquired about Dale's work ethic, why Dale thought he was qualified to work for AACC, and how he would go about making a sale. The rest of the time was spent talking about competitive leisure sports. (Dale suspected that the interviewer was trying to measure his level of competitiveness. Yet, this line of inquiry did not bother him; he was just relieved to be off the restaurant topic.) The interview ended abruptly after 45 minutes following a brief review of AACC's benefits and expectations related to the sales job for which Dale had applied. Dale was told to expect to hear from them within a week.

Four days later, Dale received a letter offering him a sales job with AACC. Dale telephoned his acceptance and made plans to begin work in a week's time.

Entry

Going to work that first day, Dale was as apprehensive as a new kid on the block. This was his first "real" job in his chosen field, and he was concerned that he actually knew little about how to sell AACC's products. Moreover, while they told him he would be trained, he did not know how long the training was to last, who would be training him, or even how he would be trained. He did not have to wait long to find out. When he arrived at work, Bill Kramer quickly showed Dale to his office and introduced him to the members of the sales staff he had not yet met. Bill and Dale then climbed into Bill's car and set out on the day's sales calls.

Driving out of the parking lot, Bill described their day's schedule. "Dale," began Bill, "I just want you to watch me. I'll brief you on the customers we'll see, but observe the different ways I sell our products. Later this afternoon, we'll see how well you paid attention when we talk about the principles behind my approaches." Dale was also told to *ask* when he had a question. The only thing wrong with a question, as far as AACC was concerned, was when it was not asked. His boss even told a couple of stories about situations in which he felt awkward about asking questions, but in each context he demonstrated how important it was that he did make inquiries. Dale kept these stories in mind. While his boss's questions seemed quite logical, Dale was still concerned that he would end up asking dumb questions.

Dale's first day on the job was typical of his schedule for the next 3 weeks. He and Bill would see an old customer, talk about the call, visit a prospective client, talk about it, and then repeat the cycle. Bill demonstrated how he cultivated old accounts for new business and the different ways to find new accounts. Dale learned how to dress (the AACC uniform consisted of blue or gray suits with solid colored button-down shirts), conduct himself in the office (e.g., when to be at work in the morning, how long to take for lunch), make a sales presentation the "AACC way," complete order forms, and cultivate friendships with clients. In short, his boss was chiseling him into the AACC mold.

Bill initiated most of their discussions and was especially helpful in explaining the events and activities Dale observed. His boss also shared with him what the company objectives were for the rest of the year, how he would be evaluated, how people moved up, and what lateral-move options he would have in the coming year. In turn, Dale usually did not beat around the bush when asking questions. For instance, when Bill seemed to deviate from his normal sales routine, Dale would ask specific, straight-to-the-point questions. Whenever Dale would "lead" in a presentation to a prospective customer, he felt free to ask later how he did and how he could improve. While Dale always found his boss easy to approach and willing to listen to his questions, there were some questions that Dale wanted answered but did not want to ask his boss. For example, while Bill said that work started at 9 A.M., often he did not come into the office until 10 A.M. Was 9:00 the rule or just an approximate starting time? Since Dale did not really know any coworkers beyond their names at that point (he was spending all of his time with his boss), he did not feel comfortable asking them questions. There were also times when Dale would ask a question in such a way that it would not seem like a question. Once when he wanted to find out how long his training period would last, he made references to how how long it usually took someone to catch on to the AACC sales method and remarked about the amount of time Bill was spending training him. Unfortunately, Dale did not find that this indirect approach generated much useful information.

On Monday morning of the fourth week, Dale sat down in Bill's office and set sales goals for himself for the next 6 months. He was now on his own. He spent the better part of his first day on his own dropping in on regular customers to "grease the wheels" and to see if there was anything they needed. The next morning he gathered up his courage and copied his boss's cycle of "old customer, new customer." By the end of the week, two significant events had occurred. First, he had success in getting orders from two regular customers and three new ones. (By then his boss was out of town on business, but Dale called him and told him the news. His boss was very pleased and told him to go celebrate.) These successes made Dale more confident and enabled him to try a few new things in his sales pitch to suit his personality better. Second, he felt somewhat ill on Friday morning of that week and decided to do paper work in the office rather than make sales calls. However, after a short time in the office, several of the sales staff noticed his presence and invited him to lunch. Up to this point, Dale hardly knew any of the sales staff. In part, he had consciously avoided taking the initiative to get to know them because he still felt unsure of his abilities. They were successful at selling while he had yet to prove himself. However, emboldened by his successes in the last few days he felt ready to meet them. Over lunch, he found them to be friendly and quite talkative about AACC, the office, and other salespersons. They started to give advice about breaking into sales. He even got them to talk about their best and worst sales experiences. Driving around after lunch, he reasoned that he was off to a pretty good start. Judging by what others had said, he felt that he had a good idea of what was expected of him and that he was dividing his time at work properly.

When his boss returned to town, Dale found himself only occasionally checking in with Bill Kramer and spending more of his time talking with his coworkers. Coming into the office and saying hello to friendly faces and joining them for lunch (all but three of the office's 13 sales staff were "regulars"), Dale began to consider himself "one of the guys." His AACC experience was so different from his job at USA where the established employees kept to themselves and everyone went home at 5 P.M. In contrast, the sales staff at AACC routinely walked back and forth between each other's and the regional manager's offices asking questions or sharing the latest news. They also went together to the Texas Cowboys' and Southwest Rangers' games; in these contexts, work issues were not usually discussed.

Lunch was the major meeting ground for sharing information. If they did not go out, they would eat in the company cafeteria. They typically talked about what was going on in the company (e.g., discussing items in the corporate magazine or on the computer bulletin board that day, swapping "insider" information) and shared how they were doing in their sales and social lives. Though still close to his boss, Dale generally asked his coworkers about routine, day-to-day operations instead of bothering Bill. Further, when he asked work-related questions, they never chastized him or said, "Well, you should know this by now."

After 4 months on the job, AACC sent Dale to their corporate headquarters on the West Coast for a 2-week orientation and training program. Along with about 30 other new employees, he reviewed the company policy and benefit manuals, dined with some of AACC's top executives, and was given a tour of relatively "sensitive" product research areas. Dale could not believe how big yet personable AACC was. By his 9th month, Dale's self-image was changing. An old college roommate, when he visited Dale, could not believe the transformation. Before he graduated from Midwestern State, Dale talked negatively about companies like AACC. Now, Dale was a living advertisement. He talked up the company to anyone who would listen. Their success was his success; their values were his values. Dale saw himself as a representative of AACC to the public.

Metamorphosis

When Dale arrived at AACC, they were in the midst of expanding their marketing and sales efforts. While they had great success in most areas (posting a 47% increase in total sales over the previous year), corporate headquarters began to have trouble keeping track of decisions and emphases at lower hierarchical levels. AACC felt that they had become too decentralized in many areas, marketing and sales being examples. Subsequently, a major reorganization was implemented that added hierarchical levels to the organization. For the Dallas branch of AACC, the reorganization meant that Bill Kramer was promoted to a higher rank and two new supervisors were brought in under Bill to coordinate the sales staff of the Dallas office. In addition, the company altered the commission system for its sales personnel, making the upper limits of their salary package more difficult to obtain. These changes coincided with Dale's need to redefine some elements of his job.

The restructuring introduced in the Dallas office upset Dale. While he could tolerate the prospect that his earnings for his second year at AACC would be a little more difficult to achieve, Dale disliked his new supervisor, Ken Dolman. Ken tended to antagonize Dale and the other six sales staff under his charge. Unlike his previous boss, Ken was not concerned with integrating into the social network and seemed aloof. Dale also sensed that his new boss did not have much respect for his staff's past sales and productivity levels. They would have to prove themselves all over again.

To make things worse, Dale's new boss acted as if he were keeping tabs on their activities. They began to have to document all their phone calls and travel expenses. Whereas Bill's office had been open to the sales staff to stop by at any time, Ken's secretary made appointments for them or wrote down their questions. New paperwork procedures were introduced and consumed about an hour of their time daily. Instead of receiving an occasional memo through the computer mail, Dale began to receive three or four memos a day from top management about issues that previously had been handled by walking across the hall and talking with managers. With the sales staff traveling more, Dale began to spend more time on the computer reading the mail and checking the bulletin board to learn about the latest developments within the company and, specifically, within his best-selling product lines. If he had a question, he would wait and ask a coworker rather than approach his boss; he did not want to risk giving his boss a reason for thinking badly of him.

With the recent voluntary transfers of three of the "regulars," Dale is beginning to wonder if he should leave also. He is not looking forward to his 18-month evaluation. Dale set his goals with Bill, but he is going to be evaluated by Ken who is unlikely to agree with Dale's self-assessment. When Bill Kramer was still his boss, Dale had planned to talk to him about taking on more responsibility within the sales group. Ken's arrival, however, changed those plans. Dale is now thinking that he would be satisfied with a little more respect from Ken and a return to the open climate that once pervaded the office.

BOB HOFFMAN (Denver, Colorado)

Vocational Socialization

To hear Bob Hoffman tell it, he was raised to become an engineer. As a youngster, Bob was regularly brought to visit his grandfather's and father's engineering offices and encouraged to play with their drawing instruments and drafting boards. He was even given his own miniature drafting table to play with at home. Moreover, the conversation at family gatherings often drifted to engineering stories or problems. Due in part to this exposure, Bob would generally take charge of "engineering" the fortifications, giving instructions and measuring progress, whenever he and his friends built forts in their backyards.

His parents' attitudes toward work also shaped his views. For instance, Bob's mother was a premier high school math teacher, so consequently Bob frequently observed his family change their routines to accommodate each parent's work projects. He assumed that everyone's parents worked late into the evenings because he often heard his parents discussing how they "burned the midnight oil" in order to finish a project.

By his 15th birthday, Bob made two decisions that greatly shaped his career plans. First, he decided to take engineering preparatory classes while in high school. He found the classes to be easy to master and enjoyable. By the time Bob went to college, he had the equivalent of 2 years worth of college-level mechanical engineering courses. Second, he decided that he wanted to work for AACC. Most of his father's friends were in mechanical engineering and many worked for AACC, which was headquartered in his home town. From his father's friends, he heard stories about the projects they were working on, how impasses were resolved, and how the company took care of its employees. In addition, the townspeople looked on AACC with pride. They were intrigued by AACC's products and by the "computerese" AACC's employees talked.

During his sophomore year at West Coast University, Bob had his first work experience through a university and industry cooperative program. He applied to and was thrilled when he was accepted into AACC's coop program. Further, due to his advanced academic standing in engineering courses and high grade-point average (and, possibly, his connections), Bob was selected as one of six "elite" interns to participate in a special job/department rotation program.

Through his sophomore and junior years, he learned the ins and outs of the workings of four different AACC departments. Meeting once a week with the other interns, Bob was able to discuss his experiences and receive feedback about his own activities. In addition, a manager assigned to meet with these interns evaluated and provided feedback on their memos and proposals. (They were expected to write about what they observed and, when feasible, propose changes in current operations or project designs.) For Bob, it was exciting to know that his observations and/or suggestions were benefitting on-going projects.

At the end of his 2-year coop with AACC, Bob wrote a positive evaluation of his experiences. Though he valued the technical expertise he gained, he most appreciated learning how a company should treat its employees. For instance, while his group of interns were called "boy wonders" (or "girl wonders," for female students) by the employees, they were nonetheless treated with respect and never "talked down to" by full-time employees. Although it had been difficult to adjust to working in a new department every 6 months, Bob felt that these experiences had provided him with a good idea of how AACC worked and what it took to get ahead in the company.

Anticipatory Organizational Socialization

When the major computer firms interviewed on campus in the spring semester of his senior year, Bob decided to see all of them and not take any chances on getting a job. While AACC was his only real consideration and he felt very confident about the probability of receiving a job offer from them, he had heard their new CEO was making a lot of changes. Since AACC would be the last of the computer firms to come to campus, he set out to enjoy interviewing with the various firms and see what would happen.

In the end, Bob received four second-interview offers out of a possible eight. He even went on two second interviews with AACC's direct competitors (much to the chagrin of his parents) and received job offers from both of them. However, he ultimately accepted AACC's offer because it seemed that they really wanted him to work there. In his first interview with AACC, the representative made a big deal over his coop experience, described two or three projects in which he might work, indicated who his departmental supervisors might be, and discussed AACC's growth and how someone with Bob's background might grow along with the company. The interviewer also listened carefully to Bob's answers to questions, asked lots of open-ended questions, and was not in a hurry to end the interview. Moreover, the interviewer talked about his own experiences at AACC and even mentioned working with some of the people Bob knew. At the conclusion of their 35-minute interview, Bob was excited. He felt that his dream about working for AACC might be coming true.

A few days later AACC invited Bob to come to the site where, if hired, he would be working. They flew him to Denver, Colorado over his spring break and paid for his room at the Five Star Hotel. Bob could not believe the company was paying his way for 5 days, even though he was only scheduled to visit the Denver facilities for 2 of them. AACC even rented him a car, provided him with a per diem, and gave him a list of the best night spots in town to visit.

On Tuesday and Wednesday, he met with several senior associates who gave him a tour of their buildings or areas, introduced him to various people, and spent about 50 minutes each formally inquiring about his computer and engineering knowledge. For instance, after explaining the situation of a hypothetical client with a real piece of AACC's equipment, they asked him what alternatives were available in implementing the client's desired computer uses, how best to install each alternative, and what the advantages and disadvantages of each alternative were. Although Bob thought these interviews were "brutal" (he was asked some questions that were beyond him), he reasoned that perhaps it was to be expected since he had been part of the "boy wonder" group at headquarters. It was clear that Bob had done fine in answering questions since, on his last afternoon at the facility, one of the interviewers let him know that within 2 weeks he would be receiving a job offer in the mail. To Bob's amazement, the interviewer asked whether Bob would be interested in working in his department of "applied systems." Responding affirmatively, Bob hurried off to call his parents and best friends in California.

En route home, Bob realized that he had not met anyone in his future work group. He did not even know his supervisor's name. From what the first interviewer told him, Bob decided not to let it bother him. He assumed that he would be working on the same sort of projects he had been exposed to in school and in his coop experiences. He also expected his supervisor to be similar to those in the coop program where employees were respected for their opinions, questions were encouraged, workers were treated like adults, and so on. In light of his experiences in Denver, he reasoned that AACC must have big plans for him.

During the next 3 months, Bob occasionally talked with his father's friends who worked at AACC and twice dropped by corporate headquarters to see the manager who coordinated his coop group. He was informed that four of his fellow interns had taken jobs in various positions within AACC. While these visits provided him with little new information about his job or AACC, he liked renewing old contacts and was reaffirmed in his impressions of AACC as a quality organization.

Entry

On the second Monday in July, Bob showed up at the personnel office at 8:30 a.m., 30 minutes early. A personnel staff member welcomed him to AACC and gave him a packet of materials and forms that he needed to read and complete, a set of keys to the building and his office, as well as directions to his office. They told Bob that his supervisor, Sam Hickson, knew he was arriving today and that he should stop by and check in with him. Bob was also instructed to be in the personnel conference room at 11:30 for lunch and the beginning of his orientation.

In room B12403, Bob found a man in his early 50s, dressed in AACC's "uniform," feverishly packing his briefcase and shuffling through papers on his desk. Making sure he was in the right office, Bob reached out his right hand and introduced himself. Startled, his new boss looked up, shook Bob's hand, and explained as he went back to sorting through papers, "They told me you'd be here today, but I didn't think I would get a chance to meet you before I left. My plane leaves for Germany in 2 hours." In the next few minutes, his boss briefly explained the purpose and length of his trip, and told Bob to get to know the others after the orientation programs were finished. Bob said, "No problem. I'll find out from the other team members how I can assist in their projects."

"Team?" Sam Hickson replied, "What team? Our work is not done by teams around here. Let me see your file again." Pulling Bob's file from a cabinet behind him, his boss mumbled as he glanced through it. "Yeah, the northern California branch. Hmmm. A 'boy wonder' . . . graduated second in the engineering school at West Coast. . . ." Displaying irritation, Sam quickly went through his standard review of department policies and procedures. Closing his briefcase and walking out of his office toward the exit, he concluded by saying that AACC had an "open door" policy and that Bob should feel free to come in and ask questions any time. As his boss turned and walked down the hall, Bob felt reservations about ever asking his boss for anything. Making his way to his office, he shrugged Sam's behavior off as pretravel jitters and began flipping through his personnel packet.

After completing the necessary forms and glancing at the other materials in his personnel packet, Bob went looking for others who might be in his work group. At the third office, he found someone working at a desk. After Bob introduced himself and explained that he was looking for others who worked under Sam Hickson, Pat DeBernardi put down his pen and computer print-outs and invited Bob to sit down and chat. Discovering that Pat was a member of his work group, Bob said he was new to AACC and was just trying to get familiar with the surroundings and the work. (He did not mention that he had been at AACC on the West Coast and that he had family friends who worked at AACC headquarters. He thought it best to hold off on the "boy wonder" experience until he knew how Pat would react.)

What Pat told Bob was a little disconcerting; things were quite different from what he expected. Evidently, most work was completed independently of other group members. Pat said Bob would eventually be given an assignment and a list of names of people throughout the organization (usually located somewhere in the Denver office) who would be working on the project. One person would develop the program. Another would install it. Someone else would write the documentation. A fourth person would see that the other persons did their job correctly and make sure the customer was satisfied during implementation and afterward. Until he had the "lead" role, Bob would probably work on portions of the first three tasks.

Most of the people in their work group had been with AACC for 15–20 years. Since Bob was the first "rookie" he knew to be placed in this setting (most persons had 2–3 years experience in the company before being placed in the applied division), Pat figured top management must have thought highly of Bob's credentials. Bob shrugged at the compliment and thanked Pat for his time. As Bob was leaving, Pat suggested that Bob join him for lunch the next day when the others in the work group would be back in the office.

Orientation began with the two personnel staffers and 10 new or newly transferred employees (every level of the hierarchy seemed to be represented from a new custodian to a transferred senior associate) eating chicken and fruit salads brought from the cafeteria. After everyone was introduced, the newcomers were presented with the basic tenets of the company's philosophy (i.e., respect for the "individual"; any question can be answered within three phone calls; the importance of quality workmanship; and an "open door" policy all the way up to the chief executive), instructed on how to use the company's electronic mail system, and introduced to the first of four sections of the firm's policy handbook. The next day, they reviewed the other three sections of the policy handbook, and the following day they received a short course on company benefits and employee options.

Tuesday's meeting over lunch with the other members of his work group was helpful to Bob in several ways. First, it gave him a needed break from the boring policy handbook review as well as something to think about during the rest of the sessions. Second, several work-group members went out of their way to make Bob feel at home and invited him to drop by their offices and visit any time. They said not to worry about feeling lost; everyone in the applied section at the Denver office had experienced that. They would be glad to answer any of his questions. Third, he had a chance to listen to the group share "insider" talk. While they seemed at ease in talking with each other, Bob inferred from their comments that they felt freer than usual to state their opinions since Sam was not around to drop in and/or monitor their conversations.

Bob heard that Sam was an ex-Air Force colonel who apparently had strong opinions about how things should be run. To Sam's credit, however, he evidently was willing to listen to others' opinions and act on them. Yet, it bothered some (and Bob as he listened) that Sam played favorites and tended to provide directive supervision in areas where he was lacking in expertise. To make matters worse, Bob thought he heard an aside that engineering was not Sam's strong suit. Bob made a mental note to ask someone later in private about this comment.

Bob soon uncovered other sources of information as well. During the next couple of days, Bob began to notice billboards set up in different locations throughout AACC's facilities. In contrast to billboards at headquarters and at West Coast U, which only had official announcements, these billboards were mostly filled with employees' comments. They contained a great deal of dry, engineering humor and were fun to read. The quarterly corporate magazine was also interesting to read, but for different reasons. Arriving in his apartment mailbox, the magazine provided a corporation-wide view of the organization. It was generally filled with about a dozen interesting articles highlighting different individuals' accomplishments and the corporation's performance with regard to production goals and stock exchange yields.

For 2 weeks, Bob considered himself an outsider. Although he had experience in the field and followed a couple of people around on their assignments, he found that "meshing in" was difficult. It did not help that he did not have a formal assignment. Further, Bob did not want to ask too many questions lest his new colleagues become tired of him. However, he got to know his coworkers pretty well during this time and learned how they got things done, sometimes with and sometimes in spite of their boss. It was not until his supervisor returned and he was given a specific assignment (albeit small) that Bob felt he was officially a part of the company. Along with his assignment, Bob's supervisor set 6-month work goals for him to achieve.

Before starting work in Denver, Bob expected his relationship with Sam to be like those with his other supervisory relationships (i.e., warm and friendly, with lots of encouragement and opportunities for the exchange of ideas). Unfortunately, this was not the case. Bob felt that his extra-hard work on projects went unnoticed by Sam. The first time he tried to suggest a new engineering idea to his boss, it was like talking to a stone-wall. Since Sam never seemed to have time to talk about engineering matters with him, Bob wondered whether he intimidated Sam because he knew so much more about engineering. In addition, Bob began to see the weaknesses in Sam that his coworkers warned him about.

Bob was also bothered by two other facets of his supervisor's behavior. As Bob proved himself and was given tougher assignments, he needed more technical information about several of AACC's products. Since this information was somewhat "sensitive" (AACC did not want the data to make their way to competitors), the information ordinarily needed to be requested by a supervisor. Although his boss always said he would have the information to him in a few days, Bob never received any of the data he requested. Moreover, Sam objected to being asked about the materials a second time. As a consequence, Bob soon stopped "bothering" Sam with requests for information. Bob was also perturbed at Sam's version of the "open door" policy; what was said in confidence became public knowledge. For instance, Sam told Bob in confidence that his apparel was not suitable for AACC. Specifically, Sam objected to Bob's practice of not wearing socks with his top-siders. Bob decided to not tell anyone about the incident, but was surprised when, 2 days later, a coworker asked whether it were true that nonsales personnel at headquarters frequently came to work in the summertime in t-shirts, blue jeans, and sandals. Shortly after this incident, Bob's appearance around the office became more casual and less businesslike. He began trying to get on Sam's nerves to see how he would react.

For Bob, the final straw came at his 6-month evaluation. While he thought that he had been doing excellent work because he had rated increasingly tougher assignments and received the verbal approval and praise of those with whom he worked, his supervisor seemed to identify critical weaknesses in everything he had done. There were even flaws in his first couple of assignments, although Sam had said nothing when Bob had asked for performance feedback. Bob could not believe he received only an "average" evaluation and a recommendation that his goals for the next 6 months stay at the same level. Bob no longer felt he knew what was expected of him or even what it took to please his supervisor. He decided it was futile to ask his coworkers about it. The next day Bob began inquiring into job openings in other departments. Communicating with contacts he had made through the company's electronic mail system, he stated that he felt stifled in his present work and was looking for something more challenging. In addition, he listed as references several persons from different departments with whom he had worked.

In talking (through the electronic mail) with his "boy/girl wonder" cohorts, he discovered that others had been "lured" by their college representatives into believing their work would be more challenging and autonomous than it turned out to be. Comparing entry experiences, Bob also discovered that the others had undergone a set of training experiences that were specifically designed to give newcomers a thorough set of job-related skills. Bob wondered why he had not received similar training.

Within a month, Bob transferred to another department within the Denver facility. Since his old supervisor was angry that Bob had "transferred out from under him," Bob approached his new supervisor, Richard Brill, cautiously. Although he had worked on a project with Richard through the electronic mail, Bob worried that he might be carrying a reputation with him. Consequently, he was very conscious of his behavior (even the way he dressed). At the same time, however, he also made an effort to establish a relationship with his supervisor that was more open than the one he had experienced with Sam. When he wanted performance feedback, he told

Richard that he had done a poor job of picking up his last supervisor's expectations and wondered if Richard might tell him how he was doing so far. He also actively sought the opinions of coworkers who might be acquainted with his supervisor's feelings about his performance.

Metamorphosis

After 4 months in his present job and more experience interacting with customers, Bob began to see the value of conveying a positive image to AACC's customers. The importance of image was reinforced when he became friends with several marketing and sales representatives through the company's tennis tournaments. Their fairly stringent social and work codes (covering what you should wear, the kind of car you should drive, and what restaurants you should frequent) began to influence him as he developed friendships with them. Soon Bob began to wear socks and come to work more often in a suit and tie.

Following a "superior" rating in his second 6-month review, Bob was given an assignment as a project head. He assigned responsibilities to each work group member and set deadlines for task completion. He also tried to monitor their progress and serve as a resource whenever troubles were encountered. In addition, his manager began directing others to ask Bob all "technical" questions.

About this time, he was also asked to take several departmental newcomers to dinner. When the topic of commitment to AACC arose, Bob thought they would benefit from hearing about his "rebellion" against his first supervisor, which was expressed through his dress and appearance. While he doubted that he would have ever knowingly rebelled against the company, he told them that he now saw that his actions caused potential problems for the corporation. He specifically referred to others' copying his *sans* socks look. They all laughed about how silly it might look to see 45-year-old men in polished loafers and pressed slacks sporting no socks and 3 days worth of facial hair! Subsequently, Bob told the newcomers that the longer he was with the company, the more he appreciated its values.

After a year and a half with AACC, Bob is again faced with the dilemma of leaving his present job for one with more autonomy and pay. This time, another supervisor has sought him out and asked if he would like a new job. However, Bob is concerned. While the job sounds challenging, he is unsure of the supervisory relationship he may encounter. He considers himself fairly lucky now. He has "lucked" into a good supervisor. While his present job is not perfect, he is able to talk about changing the nature of his job with his supervisor. He figures that there is more to a job than just the job description.

CONCLUSION

The experiences of Dale Zuzick and Bob Hoffman reflect a repetitive cycle of role learning, adjustment, and negotiation. To some extent, all individuals throughout their careers find themselves having to perform new roles and to discover and adjust to the expectations of their role set (i.e., their supervisor, coworkers, and subordinates) concerning how their role should be performed. At the same time, there are attempts to modify others' expectations so that the role can be performed in a manner better suited to the role performer. This cycle of discovery and reciprocal influence often takes place in evolving organizational environments in which the nature and pressure of work change in a regular but unpredictable pattern. In sum, this case study only provides a glimpse of the initial segments of two employees' careers. Yet, it is important to note that these newcomers have already encountered experiences that may have a major impact on the way they relate to others in the office (e.g., manner of seeking role-related information). Moreover, their patterns of role-making behaviors reveal strengths and weaknesses that may aid or alternatively constrain their career advancement.

NOTES

1. The story of the two main characters in this case study are derived from field interviews with the subjects. While the events recorded here are generally representative of their experiences, data from three additional interviewed subjects are occasionally utilized in order to present equivalent accounts of the main characters' assimilation experiences.

KEY TERMS

organizational assimilation
realistic job preview
investiture–divestiture socialization tactics
collective–individual socialization tactics
fixed–variable socialization tactics
formal–informal socialization tactics
information-seeking strategies (overt, observe, third party, indirect, testing)

role ambiguity
role conflict
vertical dyadic linkages
role-taking
role-making
individualization
role negotiation
organizational life cycle

DISCUSSION QUESTIONS

1. Describe how Bob and Dale adjusted to their roles during entry *and* metamorphosis. What accounts for differences between these new employees' experiences during entry? During metamorphosis?

2. Although these newcomers joined the same organization, they had a completely different set of experiences. Why?

3. What factors influenced these new employees' expectations about work, AACC, and the manner in which they adjusted to their new roles?

4. Evaluate AACC's efforts at assimilating new employees.

5. What were the major factors contributing to these newcomers' role ambiguity and role conflict? Identify these newcomers' efforts to reduce their levels of role ambiguity and role conflict.

6. Identify and evaluate newcomers' use of information-seeking strategies to develop role clarity.

SUGGESTED READINGS

Jablin, F. M. (1987). Organizational entry, assimilation, and exit. In F. M. Jablin, L. L. Putnam, K. H. Roberts, & L. W. Porter (Eds.), *Handbook of organizational communication: An interdisciplinary perspective* (pp. 679–740). Newbury Park, CA: Sage.

Jones, G. R. (1986). Socialization tactics, self-efficacy, and newcomers' adjustments to organizations. *The Academy of Management Journal, 29,* 262–279.

Miller, V., & Jablin, F. M. (1987). *Newcomers' information seeking behaviors during organizational encounter: A typology and model of the process.* Paper presented at the 73rd Annual Meeting of the Speech Communication Association, Boston.

Quinn, R. E., & Cameron, K. (1983). Organizational life cycles and shifting criteria of effectiveness: Some preliminary evidence. *Management Science, 29,* 33–51.

Van Maanen, J., & Schein, E. H. (1979). Toward a theory of organizational socialization. In B. M. Staw (Ed.), *Research in organizational behavior* (Vol. 1, pp. 209–264). Greenwich, CT: JAI.

PART II

Organizational Culture

CHAPTER 3

Organizational Culture and Counterculture: An Uneasy Symbiosis

JOANNE MARTIN
Stanford University

CAREN SIEHL
Arizona State University

Four sentences capture the essence of much of the recent organizational culture research. First, cultures offer an interpretation of an institution's history that members can use to decipher how they will be expected to behave in the future. Second, cultures can generate commitment to corporate values or management philosophy so that employees feel they are working for something they believe in. Third, cultures serve as organizational control mechanisms, informally approving or prohibiting some patterns of behavior. Finally, there is the possibility, as yet unsupported by conclusive evidence, that some types of organizational cultures are associated with greater productivity and profitability.

Most of this research shares a single set of simplifying assumptions. First, the perspective of the organization's top management is assumed because the functions studied serve to (1) transmit top management's interpretations of the meaning of events throughout the organization, (2) generate commitment to their practices and policies, and (3) help them control behavior in accordance with their objectives. Second, the functions of culture are portrayed as integrative, unifying the diverse elements of an organization. Third, organizational culture is treated as a monolithic phenomenon—one culture to a setting. Finally, many of these studies implicitly assume or explicitly assert that culture can be managed by using direct, intentional actions not unlike those used in other management tasks.

This particular set of simplifying assumptions may blind us to some important aspects of organizational culture. For example, studies of blue-collar workers' practices, such as "hassling" ratebusters, clearly indicate that cultural mechanisms can be used to undermine top-management objectives. Cultures can serve differentiating rather than integrating functions by, for example, expressing conflicts among parts of a society. Instead of being monolithic phenomena, organizational cultures are composed of various interlocking, nested, sometimes conflicting subcultures.

Finally, it is likely that cultural development, like other aspects of organizational functioning, is not as responsive to direct managerial attempts at control as many would like to believe. It may be that cultures cannot be straightforwardly created or managed by individuals. Instead, cultures may simply exist and managers may capitalize on cultural effects they perceive as positive or minimize those perceived as negative. Perhaps the most that can be expected is that a manager can slightly modify the trajectory of a culture, rather than exert major control over the direction of its development.

This article assumes that cultural mechanisms can underline as well as support the objectives of the firm's top management. We argue that in addition to serving integrative functions, cultures can express conflicts and address needs for differentiation among organizational elements. Instead of treating culture as a monolithic phenomenon, we explore a counterculture's uneasy symbiotic relationship with the rest of an organization. Finally, we address the relationship between cultural development and managerial action by asking what a leader does, inadvertently or advertently, that seems to affect the development of a counterculture.

To examine a subculture in some depth, a few conceptual distinctions are needed. Edgar Schein has distinguished three levels of culture: basic assumptions, values or ideology, and artifacts (such as special jargon, stories, rituals, dress, and decor). We would add a fourth category, management practices. These are familiar management tasks, such as training, performance appraisal, allocation of rewards, hiring, and so forth. (Practices may or may not include artifacts. For example, a training program for new employees may be an occasion for telling organizational stories and may conclude with a ceremony.) Artifacts and practices express values, which may also be expressed as a corporate ideology or management philosophy. Underlying those values are even deeper assumptions, which rest at a preconscious level of awareness. Schein argues persuasively that because assumptions are taken for granted, they are difficult to study except through the use of long-term observation and in-depth, clinical interviewing techniques. (See Wilkins, 1983, for a description of such a technique.) Because of the methodological difficulty of studying assumptions, we restrict our attention to artifacts, practices, and values, reserving some tentative speculations about assumptions for the concluding discussion.

Next, a distinction needs to be drawn between an organization's dominant culture and the various subcultures that might coexist with it. A dominant culture expresses, through artifacts, core values that are shared by a majority of the organization's members. At least three types of subcultures are conceivable: enhancing, orthogonal, and countercultural. An enhancing subculture would exist in an organizational enclave in which adherence to the core values of the dominant culture would be more fervent than in the rest of the organization. In an orthogonal subculture, the members would simultaneously accept the core values of the dominant culture and a separate, unconflicting set of values particular to themselves. For example, an accounting division and a research and development (R&D) department may both endorse the values of their firm's dominant culture, while retaining separate sets of values related to their occupational identities, such as "going by the numbers" for the accounting department and "valuing innovation" in the R&D department.

The third type of subculture, a counterculture, is the focus of this article. We propose that some core values of a counterculture should present a direct challenge to the core values of a dominant culture. Thus a dominant culture and a counterculture should exist in an uneasy symbiosis, taking opposite positions on value issues that are critically important to each of them. This article explores the adequacy of this proposition by collecting artifacts from a dominant culture and a counterculture and determining what values those artifacts express. We expect that some artifacts from a counterculture will ridicule a subset of the dominant culture's values, whereas other countercultural artifacts will express support for an alternative set of values.

To find a setting in which we can study this issue, we need to know what types of organizational conditions are likely to give rise to a counterculture. Ruth Leeds Love's (1974) discussion of the absorption of protest offers a solution. She posits that organizations that are strongly centralized, but permit a decentralized diffusion of power, are likely to spawn what she terms a "nonconforming enclave." An organizational member challenges some aspect of the dominant culture. If the challenger is a charismatic leader, Love proposes that the organization will absorb the potential for protest by giving the charismatic person limited power, some formal structural autonomy, and a tacit mandate to gather followers and create a nonconforming enclave. This strategy has advantages from the dominant coalition's point of view. If the enclave functions innovatively, within the institution's latitude of tolerance, the institution benefits. If not, the institution has isolated the deviance. The structural autonomy serves as a boundary, defining the limits of acceptable behavior and possibly making the unwanted enclave easier to destroy.

To translate Love's proposition into the terminology introduced above, a counterculture should be most likely to arise in a strongly centralized institution that has permitted significant decentralization of authority to occur. The counterculture will be likely to emerge within a structural boundary and, interestingly, it may well have a charismatic leader.

THE GM CASE

Organizational Setting

General Motors (GM) is a well-documented case that fits the description outlined by Love. The firm is strongly centralized in that authority and responsibility for financial control and the long-range strategy of the firm rest in the hands of corporate headquarters. Nevertheless the divisions, such as Pontiac and Chevrolet, have considerable autonomy on operating issues. The rationale for this structure was provided in former GM president and chairman of the board Alfred P. Sloan Jr.'s famous "Organizational Study" (released in 1920). The plan's description of an inevitable tension between centralization and decentralization accurately describes the firm today.

One division of GM was headed for some years by John DeLorean. This formal position of leadership gave him visibility, resources, and power; these were apparently augmented by such charismatic attributes as personal magnetism and dramatic flair. (Although DeLorean encountered business and personal difficulties after his departure from GM, this article focuses exclusively on his years with GM.)

Procedure

In the first stage of this research, the available published literature on GM was surveyed and several present and former GM employees interviewed by means of an open-ended format. The objective of this stage of the research effort was to gain a relatively broad base of knowledge about the corporation, with particular focus on the dominant culture.

In the second stage of the research effort, two views of the corporation were selected for an in-depth content analysis. The first is a "corporate history" of GM, Ed Cray's *Chrome Colossus: General Motors and Its Times* (1980). This book was selected for several reasons. It is fairly recent. Unlike many others, it reports some information that is critical of the firm. It is comprehensive and provides a detailed picture, particularly of the firm's dominant culture. The second view selected was J. P. Wright's description of DeLorean's activities, *On A Clear Day You Can See General Motors* (1979). This book was selected because it is the most thorough published account of DeLorean's activities at GM.

Because culture is a socially constructed reality, it would be an exercise in futility to try to capture a single "objective" picture of a culture or subculture. Undoubtedly, Cray and Wright have views of the issues and events discussed below that are somewhat different from others' views. It is impossible to avoid bias in the perception of a socially constructed reality; indeed, in some senses, that bias is the focus of this investigation.

One important limitation of these data sources merits mention. Cray and Wright focus primarily on the activities of relatively high-ranking executives. They do not attempt to explore how these leaders' activities were perceived by their subordinates. Hence, the present article focuses on leader activities rather than subordinate reactions to such activities.

Core Values

Three related core values were repeatedly stressed (although terminology varied) in the various portrayals of the dominant culture at GM: respecting authority, fitting in, and being loyal. The description below begins with the dominant culture and describes the cultural artifacts that express these three core values. Next, the artifacts from DeLorean's division are examined to determine if they ridicule the dominant culture's values or express an alternative set of values, thus providing evidence of an uneasy symbiotic relationship between a dominant and a counterculture. In this latter part of the article, DeLorean's activities are studied to determine how they contribute, deliberately or inadvertently, to the development of a counterculture.

Respecting Authority: Jargon and Rituals of Deference

One core value of GM's dominant culture involved the importance of paying deference to the top corporate management. The special language or jargon used to refer to these executives' domains and activities reflected this core value. The top team's offices were located in an I-shaped end of the 14th floor of the huge GM headquarters building. Company jargon referred to this domain as "the 14th floor" and to these offices as "executive row." Apparently even GM's critics spoke these words with some deference. The high status of these top executives was also evident in the derogatory terms used to refer to their subordinates. Each member of the top management team was assigned a junior executive, who acted as an assistant and secretary. These subordinates were called "dog robbers," a term that originally referred to the servants in large households who were assigned the undesirable task of cleaning up dog droppings.

Another type of cultural artifact is a ritual—that is, an activity composed of a formalized or patterned sequence of events that is repeated over and over again. GM had many rituals that supported the core value of deference owed to authority. For example, subordinates were expected to meet their superiors from out of town at the airport, carry their bags, pay their hotel and meal bills, and chauffeur them around day and night. The higher the status of the superior, the more people would accompany him on the flight and the larger the retinue that would wait at the airport. A chief engineer would be met by at least one assistant engineer and perhaps a local plant official; a divisional general manager would travel with at least one executive from his office and would be met at the airport by the local plant manager, the heads of the regional and zone sales offices, and the local public relations director. If the chairman of the board decided to visit field offices, dozens of people would be involved in accompanying and meeting him.

Adherence to the airport ritual was not merely a social nicety, as DeLorean learned to his dismay on an occasion when he failed to meet his boss, Peter Estes, at the airport. Estes stormed into DeLorean's shower, nearly tearing the shower door off its hinges, shouting with atypical rage. "Why the hell wasn't someone out to meet me at the airport this morning? You knew I was coming, but nobody was there. Goddamnit, I served my time picking up my bosses at the airport. Now you guys are going to do this for me" (Wright, 1979, p. 35). The airport ritual communicated the message that no part of an executive's work was more important than helping superiors, even by meeting their most mundane needs. It is hardly surprising that Estes was somewhat perturbed, since DeLorean's refusal to adhere to the ritual clearly flouted a core value of GM's dominant culture and sent a crystal-clear message of disrespect for Estes' authority.

Fitting In: Communicating Invisibility by Visible Cues

It is no accident that few people could have recognized GM's chairman of the board, Thomas Murphy, although the faces of his peers, such as Henry Ford of Ford and William Paley of CBS, frequently graced the television screen, the front pages of newspapers, and the covers of news magazines. GM employees who found themselves the object of attention from the news media could expect a severe reprimand for disregarding another core value of GM's dominant culture: Ideal GM employees were invisible people who could fit in without drawing attention to themselves.

The core value of invisibility was expressed through such visible cultural artifacts as dress and decor. GM's dress norms in the 1960s required a dark suit, a light shirt, and a muted tie. This was a slightly more liberal version of the famous IBM dress code that required a dark suit, a sparkling white shirt, and a narrow blue or black tie. When all employees wear the same uniform, no single employee stands out.

Rules on office decor also expressed the value of invisibility. Even on the 14th floor, office decor was standardized. The carpeting was a nondescript blue–green, and the oak paneling was a faded beige. When DeLorean was promoted to headquarters, he requested brighter carpeting, sanding and restaining of the paneling, and some more modern, functional furniture. The man in charge of office decoration was apologetic, but firm: "We decorate the offices only every few years. And they are all done the same. It's the same way with the furniture. Maybe I can get you an extra table or a lamp . . ." (Wright, 1979, pp. 18–19).

The invisible GM employee was a "team player." Executives signaled their willingness to be team players by engaging in public, symbolic acts of conformity. Many of these activities centered on the act of eating. When executives were in town, for example, they were expected to eat in the executive dining room, where conversation usually consisted of bitching and office gossip, apparently irrelevant to serious business issues.

These meals were rituals. The executives were isolated in a separate room at predictable times. They said predictable sorts of things. Although at the manifest level these activities may have seemed irrelevant to the company's business, at a deeper level the eating ritual communicated several important aspects of the value of fitting in. Participation in the ritual required sacrifice of one's personal time that could have been spent having lunch with friends from outside GM or with one's family. When the conversation concerned gossip or complaints about GM, the talkers were taking personal risks by exposing themselves as "back-biters" or "tale-tellers," while listeners were initiated into an "in-group" of confidants sharing private knowledge. Precisely because topics of conversation were private and in a sense forbidden, the eating ritual was important. It signaled a willing sacrifice of time, an extension of the company into the more private and personal aspects of employees' lives, and a visible manifestation of willingness to fit in.

Failure to participate in the eating ritual was seen as a direct and unambiguous challenge: "Why doesn't he have dinner with the other executives? He's not acting like a team player" (Wright, 1979, p. 9). Costs of such a challenge were clear. Standard management practices punished those who failed to fit in. For example, performance appraisals were not based solely on objective criteria—the work records of those who were promoted were often inferior to those of people who languished in lower-level positions. Performance appraisals relied heavily on subjective criteria, which included an assessment of an employee's private life. Top executives were expected to behave in a decorous fashion, avoid fads, and (at least publicly) maintain the appearance of a stable married life. "He's not a team player," was a frequent, and many times the only, obstacle to an executive's promotion (Wright, 1979).

Being Loyal: Inferring the Dominant View from What Is Absent

Another core value central to the GM philosophy was loyalty to one's boss, which was a special case of loyalty to GM's management, which in turn was sometimes portrayed as a special case of loyalty to the country. For example, a top GM executive testifying before Congress in the 1950s drew no distinction between what was good for GM and what was good for the entire country [from Ed Cray's *Chrome Colossus: General Motors and Its Times* (1980)].

One artifact of the dominant culture that expressed the value placed on loyalty was the retirement dinner. At these dinners, as at other rituals, the content of what was to be said and the sequence of events was prescribed. A prototypical retirement dinner began with a description of the retiree's early background, perhaps with evocations of his hard-working parents and the elm-lined streets of his hometown. His first job, perhaps as a newsboy, would be recalled, followed by a brief recap of the halcyon days of his undergraduate career when, inevitably, he was a uniformed member, if not a star, of some sport team. The retiree's history as a GM employee would then be recounted in detail, beginning with his first job, typically a humble one that preserved the purity of the Horatio Alger aspect of his story. Next, his steady (always steady) rise through the corporate hierarchy would be counterpointed with allusions to his charming wife and lovely children.

Usually retirement dinner programs ended with a few joking allusions to the retiree's idiosyncracies and a promise. The retiree and the company representatives pledged continuing mutual respect, admiration, and loyalty. This pledge included a kind of proto-immortality, as the organization promised not to forget the retiree's invaluable contributions and offered him a safe passage to life outside the corporation's doors.

If the content of what is said and the sequence of what is done is prescribed in a ritual, then departure from these routines should cause consternation, as in DeLorean's failure to perform the airport ritual for his boss. If the primary purpose of the retirement dinner at GM was to reward past and insure future loyalty, then reactions to deviations from the expected behavior pattern should make this purpose clear.

A speaker at one GM retirement dinner committed two cardinal sins. He admitted that the company had once been in severe trouble, and he blamed the debacle on the ill-considered decisions of a top GM executive. Even the usually critical DeLorean was shocked by the speaker's behavior, which he criticized as a "vicious verbal attack," "un-called-for," and "vituperative." Others present were also dismayed, "shaking their heads and looking puzzled," and ". . . caught between modest surprise and downright embarrassment." Such a departure from the ritual protocol was exceedingly rare: "It was the first time I had ever heard a General Motors executive openly criticize another one, past or present, in front of corporate management" (Wright, 1979, pp. 206–207). The critical speech was so disruptive because it contradicted the ritual's basic purpose: to celebrate retiring and present GM employees for their loyalty to top GM executives and to the firm as a whole.

One cultural artifact, not yet discussed, is the organizational story. Such stories are anecdotes, ostensibly true, about a sequence of events drawn from the company's history. The stars of an organizational story are company employees, and the stories' morals concern the firm's core values and underlying assumptions.

Loyalty was so central to the GM philosophy that it is evident in what is absent from, as well as what is included in, the dominant culture's artifacts. Students of Japanese corporate cultures have noted the difficulty of interpreting cultural phenomena. To appreciate the shape and placement of a rock in a Japanese garden, the educated viewer focuses on the empty spaces around the rock. Similarly, the process of "reading" the content of a culture requires attention to disruptions and to what is absent or unsaid, because these are also clues to what is expected.

Thus reinforcement of the value of loyalty can also be seen in the type of organizational stories that were not found in this organizational setting. For example, Wright began his discussion of the loyalty issue with the telling observation that GM had no "prodigal son returns" story about an executive who left his "corporate home," because those who left were considered deserters and were not generally welcomed back.

The Development of a Counterculture: Questioning Deference to Authority

DeLorean expressed his opposition to deference to authority by telling this organizational story:

> In preparing for the sales official's trip to this particular city, the Chevrolet zone sales people learned from Detroit that the boss liked to have a refrigerator full of cold beer, sandwiches, and fruit in his room to snack on at night before going to bed. They lined up a suite in one of the city's better hotels, rented a refrigerator, and ordered the food and beer. However, the door to the suite was too small to accommodate the icebox. The hotel apparently nixed a plan to rip out the door and part of the adjoining wall. So the quick-thinking zone sales people hired a crane and operator, put them on the roof of the hotel, knocked out a set of windows in the suite, and lowered and shoved the refrigerator into the room through this gaping hole.

That night the Chevrolet executive wolfed down cold-cut sandwiches, beer, and fresh fruit, no doubt thinking, "What a great bunch of people we have in this zone." The next day he was off to another city and most likely another refrigerator, while back in the city of his departure the zone people were once again dismantling hotel windows and removing the refrigeration by crane (Wright, 1979, p. 37).

The "refrigerator story" carries at least two messages. First, it is common practice at GM to engage in expensive and time-consuming efforts to defer to even minor wishes of people in authority positions. Second, the tone of the story implies that people who engage in these activities sometimes go to ridiculous extremes.

The "refrigerator story" is an example of a cultural artifact that has "boomeranged" against the dominant culture. At first the story appears to be another illustration of the importance of deference to authority, then it becomes clear that the story portrays a situation in which this value has been carried to a ridiculous extreme. When cultural artifacts boomerang, they call into question those core values that at first they seem to reinforce. Boomeranging cultural artifacts can breed a deep alienation from the dominant culture's core values, undermining rather than supporting top management's objectives.

We posited that a counterculture would undermine the dominant culture's values, as evident in the "refrigerator story," and that it would produce cultural artifacts supporting an alternative set of core values. The story-creation process is one means of expressing alternative values. The process begins when a visible, often powerful and charismatic figure responds to a situation in a dramatic fashion, role modeling the behavior that would be expected of employees who might someday face a similar situation. If the central character is sufficiently noteworthy, the event sufficiently dramatic, and the behavior clearly relevant to future activities, then the role-modeled event may be recounted and eventually transformed into an organizational story.

The story-creation process is one way in which an individual actor can help create a counterculture, though it is important to note that the process can occur without the central actor's intentional cooperation. Even if an actor does intend to create a story, the transformation of an event into a shared organizational story depends largely on whether organizational members find it sufficiently interesting to repeat.

DeLorean, for example, repeatedly created such stories. For example, wanting to replace deference to authority with task-oriented efficiency, he decided to discourage the practice of meeting superiors at airports. Instead of issuing an edict by memo, he role-modeled the behavior he wanted on an occasion when he was scheduled to speak to a luncheon of McGraw-Hill editors and executives in midtown Manhattan. DeLorean found his own ride from the airport to the McGraw-Hill offices. The McGraw-Hill people were used to GM executives who traveled with "retinues befitting only the potentates of great nations"; when they questioned DeLorean about the whereabouts of his subordinates, DeLorean complacently replied that he hoped they were back in Detroit getting some work done. DeLorean noted with some pride that he subsequently heard that the "McGraw-Hill incident" had been retold many times, both by his subordinates and by McGraw-Hill employees (Wright, 1979).

This incident was transformed into an organizational story for several reasons. The star was DeLorean, a controversial and powerful figure. The events were sufficiently dramatic to be interesting and had clear implications for the types of behavior that would be considered appropriate for De-Lorean's subordinates. If a similar situation arose, subordinates surmised that they should not meet DeLorean at the airport unless there was specific business to conduct en route. Finally, the events were noteworthy because they expressed a value that contradicted a core value of the dominant culture. In DeLorean's division, job performance was more important than deference to authority.

An Alternative to Fitting In: The Limits
of Acceptable Deviance

DeLorean was opposed to the value placed by the dominant culture on team play and fitting in. Instead, he valued dissent and independence. Sensibly, he backed his values with practices—changing, for example, the performance appraisal system in his division. No longer were subjective criteria, indicating willingness to fit in, considered relevant. Instead, performance was measured on the basis of criteria that were as objective as possible.

DeLorean reinforced this value with cultural artifacts as well as practices. For example, he made a point of claiming that he would rely on objective performance appraisal criteria, even when the results ran counter to his own subjective opinions. He backed this claim with an anecdote, which he claimed became a shared organizational story. The central figure in the story, aside, of course, from DeLorean himself, was a disagreeable man whose performance record was superlative. Despite his personal dislike of the man, DeLorean promoted him several times, admitting that he tried to "stay the hell away from him" (Wright, 1979, p. 32).

This anecdote has two intriguing central characters. DeLorean's strong dislike of his subordinate adds an element of personal interest. In addition, the anecdote clearly prescribes how DeLorean would have his subordinates behave when they assessed the behavior of a disliked subordinate. In this example, DeLorean articulated a core value that was counter to the core values of the dominant culture, he backed that new value by implementing consistent performance appraisal practices, and he dramatized and illustrated the value by role modeling the desired behavior. Although DeLorean's retrospective account may exaggerate the intentionality and impact of his behavior, it is plausible that these activities contributed to the development of a counterculture among DeLorean's subordinates.

DeLorean also used other techniques to facilitate the development of a counterculture. For example, when he was promoted to head the Chevrolet division, he used decor changes to symbolize his declaration of independence. The division's lobby and executive offices were refurbished with bright carpets, the paneling was sanded and restained, and modern furniture was brought in. In accord with the espoused values of independence and dissent, executives were allowed, "within reasonable limits," to decorate their offices to fit their individual tastes.

In his own dress DeLorean role-modeled an apparently carefully calibrated willingness to deviate from the dominant culture's emphasis on fitting in. DeLorean's dark suits had a continental cut. His shirts were off-white with wide collars. His ties were suitably muted, but wider than the GM norm. His deviations were fashionable for the late 1960s, but they represented only a slight variation on the executive dress norms of the dominant culture.

If a counterculture is to survive within the context of a dominant culture, a delicate balancing act must be performed. DeLorean apparently did not hesitate to initiate stories and implement practices that directly challenged the dominant culture's core values. His use of visible cultural artifacts (not easily hidden from visiting outsiders) was more subtle, perhaps deliberately more circumspect. Although the extent of his intentionality is unclear, DeLorean's deviance appears carefully calibrated to remain within, but test the limits of, the dominant culture's latitude of acceptance.

Opposing Demands for Unquestioning Loyalty

The Corvair disasters provided superb raw material for a "boomerang" challenge to the dominant culture's emphasis on loyalty. The story begins as a seemingly straightforward presentation epitomizing GM's finest characteristics. Initially, the Corvair was seen as an innovative, appealing product— the best that GM minds could produce. The rear placement of the engine, the independent swing-axle suspension system, and the sporty styling gave the Corvair a racy image designed to appeal to the young.

At this point the Corvair story boomerangs: It takes a sudden turn and becomes a scathing indictment of the values it first appeared to endorse. Several GM employees raised objections to the car because of their concern about the lack of safety of the rear engine and the fact that the swing-axle design had a tendency to make the car directionally unstable and difficult to control, with a propensity to flip over at high speeds (Cray, 1980). Despite evidence supporting the validity of these objections, GM management told the dissenters to stop objecting and join the team or find some other place to work (Wright, 1979).

DeLorean concluded the Corvair story by enumerating the deaths caused by its faulty design and the negative effects its production had on the firm. These disastrous consequences included a "Watergate mentality" that led to attempts to buy and destroy evidence of owner complaints about the car, millions of dollars in legal expenses and out-of-court settlements, and extensive damage to GM's reputation. DeLorean explicitly stated the moral to the Covair story in terms of the "group think" dangers of an overemphasis on loyalty:

> There wasn't a man in top GM management who had anything to do with the Corvair who would purposely build a car that he knew would hurt or kill people. But, as part of a management team pushing for increased sales and profits, each gave his individual approval in a group to decisions which produced the car in the face of serious doubts that were raised about its safety, and then later sought to squelch information which might prove the car's deficiencies. (Wright, 1979, p. 56)

It is noteworthy that this contribution to the creation of a counterculture within DeLorean's division includes no direct action. Instead, DeLorean merely offers, in this boomeranging story, a reinterpretation of past events.

CONCLUSION

This analysis of the dominant culture at GM revealed three core values. Deference to authority was represented in the airport ritual and jargon, such as "dog robbers." The value of being invisible was expressed through management practices, such as subjective performance appraisal criteria, and through visible artifacts, such as conservative dress, standardized office decor, and public eating rituals. The value of loyalty was so central that it was evident in what was absent—a retirement dinner ritual that was disrupted and a prodigal son story that was missing.

Evidence of a counterculture was also found. In addition to ridiculing the values of the dominant culture, DeLorean articulated an alternative set of core values, preferring productivity to deference, objective measures of performance to subjective indicators of conformity, and independence to blind loyalty. Clearly the dominant and countercultures took opposite positions on value issues of central importance to both.

Several of DeLorean's activities apparently influenced the development of this uneasy symbiosis. First, he used "boomeranging" cultural artifacts, such as the "refrigerator" and "Corvair" stories, to ridicule the values of the dominant culture. Second, he articulated the countercultural values openly, through management practices such as objective performance appraisal criteria, and through the story-creation process, as in the "McGraw-Hill" story. In addition, his use of such visible cultural artifacts as dress and decor communicated more subtly the limits of acceptable deviance.

While a manager alone may not be able to create or "manage" a culture, DeLorean's activities suggest that several managerial techniques may have a detectable impact on the trajectory of a culture's, or a subculture's, development. Those techniques include implementation of practices that are consistent with preferred values, articulation of "boomerangs," attempts to create organizational stories, and carefully calibrated uses of visible artifacts.

If DeLorean's activities are to serve as a source of cultural management ideas, it is important to discuss the limitations of his achievements at GM. It is true that for a time he maintained a delicate balance, fostering the development of a counterculture that rested within the dominant culture's latitude of tolerance. Eventually, however, DeLorean's dissent met with disfavor, and he left GM to found a company of his own.

DeLorean's history at GM raises some interesting questions that are addressed in Love's analysis of the absorption of protest. A counterculture can serve some useful functions for a dominant culture, articulating the boundaries between appropriate and inappropriate behavior and providing a safe haven for the development of innovative ideas. Did GM's top management want DeLorean's counterculture to succeed, and were they disappointed when his deviance went beyond their latitude of tolerance? Or, as implied in the analysis of the basic assumptions underlying the dominant culture's core values, had GM permitted DeLorean's counterculture to grow and die in order to provide an object lesson for other potential deviants? Or was the strength of the counterculture an unanticipated and unwelcome surprise to the dominant culture? No matter which of these alternatives comes closest to the truth, clearly it is a complex process, beyond the control of any one individual, to maintain the uneasy symbiotic relationship that exists between a dominant culture and a counterculture.

Acknowledgments. The authors wish to thank the following people who gave us particularly helpful comments on an earlier draft of this article: Susan Kreiger, Hal Leavitt, Meryl Louis, Gerald Salancik, and Edgar Schein. A preliminary version of this article was presented as part of the symposium "Can Culture Be Managed?" at the annual meeting of the Academy of Management in New York City in August 1982.

KEY TERMS

organizational culture	dominant culture
artifact	subculture
corporate values	enhancing subculture
basic assumptions	orthogonal subculture
organizational story	counterculture
ritual	boomeranging cultural artifact

DISCUSSION QUESTIONS

1. What is meant by the phrase "uneasy symbiosis" between dominant cultures and countercultures? What benefits do countercultures provide for members of dominant cultures? What problems do countercultures create for members of dominant cultures?

2. Under what conditions are countercultures likely to arise? Do you think a charismatic leader is essential?

3. To what extent can organizational cultures (or subcultures) be managed? What can leaders do to influence culture? What constraints make it difficult for leaders to influence culture?

4. Some people say that managing culture is unethical "value engineering." What do you think?

SUGGESTED READINGS

Organizational culture research has its roots in Philip Selznick's *Leadership and Administration* (Row, Peterson, 1957) and Burton Clark's *The Distinctive College: Antioch, Reed, and Swarthmore* (Aldine, 1970). Four books, oriented toward the professional manager, are largely responsible for the recent renaissance of interest in this topic. William Ouchi's *Theory Z: How American Business Can Meet the Japanese Challenge* (Addison-Wesley, 1981) and Richard Pascale and Anthony Athos's *The Art of Japanese Management* (Simon & Schuster, 1981) drew heavily on Japanese models of corporate culture. Thomas Peters and Robert Waterman studied the cultures of unusually profitable American companies in *In Search of Excellence* (Harper & Row, 1982), as did Terrence Deal and Allan Kennedy in *Corporate Cultures* (Addison-Wesley, 1982).

Some have taken a critical view of the work that aroused this interest in culture. Edgar Schein disputed the reliance on Japanese models in "Does Japanese Management Style Have a Message for American Managers?" (*Sloan Management Review*, Fall 1981, pp. 55–68). The claim that cultures express an institution's distinctive competence or unique accomplishment was questioned by Joanne Martin, Martha

Feldman, Mary Jo Hatch, and Sim Sitkin in "The Uniqueness Paradox in Organizational Stories" (*Administrative Science Quarterly,* September 1983, pp. 438–453).

Others have taken a closer look at particular cultural phenomena. Organizational stories, legends, and myths have been studied by Alan Wilkins (see, for example, his article "The Culture Audit: A Tool for Understanding Organizations" [*Organizational Dynamics,* Autumn 1983, pp. 24–38]) and Joanne Martin—for example, see "Stories and Scripts in Organizational Settings" in Albert Hastorf's and Alice Isen's (editors) *Cognitive Social Psychology* (Elsevier-North Holland, 1982, pp. 255–305). For an excellent sampling of papers about a wide range of cultural phenomena, including organizational stories, rituals, humor, and jargon, see the collection edited by Louis Pondy, Peter Frost, Gareth Morgan, and Thomas Dandridge. *Organizational Symbolism* (JAI Press, 1983). Ruth Leeds Love's discussion of absorption of protest appears in Harold Leavitt and Louis Pondy's *Readings in Managerial Psychology* (2nd ed.) (University of Chicago Press, 1974).

Another approach has been to study the functions served by different types of cultures. For example, John Van Maanen and Stephen Barley have studied occupations in "Occupational Communities: Culture and Control in Organizations" in Barry Staw and Larry Cummings's (editors), *Research in Organizational Behavior* (Vol. 6) (JAI press, 1984). Caren Siehl and Joanne Martin have studied the enculturation process for new employees, producing a quantitative, easily administered measure of culture in "The Role of Symbolic Management: How Can Managers Effectively Transmit Organizational Culture?" in James G. Hunt, Dian-Marie Hosking, Chester A. Schriesheim, and Rosemary Stewart (editors), *Leaders and Managers* (Pergamon Press, 1984, pp. 227–239). Although the recent academic research is scattered in a variety of scholarly journals, books integrating this literature are being written by a number of people, including Edgar Schein, Meryl Louis, and Joanne Martin.

This article draws evidence concerning the dominant and countercultures at General Motors primarily from two sources: Ed Cray's *Chrome Colossus: General Motors and Its Times* (McGraw-Hill, 1980) and J. P. Wright's *On A Clear Day You Can See General Motors* (Wright Enterprises, 1979). Because Wright writes of DeLorean's experiences in the first person, for the sake of clarity Wright's book is cited as representing DeLorean's point of view. Because DeLorean has disowned Wright's efforts, however, it is highly likely that their opinions differ on some issues. In such cases, the book is probably more representative of Wright's opinions than DeLorean's, in spite of the former's use of the first person. The past tense is used throughout this article's descriptions of General Motors because some information may no longer be accurate.

A number of other references on General Motors were useful, including particularly the works of A. D. Chandler, such as *Giant Enterprise: Ford, General Motors, and the Automobile Industry* (Harcourt, Brace & World, 1964) and *Strategy and Structure: Chapters in the History of Industrial Enterprise* (MIT Press, 1969). Peter Drucker's *Concept of the Corporation* (John Day Co., 1972), Ralph Nadar's *Unsafe at Any Speed* (Grossman, 1972), and Alfred P. Sloan Jr.'s *My Years With General Motors* (McFadden-Bartell Corp., 1965).

CHAPTER 4

Corporate Philosophy and Professional Baseball: (Re)defining the Texas Rangers

Nick Trujillo
Southern Methodist University

Mike Stone, president and chief operating officer of the Texas Rangers baseball franchise, sits at a table across from his desk in his office in Arlington, Texas. Stone, who has two graduate degrees in organizational psychology from the University of Michigan, was a consultant to the Rangers in 1982 and became their president on November 1, 1983.

From the window to the left of Stone's desk, you can see Arlington Stadium, the home of the Texas Rangers. On the wall to the right of his desk, you can see a framed document titled "Texas Rangers Baseball Club Philosophy and Beliefs" (see Figure 4.1). It is the same document that appears in the front of the new full-time employee handbook. Stone explained the history of this document and what it means to the Texas Rangers:

> "When Eddie Chiles bought the club in 1980, he didn't know a lot about baseball. He got into it through the back door by helping out a friend. But he's enough of a businessman to know that you have to know who you are, what you're going to operate, and what you're going to achieve. So, in late 1982, after the franchise had tried several things, he asked the Rangers the very basic question: 'Why do we exist?' Well, that was the first shake-out trying to define our reason for existence and trying to examine, what we should do.
>
> "This document called the 'Texas Rangers Philosophy and Beliefs' represents the collective thoughts that were agreed upon by members of this franchise who were involved in this process of self-

TEXAS RANGERS BASEBALL CLUB
PHILOSOPHY AND BELIEFS

The Texas Rangers Baseball Club is firmly committed to the belief that personal growth and development are the only sure ways to produce a superior organization. This belief is based on philosophies which form the framework and foundation for operation of our organization.

- We believe that Texas Rangers' baseball is a cornerstone in American sports and that, as such, it should be played with the highest ideals of competitive fair play.
- We believe that Texas Rangers' baseball is a wholesome form of family entertainment and an important means of advancing the values of American society.
- We believe that people can benefit from participating in and watching games which are played with intensity and enthusiasm.
- We believe that the future of organized baseball is linked to profitability and the free enterprise system.
- We believe that every employee should be treated as an individual and provided with reasonable working conditions, pay, and benefits.
- We believe that management bears the responsibility for providing opportunities to be the best at what each individual does.
- We believe that every employee is responsible for representing the Club and baseball in general in a manner which brings credit to themselves and The Texas Rangers.
- We believe that people should be judged and rewarded on the basis of their performance, without regard to their race, gender, color or creed.
- We believe that growth and development is essential to the successful performance of every individual employee.
- We believe that management must plan for changes in order to take maximum advantage of opportunities.
- We believe that short-term gains should not be taken at the expense of long-term loss.
- We believe that effective management must be open, honest and straightforward.
- We believe that management must demonstrate high standards and commitment to excellence in achieving tangible results.
- We believe that no opportunity is too small to advance the best interests of The Texas Rangers.
- We believe that management decisions must be thought through and consistently carried out.
- We believe that willingness to innovate and implement change is the key to our success.

H. E. CHILES
CHAIRMAN OF THE BOARD
CHIEF EXECUTIVE OFFICER

MICHAEL H. STONE
PRESIDENT
CHIEF OPERATING OFFICER

FIGURE 4.1

examination. And even though the owner and I have signed this statement, it represents the work of about 40 people in this franchise. We went through week after week of intense discussions and emotional debates. There were about 10 revisions of this document involving additions, corrections, and different word choices. All this was done so that everyone could agree upon the beliefs and it would be something into which our people had made an emotional investment.

"This document serves as a reminder to current employees and it gives new employees a sense of who we are. But there is nothing magical about writing it down on paper. . . . The key is that the behaviors of all the people in this office will fall within the context of that document. And you only get that behavioral sensitivity when they're involved in the process.[1]"

In this case analysis, we review the "process of self-examination" that was undertaken by the Texas Rangers baseball franchise. We consider how members of this franchise, troubled by years of inconsistent and unsuccessful decisions by previous administrations, redefined the mission and beliefs of the organization in order to create long-term stability and success. We also examine how the mission and beliefs were communicated and implemented inside and outside the organization and how they have helped the Rangers become a more successful organization, on and off the field.

THE TEXAS RANGERS: A BRIEF OVERVIEW

When President John F. Kennedy threw out the first pitch for the Washington Senators on April 10, 1961, he indirectly began the history of the Texas Rangers. The Senators' owner Robert Short, the former Democratic Committee Treasurer who outbid Bob Hope and purchased the Senators in December of 1968, received the necessary votes from major league owners to move the Senators from Washington to Arlington, Texas in September 1971. And so Texas fans' dream came true on April 21, 1972 when manager Ted Williams guided the newly named Texas Rangers to a 7–6 victory over the Angels, thanks to Frank Howard's towering home run, the first in the expanded and newly named Arlington Stadium.[2]

Texas Ranger Payers and Players

Since 1972, the Texas Rangers have had three majority owners: Robert Short, plastics executive Brad Corbett, and oil executive Eddie Chiles.[3] Baseball fans may be surprised to learn that the Rangers have employed 13 field managers in 17 seasons including Ted Williams, Whitey Herzog, Billy

Martin, Eddie Stanky (for 1 day), Frank Lucchesi, Don Zimmer, Doug Rader, and currently Bobby Valentine. Baseball fans also may be surprised to learn that players the likes of Bert Blyleven, Dock Ellis, Frank Howard, Fergie Jenkins, Sparky Lyle, Gaylord Perry, Rusty Staub, and Richie Zisk spent part of their careers in Ranger uniforms. The 1989 roster included future Hall of Fame pitcher Nolan Ryan (acquired as a free agent) and infielders Rafael Palmeiro and Julio Franco (acquired in trades), as well as Ranger regulars such as pitcher Charlie Hough, outfielders Pete Incaviglia and Ruben Sierra, and infielder Scott Fletcher.

The Ranger front office is similar to but smaller than that of most major league franchises. The 1988 media guide listed nine officers (chair, vice-chair, two directors, president, two vice-presidents, financial consultant, general counsel), 21 front office personnel (including assistant general managers, directors, assistant directors, field superintendents, and others), and 23 administrative personnel (including secretaries, receptionists, ticket salespeople, grounds crew, and others). During the baseball season, the Rangers employ almost 1000 seasonal employees.

In addition to their major league team, the Rangers have several minor league operations including one Class AAA club (Oklahoma City 89ers), one Class AA club (Tulsa Drillers), two Class A clubs (Charlotte Rangers and Gastonia Rangers), and two Rookie clubs (Gulf Coast Rangers and Butte Copper Kings). The scouting staff, revamped in recent years, has over 30 scouts, who cover the entire United States and a wide range of Latin American countries, especially Puerto Rico, the Dominican Republic, Venezuela, and Colombia.

Texas Ranger History: Inconsistent Teams and Inconsistent Decisions

On the Field

The Ranger baseball team has had an interesting though inconsistent history, one that has never produced a first place finish in 18 seasons. The club has finished the season in fourth place or lower nine times and has never finished closer than five games behind first place. Indeed, the Rangers share a dubious distinction with the Seattle Mariners as one of two teams (out of the current 26 pro baseball clubs) that has never appeared in a postseason playoff game.

This is not to say, however, that the Rangers have never enjoyed success on the field. The club has finished in second place five times in their 18 seasons. The 1974 Rangers, under Associated Press and United Press International American League Manager of the Year Billy Martin, finished in second place behind the World Champion Athletics. That 1974 success brought over 1 million fans to Arlington Stadium for the first time. In the strike-shortened season of 1981, the Rangers missed a chance to play in the intradivisional playoffs by one game when they lost to the Milwaukee Brewers on June 11th. The 1986 Rangers, led by UPI American League Manager of the Year Bobby Valentine, finished in second place behind California and again enjoyed record attendance (1.6 million people).

Off the Field

The Ranger organization has had an interesting and inconsistent history off the field as well. Over the years, the most inconsistent franchise decisions involved player trades and manager hirings. One reporter characterized the history of Ranger player trades: "Dead fish and cheap perfume smell better than many Ranger deals."[4] For example, in 1978, the Rangers traded young pitching prospect Dave Righetti and four others for veteran pitcher Sparky Lyle and four others; 2 years later, Righetti was the American League Rookie of the Year and on his way toward a possible Hall of Fame career while Lyle was finishing his career with the Rangers. A few years later, pitching prospects Walt Terrell and Ron Darling were traded to the Mets for veteran Lee Mazzilli. Current general manager Tom Grieve summarized the significance of these and similar past trades: "Ownership traded away so many good young players that although it helped for a year or two, it just eroded the base of talent. That led to wild fluctuations when the team went right back down to where it started."

The Rangers' history of manager hirings is also an erratic one as the club has had 13 different managers in 17 seasons. The most infamous hirings occurred during the 1977 season when then-owner Brad Corbett fired manager Frank Lucchesi on June 22nd and announced that Eddie Stanky would return to managing after a 10-year retirement. Stanky led the Rangers to a 10–8 victory over Minnesota then quit the next morning, replaced by interim manager Connie Ryan. Five days later, Billy Hunter was named as the fourth manager of a very interesting week.

Finally, the Rangers financial history has been an unstable one. From 1972 to 1986, the Ranger franchise lost money *every* year, a situation that, according to Mike Stone, "created a debt history which you tow around and have to service every year which can be quite substantial." The financial problems began when former owner Bob Short sold the Rangers' local broadcast rights to the city of Arlington for a 10-year period in order to pay off the debt that had resulted from moving the Senators franchise to Texas. These missing broadcast revenues, coupled with inconsistent attendance revenues, kept the Rangers in the red for many years. These missing revenues also led to innovative but unsuccessful entrepreneurial endeavors during the first 2 years of the Chiles reign, which will be discussed shortly.

In summary, the history of the Texas Rangers is roller-coaster reading, with different owners, different managers, inconsistent plans, and inconsistent outcomes. As Tom Grieve, who has been with the Rangers for over 20 years, first as a player and now as general manager, concluded:

> "One weak point with this organization was that it had been an organization with a lot of different plans that never stuck with one plan. There always was turmoil. There were a lot of managers, general managers, and owners. There have been philosophies to win now at all costs, then movements to draft well and develop for the future. . . . I think the fans used to look at us as a team that really didn't know in what direction it was headed."

THE ERA OF EDDIE CHILES

"To tell you the truth," as Eddie Chiles explained to *Dallas Magazine* the purchasing of the Rangers, "I sort of got involved accidentally. . . . The investors picked me out because they needed money. I bought a considerable amount of interest. Then from that point, more of the limited partners would drop out and I would buy up their interest. The process kept repeating itself until one day, Corbett wanted out. I agreed to buy his stock."[5]

When Chiles bought Corbett's stock, he also assumed Corbett's position as board chairman on April 29, 1980, even though he was still a minority owner at the time. (He later became majority owner.) And by Chiles's own admission, when he assumed the chairmanship, he was "totally unprepared for the job" and "had no real knowledge of baseball."[6] Nonetheless, Chiles embarked on a new and distinctly management-oriented course for the Rangers.

To say that Eddie Chiles is a conservative Republican businessman is like saying that Babe Ruth was a decent power hitter. Chiles was chairman of the Western Company, a former Fortune 500 company that he founded, until he stepped down in early 1988 when Western filed for Chapter 11, another casualty of hard times in the oil industry. He is best known for his "I'm Eddie Chiles and I'm Mad" ads that criticized "free-wheeling Democrats" who were "about to take over this country" with a "very wasteful government that had a philosophy of tax–tax, spend–spend, and elect–elect."[7] He is a self-made capitalist of the free enterprise system in the richest sense of that expression. And he is proud of it. Not surprisingly, he adopted a similar approach with the Rangers.

A Baseball Team Owner

A 1981 Ranger press release described Eddie Chiles in this way:

> He's an energetic man who can rant and rail at inefficiency, but he also is an approachable charmer who will invite ideas. He believes in delegating responsibility and providing authority to accomplish the mission but firmly expects results and accountability.

Chiles's approach to baseball as being "no different from any other business in this country"[8] led him in 1981 to reorganize the franchise. Specifically, he divided the franchise into two separate divisions: business operations, directed by new Vice-President Sam Meason, former president of Mattel Toys, and baseball operations, directed by Eddie Robinson, the vice-president in charge of baseball under Corbett's reign.

Meason helped develop a widely publicized "3-year plan" that was designed to create economic stability for the Rangers franchise. This 3-year plan involved many decisions, some successful, others not. First, the Rangers expanded and upgraded their clubhouse, one described by a local paper as "a luxury facility, the envy of the baseball world" with a plush clubroom, a video room and classroom, a whirlpool, and a 80-foot training room packed with Nautilus equipment.[9] They also announced plans to expand and upgrade Arlington Stadium, plans that reached fruition before the 1984 season.

Second, the team renewed interest in the farm system as a way to build a winning (and cost effective) roster. One paper reported that " 'Home-grown' is becoming a buzzword around the Rangers' minor league camps" and quoted Farm Director Joe Klein as saying "the days of just relying on the farm system may be coming back into vogue" because "if you could get three or four rookies up at a time, you might be able to keep salaries down."[10]

Finally, but perhaps most importantly, the Rangers launched several entrepreneurial ventures designed to generate revenues for a franchise that had never turned a profit and that still did not own its local broadcast rights. These ventures included starting a cable television network, developing a retail merchandise and souvenir store called "Texas FanFares," and creating an athletic drink called "RangerAde."

Reviewing the First Chiles Era (1980–1982): Disappointing Results

Unfortunately, this first era of Chiles's ownership, spanning three seasons from April 1980 through September 1982, produced mixed and ultimately disappointing results on and off the field.

Losing More Games and More Money

On the field, Chiles's team was still erratic. After finishing fourth under manager Pat Corrales in 1980, new manager Don Zimmer led the 1981 Rangers to a second place finish and the second best record in the history of the team (57–48). However, 1982 ended with the Rangers in sixth place (29 games back) and with the third worst record in team history to that point (64–98). Things got so bad during the 1982 season that Chiles asked Stone, then consultant for Chiles's Western Company, to conduct management workshops with Don Zimmer and Ranger players. Neither the workshops with Zimmer nor Zimmer himself produced results. Zimmer was fired and it was time for a change on the field.

On the business operations end, the economic ventures engineered by Meason did not generate additional revenues but rather compounded the financial losses of the franchise, especially with the start-up costs associated with the cable network. Newspapers estimated that the Rangers lost more than $4 million in 1981 and more than $7 million in 1982. It was time for a change off the field as well.

REDEFINING THE RANGERS: THE PROCESS (AND PRODUCT) OF SELF-EXAMINATION

The Rangers' 1988 media guide makes a brief mention of a "series of top management meetings for the ballclub" that took place in November 1982. Those meetings, chaired by then-consultant Mike Stone, involved members of the franchise across all hierarchical levels. When all was said and done, the Rangers emerged with a new vision of how their organization would operate. But it wasn't easy.

Business Versus Baseball: The Raging Organizational Debate of 1982

Perhaps the most difficult part of this process of self-examination was that the business operations personnel did not view the Rangers in the same way as the baseball operations personnel. Part of this discrepancy between the two divisions was a consequence of the separation (both physical and functional) that existed in the organization at that time. Tom Grieve put it this way: "The baseball guys had an office over here and the business people had an office over there. We referred to them as the IBM section. They didn't know what we did. . . . No one knew each other."

However, the discrepancy between the two divisions was ultimately a matter of a fundamental difference in organizational philosophy regarding how to run a major league baseball franchise. Mike Stone explained:

"Everybody agreed that we wanted to be a championship team and to be competitive year in and year out. The difference was that the marketing people said you need to sign a Reggie Jackson or Dave Winfield in order to be successful and reach that point. The baseball people were saying, you sign a Reggie Jackson and you have him for 2 years and while he may draw some people, the team is still going to stink. That's a short-term solution.

"The debate that raged was that the baseball people wanted to grow their own talent and the marketing people were saying that's going to take at least 5 years. During those 5 years, you're going to incur losses because you stink and nobody is going to come to the ballpark. You may be out of business in 5 years rather than poised with a young competitive team. The debate went back and forth. There were talented people on both sides who were very emotional about what they thought was the right thing to do."

Who won this raging organizational debate? "Fortunately," as Mike Stone summarized, "the baseball people prevailed." That meant that the Rangers would embark on a new era of Texas Ranger baseball.

Another New Era of Texas Ranger Baseball

The victory of baseball operations over business operations did not mean that the Rangers abandoned their view of baseball as a business. Rather, the organization shifted from the Meason view that baseball was one of several Ranger businesses to the view that *the* business of the Rangers was baseball. Chiles, by way of the ever-present local papers, summarized the Rangers new philosophy:

> We're trying to start, and I hope it will be successful, a new era for Ranger baseball. We're trying to build a winning team through our farm system, through internal development, so we won't have to go into the free-agent market and pay those million dollar salaries. From now on, the Ranger organization is just going to be an old staid operation—selling tickets, selling hot dogs, beer, and don't forget those nachos.[11]

Not surprisingly, Vice-President Sam Meason, architect of the aborted business ventures, was out, and Mike Stone, consultant during the process of self-examination, was in as president to direct these redefined Rangers. Also in as new vice-president of marketing was Larry Schmittou, owner of the minor league Nashville Sounds, who was known as "the Bill Veeck of the minor leagues" for his ballpark-oriented marketing philosophy, a philosophy that matched the Rangers' new marketing emphasis on the fans' ballpark experience. However, the key enactment of the new Ranger vision was seen in baseball operations, as guided by the new organizational mission.

The New Organizational Mission: "Build a Winning Tradition Primarily through Internal Development"

Textbooks tell us that "an organization's mission is the unique role it defines for itself," one that "distinguishes it from others in the same category."[12] Thus, although virtually all major league franchises wish to produce a championship team, the mission of each franchise, whether stated formally or informally, reveals the unique way in which each franchise will organize this intended production.

As noted above, the Texas Rangers' mission, as articulated in a formal statement of purpose, was "to build a winning tradition primarily through internal development." Mike Stone defined the key terms in this way:

> "We will achieve a *winning*—meaning we'll be competitive and win more than we lose—*tradition*—meaning we'll do it year in and year out—and we'll do it *primarily*—which doesn't preclude making trades or signing free agents—through *internal development*—through outstanding scouting of players and developing those players in our own minor league system."

Once this new mission statement was agreed upon by members of the franchise, a process that took several weeks, the Rangers needed to *communicate* this mission statement to significant insiders and outsiders and, more importantly, to *implement* the actual mission through structural and behavioral changes in the franchise.

Communicating the Mission Statement

In some ways, communicating the Ranger mission statement to various organizational audiences was relatively easy. In fact, communicating almost any Ranger statement is relatively easy. After all, baseball franchises—like other professional sports franchises—are covered by several reporters in the papers, on the radio, and on TV *every* day during the season and often during the off-season. As Media Relations Director John Blake pointed out, "A lot of industry and college PR involves trying to *create* an audience. Here, we make a trade or have a game and many people are going to write about it. The issue is trying to *manage* how you announce something rather than trying to sell it."

Indeed, soon after the Rangers redefined their mission, the Dallas–Fort Worth news media covered the story extensively. Preseason headlines from the local papers forecasted the Ranger changes: "[New General Manager] Klein aims to change Ranger trade history,"[13] "Rangers Rebuilding their Credibility,"[14] and "Rangers Farm System Receives New Hope."[15] One

1984 feature on Mike Stone, titled "This Way: Stone Gives Rangers Long-Needed Direction," covered the mission statement itself with the lead, "One of the most significant provisions [of the new Ranger 'set of principles'] is that the Rangers are committed to winning 'primarily through internal development.' "[16]

The Rangers also communicated the new mission statement in their own written materials such as media guides, programs, yearbooks, and employee manuals, and in oral presentations to local groups at luncheons and banquets. The 1984 souvenir yearbook put it this way: "'Winning through internal development.' That is the Rangers commitment. It is shared by every member of the Texas organization, from principal owner Eddie Chiles to the youngest rookie fresh from the college campus." As Tom Grieve summarized: "Everyone in this organization has heard me and Bobby [Valentine] on talk radio shows or whatever saying the same thing until it sounds like a broken record. So, if you ask them, they'll say the same thing. And the fans will too." In short, the message of the new mission was communicated quickly to organizational insiders and outsiders. The more important challenge, however, was *implementing* the mission.

Implementing the New Mission

Implementing the actual mission was not as easy or as immediate as communicating the mission statement. Mike Stone stated the initial challenge, "We literally adopted a statement of purpose that was almost antithetical to the history of the franchise [and] we had to literally build a franchise almost as if we were a new expansion franchise."

First, and foremost, there was resource reallocation, especially in the scouting and minor league departments. The Rangers went from a scouting staff of 13 scouts in 1981 to 23 scouts in 1985 to 32 scouts (including seven supervisors) in 1988. A key move was hiring Sandy Johnson as scouting director in November, 1984. Johnson, who was a member of the San Diego Padre franchise, took the job because "Tom and Mike were sincere and committed to running the organization in a way that appealed to [him] through scouting and development." The Rangers have also added two minor league teams since 1981, have hired many new minor league coaches and instructors, and have opened a new spring training facility in Port Charlotte, Florida.

Second, Ranger management needed to change its behavioral history of using the minor leagues to showcase key prospects as bait for possible trades to that of using the minors to *develop* young players throughout their farm system. As Sandy Johnson indicated, a focus on development requires a decidedly different commitment by management:

"The key is that you can't worry about winning at the minor league level. People hate to hear that but it's the truth. You've got to give the 17-year-old kids their 400 at-bats rather than sitting them on the bench and letting the college kids play so that you win the pennant and look good in the newspaper. That's not how you *develop* players."[17]

Additionally, a focus on development requires a commitment to resist trading top prospects for aging veterans, to give them a chance to make the parent club, and to exercise initial patience with these kids when they make the club. Unfortunately, the Rangers have brought up young players much more quickly than was desirable because of a lack of major league depth. Nonetheless, the fact remains that seven of the eight everyday players in the Rangers' 1988 opening night line-up included "homegrown" products. And, as Bobby Valentine quipped at a 1988 luncheon to a local business group, "Last year we averaged 26 years of age. At one point, I played a starting team on the field that had a combined 19 years of major league experience. Steve Carlton was pitching against us and he had 22 years of major league experience."

Finally, since redefining their mission, the Rangers have replaced two key management positions in the franchise: the general manager (Tom Grieve for Joe Klein) and the field manager (Bobby Valentine for Doug Rader). These two separate decisions, although widely criticized by sportswriters when they first took place, have since been lauded as very successful decisions. Joe Klein, who had been endorsed by the three local papers, resigned in September 1984 under reported pressure from Mike Stone.[18] Reporters condemned the move as "the classic example of a baseball man [Klein] having to deal with a businessman [Stone]."[19] One columnist, in a piece called "Arlington Hillbillies at it again," used Klein's firing as evidence of "Ranger mismanagement, which is no more stable than a South American government."[20] Klein was replaced by Tom Grieve, then vice-president of minor league operations, who at age 36 became the youngest general manager in baseball. Although Grieve was described by Mike Stone as "the supreme embodiment of our statement of purpose," he was reviewed by local sportswriters as "nice but not ready for the job." Six months later, the same local media people were lauding Grieve as "forceful," "impressive," and "successful."[21]

In May of 1985, manager Doug Rader was fired, a move criticized by sportswriters as too late in coming. Although Rader led the Rangers to a third place finish in 1983, the 1984 squad finished in last place and the 1985 squad started off where 1984 had left them. Rader was out and Bobby Valentine, then third-base coach for the Mets, was in. Valentine was immediately a hit with the local media. More importantly, he was, as

Tom Grieve described him, "the last piece in the puzzle" of the redefined Rangers:

> "It wasn't until Bobby was hired that we had an entire organization that believed in the same mission. It sounds simple but I'm sure there are other organizatons that have failed for the same reasons. Unless every part of the organization believes in the same thing and is pointed in the right direction, then it's just impossible."

Reevaluating the Mission and the Winter Trades of 1988

After a promising second place finish in 1986, the 1987 Rangers, plagued by injuries and poor pitching, suffered a disappointing finish in last place, tied with the California Angels. The 1988 Rangers, plagued by the ninth worst collapse by an offense in 42 years of pro baseball, finished in sixth place, a very distant 33 1/2 games behind the American League Champion Oakland Athletics. One columnist lamented that these "new" Rangers were "still trapped where next year never arrives" and that the Ranger philosophy was not working.[22] It was again time for a change on the field and, as Mike Stone put it, time for reevaluation of the entire organizational philosophy:

> "Any time you have an organization that has developed a statement of purpose and 4 or 5 years later it hasn't achieved a great deal of success that is measurable at the only yardstick level—the major leagues— you're well advised as an organization to look in the mirror and say are we doing the right thing? And we did just that."

Stone described the reevaluation of the Ranger philosophy that occurred before the baseball winter meetings of 1988:

> "On November 29, 1988, 19 people in key management roles in this franchise came to Arlington and spent the whole day talking about and reexamining our statement of purpose and our philosophies and beliefs. We started out with the questions: Should we do away with our statement of purpose? Is it working? Maybe we can't grow our own talent? And there was a resounding conclusion: *No!* This is the right thing to do! When we started into this, nobody said it was a quick fix. This is a long-term solution to a problem. And we're making progress, it's just not apparent at the major league level yet. But last year the minor leagues won more games than at any time in the history of this franchise. Scouts are saying that the best players in this franchise aren't in Arlington. They're in Tulsa, Charlotte, Gastonia, and Butte, Montana [the Rangers farm clubs].

"So the challenge that confronted us as a management team was one of making some substantial changes that we felt were necessary in our line-up and at the same time not compromising our statement of purpose. That meant that we needed *not* to get rid of *key* young players out of our system and not block developmental routes. In the meeting on the 29th, we discussed that if you're developing your own players and you have excellent scouting, at some point in time you're going to have an overflow of players and you may want to trade players and deal from that strength if you can improve the overall club."

And deal they did! The Rangers took the national spotlight at the 1988 baseball winter meetings in Atlanta by making three trades (involving 15 players, 10 from the Rangers) and by signing future Hall of Fame pitcher Nolan Ryan as a free agent; the latter move was described by manager Bobby Valentine in the papers as "the one most important transaction the Texas Rangers have ever made."[23]

Local and national sportswriters alike lauded the transactions made by the Rangers. Acquired players Rafael Palmeiro and Julio Franco were characterized by sportswriters as two of the best hitters in baseball. More impressively, writers said the signing of Nolan Ryan "gives Texas a touch of class"[24] and "gives Rangers new credibility."[25] The overall change was labelled a "Texas-sized makeover,"[26] "a severe facelift,"[27] and a "new bold look,"[28] and was characterized as revolutionary in nature. One local-beat writer summarized the winter meetings by saying that "Grieve traded the Rangers' image as an also-ran in the AL West for one of a team that has given its fans something to look forward to in 1989, and the rest of the division something to be concerned with."[29] As one *Sporting News* columnist concluded in a rare feature about the Rangers, "Grieve deals Rangers the look of a contender."[30]

Although sportswriters universally applauded the Ranger player changes, some suggested that the franchise philosophy itself had changed. Peter Gammons in *Sports Illustrated* pointed out that "after finishing 33 1/2 games behind the Athletics last season, the Rangers have realized that they can't rely entirely on their youth movement anymore."[31] Two local columnists were more explicit. One, writing after the trade for Palmeiro, before the trade for Franco or the signing of Nolan Ryan, wrote this:

> The massive Cubs deal officially signaled a change in philosophy for the Rangers, and certainly a change in philosophy for Grieve. . . . Spending the past 4 years building and strengthening the farm system was good and proper. No one will regret that decision. But after . . . the past two seasons, the biggest worry was no longer player development at Port Charlotte or Tulsa or Oklahoma City. Grieve's No. 1 concern now starts at the top—Arlington Stadium. Either he improves that area immediately, or someone else will have his job.[32]

Another columnist similarly suggested that the Rangers had abandoned their statement of purpose when he wrote that Grieve had "deserted his original stand," concluding, "It is an idealistic dream, that of raising one's own talent for every position, but it doesn't seem to be a workable plan these days. Like the sea captain going down with the ship, it is more poetic than practical."[33]

In sum, the Ranger player trades of 1988 represented a dramatic change in the history of the franchise. Even the Rangers acknowledged the dramatic nature of the player changes in their new marketing slogan for the 1989 season: "It's a whole new and improved ballgame." But do these trades represent a significant departure from the organizational philosophy to build a winning tradition primarily through internal development as suggested by some sportswriters? If so, is this organizational change a natural evolution? A timely or untimely modification? A complete revolution?

In the next section, this case study concludes by considering some of the ways in which the overall success of the Texas Ranger organization can be assessed. It begins by evaluating the Rangers' commitment to their mission of building a winning tradition through internal development then moves to other areas of concern.

EVALUATING THE ORGANIZATIONAL SUCCESS OF THE TEXAS RANGERS

Implementing the Mission: The Evolution of an Organizational Philosophy

Given their history of ever-changing organizational philosophies, the first index of Ranger success should be the extent to which they have maintained a consistent direction toward accomplishing their mission. After close examination, the record shows that they have done so. They have continued to stress (and fund) their scouting department, resulting in quality and quantity coverage across the United States and in Latin America. One sportswriter went so far as to say that "the Rangers are suddenly challenging teams such as the Dodgers, Blue Jays, Yankees, Padres, etc. in establishing scouting programs in the Latin countries."[34]

But what about the winter trades of 1988 and the so-called "severe facelift" of the "rearranged Rangers"? Clearly, the Rangers traded several of their own homegrown young players (e.g., Oddibe McDowell, Jerry Browne, Mitch Williams, and Paul Kilgus), but does this action represent a significant shift in the Ranger philosophy as some sportswriters have suggested or is it a natural progression or evolution of that philosophy? I believe these trades represent a natural evolution of the Ranger philosophy for several reasons.

First, trading players is by no means an antithetical action to the Ranger philosophy. As Mike Stone reminded us earlier, the word "primarily" is in the statement of purpose specifically so that the Rangers do not "preclude making trades or signing free agents." This reminder, however, should not suggest that the decision to trade players was merely an escape clause in case their prospects did not emerge as major league ballplayers. Indeed, the decision to trade players is ultimately a central ingredient of the Ranger philosophy. As Tom Grieve explained in December of 1987, 1 year before the trades of 1988:

> "In the early stages of the philosophy, you can't trade young players. Eventually, though, we'd love to get to the point where the Mets were when you build up such a phenomenal base of young talent that you don't have a place for all the kids to play. Then you can trade four players to San Diego for a Kevin McReynolds or to Montreal for a Gary Carter. We want to be able to do that some day if we continue to do what we want in scouting and player development."

Admittedly, Ranger management would have loved for all of their prospects to emerge as bona fide major league stars, but such is never the case with *any* team or in any organizational context. So, too, Ranger management wanted to win a championship in the 1980s with all their homegrown players, but it was not to be. Thus, the Rangers decided it was time to trade several Ranger players for top prospects from other clubs.

Second, did the Rangers trade their own young players for grizzled older veterans as they had done in their not-so-glorious past? As Stone indicated, such a move "would be in direct violation of that statement; for example, if we had traded Bobby Witt for Dave Winfield, that is exactly in diametric opposition to our philosophy." Instead, the Rangers traded their own young players for other young players who still have time to develop within the Ranger system.[35] Moreover, the Rangers did not give up anything for Nolan Ryan except, as Stone put it, "a lot of cash."

So does this mean that the Rangers gave up their youth for other youth and thus consistently maintained their philosophy? Not exactly, because all players—just like all organizational members—are not created equal, nor do they perform equally. Managers in every organization evaluate personnel and find *top* prospects who are especially valued. The same is true in baseball, as Stone argued,

> "When you've got *premium* kids that you've developed, you hold on to those. If we had dealt Ruben Sierra or Bobby Witt [two potential superstars with the Rangers] in those transactions, I would have said, 'Wow.' But you've got all kinds of other kids and if you can trade for kids that will make you better, and put those kids with your kids, you're still doing it through internal development."

In sum, from an organizational perspective, Ranger management promoted their internally developed prospects and gave them essentially 3 years to perform—to produce a winning tradition—and that winning tradition did not occur. So they made tough management decisions and kept their premium players, trading other Ranger players to obtain premium players from other organizations in order to improve their overall team. Stone contends that this is entirely consistent with their organizational philosophy. As he explained, "As I look at it, the question is: Did we give up youth critical to our statement of purpose for older players who are on the descending curve of their careers? Or, did we give up young players who are not critical to our statement of purpose to improve ourselves with young players who indeed are critical to it?" Stone argues that they did the latter. Perhaps Tom Grieve summarized it best when he offered this seemingly paradoxical statement: "I don't feel like the organization was afraid to do things the last 3 years. We had a plan and stuck with it. We needed to make some changes, but we didn't change our plan."[36]

Building a Loyal Fan Base

The numbers speak for themselves. The Rangers home attendance hit record highs in 1986 (1.69 million) and in 1987 (1.76 million) and remained high in 1988 (1.58 million); indeed, prior to 1986, the club had drawn over 1.5 million just once in 14 seasons. Perhaps the most striking aspect of these records is that although the 1986 season found the Rangers contending for the division championship and finishing in second place, the 1987 Rangers opened the season with a 1–10 mark, never occupied first or second place, and finished the season in a tie for last place. And yet they set another attendance record. Tom Grieve explained,

"As time has gone by, I think the fans have believed that this is the right philosophy. It's been amazing to everybody here how they have jumped on board. This is what they were looking for all along—their own players that they can watch develop into Rangers. They have much more of an identification with this group than they would with free agents and traded players. It's really been amazing.[37]"

Developing a Positive Public Image

We are the Worst,
We are the Rangers,
We're the ones who brighten pitchers' days.
So forget about us winning,
It's a ballteam we're faking,
We're wasting our lives.
It's true, we'll finish last again,
Just wait and see.[38]

When this passage was published in the newspaper in June 1985, Bobby Valentine has just replaced Doug Rader, and the Rangers were still in last place, where they had finished in 1984. It was another low point in a (sometimes) up and (mostly) down history of media coverage. But Valentine's "fresh" and "positive" approach with his young team soon paid dividends, both on the field and in the papers. The 1986 winning record did wonders for the team's positive coverage, both locally and nationally. Ray Gandolph of *ABC News* and Ken Picking of *USA Today* found themselves at Arlington Stadium, doing features on "V-Ball." Local-beat writers celebrated with "Rangers Have Organization on Right Road,"[39] while feature writers did profiles on Ranger announcers, promoters, groundskeepers, policemen, vendors, fans, and even the video dot race that runs on the Diamond Vision screen in center field during the sixth inning. It was a time to celebrate Ranger baseball.

Not surprisingly, the Ranger who has been the most visible catalyst of the Rangers' positive image is the field manager, Bobby Valentine. Valentine has been a hit with the local media, community leaders, and fans alike. *Sports Illustrated* described him as one of the top four managers in dealing with the media.[40] Valentine, who learned about representing the franchise from his mentor, Dodger skipper Tommy Lasorda, also has one of the busiest schedules of public appearances in the major leagues and is willing to attend almost any function, regardless of the number of people in attendance or the possibility of remuneration. Tom Grieve told one of many stories about Valentine:

> "I had scheduled a luncheon 5 months in advance and never looked at the calendar and it turns out that it's on the first day of the June draft. So the day we're going to make our first three draft choices, I have to go to this luncheon. I'm upset but it's too late to call it off. Bobby came up here to watch the draft and said, 'Hey, what's the matter?' I said, 'Oh, I've got to go to this luncheon.' He said, 'Stay here, I'll go get a tie on and do it for you.' Turns out there were about 10 people there, a little dinky club. They didn't even have a microphone, he just sat there and ate with them. It took 2 hours of his day, the day of a game, and he never even thought twice about it."

The accessibility of Valentine and other Ranger representatives has contributed to the development of the Rangers' positive image in the press. Indeed, media coverage of the team has continued to remain positive for the most part despite very disappointing seasons on the field in 1987 and 1988. Although some sports columnists occasionally harpoon the team, as sports columnists are wont to do, most stories have focused on the "qualified successes" of the past few seasons. Perhaps the most striking evidence of favorable coverage came before the 1988 season when the Rangers released pitcher Steve Howe, who had been signed by the Rangers in 1987 despite his long history of drug problems and multiple releases by previous clubs. Howe's release, motivated by his violation of certain conditions of his after-care program, could have provided grist for "we told you so" assaults in the press. Instead, one columnist, known for his regular assaults on past Ranger teams, said this:

> "Take a look at how the Rangers handled the Howe release, and you can see clearly that a big-league problem was handled in a big-league fashion. It wasn't too many years ago when seemingly everything the Rangers touched turned to bush, bush, bush. But even Steve Howe didn't drag the organization back to those sad, old days, which is a credit to leadership.[41]"

The Bottom Lines: Turning Profits and Winning Games

Turning Profits

Baseball purists (especially sportswriters) often express a distaste for the idea that baseball owners should make profits and control costs. Surprisingly, organizational communication researchers often share a similar distaste in discussing company profits. For all the talk generated by *In Search of Excellence* about "productivity through people," "value-driven action," "loose–tight properties," and "cultural excellence," researchers forget that the companies examined by Peters and Waterman "were not truly excellent unless their financial performance supported their halo of esteem."[42] Quite simply, from an organizational perspective, it is difficult to evaluate a company without considering its balance sheet.

This is not to say that the Ranger organization is an "excellent" company (though one could illustrate many of Peters and Waterman's principles with Ranger examples), but from a financial standpoint, they are moving in a profitable direction. After losing money every year since 1972, the Rangers finally turned a profit in 1986 and made money in 1987 and 1988. Record attendance figures, local broadcast packages, and one of the lowest player payrolls in the major leagues were the main contributing factors. Purists, of course, would respond by saying that major league franchises who control player salaries usually remain losers. But the fact remains that the Rangers in recent years have had one of the best cost-per-victory ratios in the majors.[43] Of course, purists would probably reject this equation too. Nevertheless, the Rangers have been profitable in the past 3 years and, thus, are a more successful company than if they were still losing money.[44]

Winning Games

And finally, in regard to the bottom line for baseball purists—winning games and winning championships—Ranger management is well aware of the need to win. As Tom Grieve put it in December of 1987:

> "What we have to do is stick with our philosophy and eventually prove that we can win, whether it is next year or the year after. We need to prove that we have good scouts and good minor league people and good management by taking these young players that we're bragging about and turning them into winners. You can't always be building. Eventually you have to win."

Unfortunately, the Rangers have not yet accomplished their mission to build a *winning* tradition. They enjoyed a taste of hopeful things to come in 1986 when a very young Ranger team stayed in the pennant race into September and finished in second place, behind the California Angels. The 1987 team, plagued by injuries, suffered a disappointing finish in last place, tied with the California Angels; even so, they ended the season only 10 games behind the eventual World Champion Minnesota Twins, the second smallest Ranger deficit in a full season since 1979.

The 1988 Rangers, plagued by a surprising lack of offense, finished with a record of 70–91 (.435), in sixth place, 33 1/2 games behind the American League Champion Oakland Athletics. The 1988 season was especially disappointing since the Rangers youth movement was expected finally to "come of age." Indeed, the disappointment of the 1988 season, along with the development of major league prospects in the Ranger farm system, led the Rangers to make the trades in the 1988 winter meetings described earlier.

The 1989 Rangers enjoyed their best ever start by compiling a 17–5 record to lead their division in the month of May; by September, however, the Rangers had fallen to fourth place, where they finished with a record of 83–79. In terms of media coverage, however, 1989 was a banner year, thanks largely to the performance of pitcher Nolan Ryan whom the Rangers had signed as a free agent during the winter of 1988. The Rangers enjoyed rare cover stories in the March 6, 1989 and August 21, 1989 editions of *The Sporting News* and the May 1, 1989 edition of *Sports Illustrated*. And when Nolan Ryan became the first pitcher in major league history to register 5,000 strikeouts when he threw a 96 mile per hour fastball past a swinging Rickie Henderson of the Oakland Athletics on August 21, 1989, over 200 reporters were at Arlington Stadium to cover the event. Ryan's 5,000th strikeout was featured on national sports newscasts such as ESPN and CNN as well as on the national CBS and ABC nightly news reports. In short, Nolan Ryan's 1989 season helped to put the Rangers on the national map; Ranger management hopes a 1990 championship will keep them there.

Acknowledgments. The author expresses appreciation to members of the Texas Rangers organization, especially to President Mike Stone for his permission to study the Ranger franchise for this case analysis.

NOTES

1. Unless otherwise noted, all quotations were obtained in personal interviews with Ranger personnel that were conducted over a 15-month period from October 1987 to December 1988. These quotations have been edited and condensed for this case analysis.

2. The Rangers were to play their first home game a week earlier but the first baseball strike postponed the home opener until April 12. The Rangers played their first game on April 15 in Anaheim against the California Angels, losing by a score of 1–0.

3. In March 1989, the Rangers were sold to a group of investors led by George W. Bush, the son of President George H. W. Bush.

4. Steve Pate, "Klein aims to change Ranger trade history," *Fort Worth Star-Telegram* (February 26, 1983).

5. Robert Vernon, "Thrill of victory," *Dallas Magazine* (Winter, 1988), p. 34.

6. Steve Pate, "Eddie Chiles," *Dallas Morning News* (July 5, 1987).

7. Ibid.

8. Ibid.

9. Claire Eyrich, "Rangers leading the league in luxury clubhouse department," *Fort Worth Star-Telegram* (April 23, 1981).

10. Bill DeOre, "Rangers revive belief in strong farm system," *Dallas Morning News* (April 12, 1981).

11. Randy Youngman, "Meason, Rangers, part ways," *Dallas Morning News* (February 1, 1983).

12. Craig Aronoff and Otis Baskin, *Public Relations: Profession and Practice* (St. Paul, MN: West, 1983), p. 119.

13. Steve Pate, *Fort Worth Star-Telegram* (February 26, 1983).

14. Galyn Wilkins, *Fort Worth Star-Telegram* (March 13, 1983).

15. Steve Pate, *Fort Worth Star-Telegram* (March 21, 1983).

16. Paul Hagen, *Fort Worth Star-Telegram* (July 1, 1984).

17. Even so, the 1988 Class AA Tulsa Drillers won the Texas League Championship.

18. Klein had also engineered a few unsuccessful player moves, especially the trade of pitchers Mike Smithson and John Butcher for outfielder Gary Ward and catcher Jim Sundberg for catcher Ned Yost.

19. Randy Galloway, "Rangers get messier with Klein firing," *Dallas Morning News* (September 2, 1984).

20. Skip Bayless, *Dallas Morning News* (September 1, 1984).

21. Phil Rogers, "Erasing doubt: Grieve casts forceful image in GM role," *Dallas Times Herald* (March 5, 1985).

22. Blackie Sherrod, "Rangers in Review: Rangers still trapped where next year never arrives," *Dallas Morning News* (October 3, 1988).

23. Phil Rogers, "Team wins bidding war over pitcher," *Dallas Times Herald* (December 8, 1988). At the time of this writing, the Rangers were expected to make additional trades for another designated hitter and/or outfielder.

24. Phil Rogers, "Rangers purchase an image," *Dallas Times Herald* (December 11, 1988).

25. Randy Galloway, "Ryan gives Rangers new credibility," *Dallas Morning News* (December 8, 1988).

26. Peter Gammons, "And here we go again," *Sports Illustrated* (December 19, 1988), p. 53.

27. Phil Rogers, "Grieve: You can't run scared," *Dallas Times Herald* (December 9, 1988).

28. Skip Bayless, "Who will pay for Rangers new bold look?" *Dallas Times Herald* (December 9, 1988).

29. Tracy Ringolsby, "Rangers accomplish Atlanta mission," *Dallas Morning News* (December 9, 1988).

30. Moss Klein, "Grieve deals Rangers the look of a contender," *The Sporting News* (December 19, 1988), p. 47.

31. Peter Gammons, *Sports Illustrated* (December 19, 1988), p. 53.

32. Randy Galloway, "Grieve curbs front-office wait problem," *Dallas Morning News* (December 6, 1988).

33. Blackie Sherrod, "Rangers agree to outside help at last," *Dallas Morning News* (December 9, 1988).

34. Randy Galloway, "Latin flavor will spice up Rangers' image in big leagues," *Dallas Morning News* (March 9, 1986).

35. Rafael Palmeiro is 24 and Julio Franco is 27.

36. Tracy Ringolsby, *Dallas Morning News* (December 9, 1988).

37. In a study conducted before the 1988 season, this fan identification was confirmed. Of the 434 Dallas–Fort Worth residents interviewed, 60% considered themselves Ranger fans, 76% said the Rangers had a positive image in the community, and 54% felt pride in the Rangers. Still, only 20% believed the 1988 Rangers would win the division. For more information about the study, please contact the author.

38. Dave Scott, "Ranger-Aid to benefit starving fans," *Arlington Daily News* (June 17, 1985).

39. Randy Galloway, "Rangers have organization on right road," *Dallas Morning News* (June 12, 1986).

40. Peter Gammons, "Best of the Bosses," *Sports Illustrated* (May 2, 1988), pp. 46–51.

41. Randy Galloway, "Look Howe far the Rangers have come," *Dallas Morning News* (January 21, 1988).

42. Thomas J. Peters and Robert H. Waterman, *In Search of Excellence* (New York: Harper & Row, 1982), p. 22.

43. One business report estimated that the Rangers were one of the seven most cost effective teams that held the cost per victory under $100,000 (compared with the Dodgers and Orioles who paid over $190,000 per victory). See Tom Steinert-Threlkeld, "Baseball needs penny pinchers," *Fort Worth Star-Telegram* (May 19, 1988).

44. Even so, Eddie Chiles has tried unsuccessfully to sell the Rangers for the past 3 years before he sold the club in March 1989.

KEY TERMS

organizational philosophy	public image
mission	internal development
statement of purpose	

DISCUSSION QUESTIONS

1. Why do you think so much effort was invested in developing the mission statement and the philosophy and beliefs document (see Figure 4.1)? Do you believe this kind of written document is important? Why or why not?

2. Rank or rate each of the Ranger beliefs in terms of its importance to the ultimate success of the franchise. Select the three most important and the three least important and discuss your rankings.

3. List the many ways that Ranger employees helped shape and communicate the corporate philosophy to organizational insiders and outsiders. How can companies that do not receive the public attention that sports franchises receive do this?

4. How did the Rangers deal with an organizational mission that did not appear to be working? Do you think the 1988 player trades are consistent with the Ranger philosophy to build a winning tradition primarily through internal development as argued in this case analysis? Why or why not? How do organizations deal with what appears to be inconsistent behavior regarding their publicized belief system?

5. Do the Rangers' values and beliefs apply to other nonsports businesses? Which of the 16 beliefs seem most relevant to other businesses and which seem peculiar to sports franchises? Why?

SUGGESTED READINGS

Beyer, J. M. (1982). Ideologies, values, and decision making in organizations. In P. Nystrom & W. Starbuck (Eds.), *Handbook of organizational design* (Vol. 1, pp. 166–202). London: Oxford University Press.

Deal, T. E., & Kennedy, A. A. (1982). *Corporate cultures*. Reading, MA: Addison-Wesley.

Kruse, N. W. (1981). Apologia in team sports. *Quarterly Journal of Speech, 67,* 270–283.

Posner, B. Z., Kouzes, J. M., & Schmidt, W. H. (1985). Shared values make a difference: An empirical test of corporate culture. *Human Resource Management, 24,* 293–309.

Trujillo, N., & Ekdom, L. R. (1985). Sportswriting and American cultural values: The 1984 Chicago Cubs. *Critical Studies in Mass Communication, 2,* 262–281.

CHAPTER 5

Past and Present Images of Challenger in NASA's Organizational Culture

Mary Helen Brown
Auburn University

The story of Challenger reveals much about the NASA culture. The explosion that destroyed the craft also rocked the image the public had of the National Aeronautics and Space Administration and the image NASA had of itself.

Studies in organizational culture focus on the aspects of an organization that work to make it special to its members. Culture goes beyond "something an organization has; a culture is something an organization is" (Pacanowsky & O'Donnel-Trujillo, 1983, p. 146). In general, an organization's culture is marked by critical events, that is, occasions notable enough to capture the "minds and actions" of members (Pettigrew, 1979). As such, a case analysis of a culture before, during, and after a critical event should increase understanding of the very essence of an organization.

With this in mind, this case study explores NASA's culture and the Challenger disaster. Culture played a major role throughout Challenger's saga, in that NASA was then facing a contradictory cultural situation: The shuttle that had helped make NASA special had also made NASA routine. The role of this cultural situation will be examined in (1) the background of Challenger and the space shuttle program, (2) the immediate reaction to the explosion by NASA and its public, (3) the investigations into the event, and (4) the role of Challenger in NASA's future.

THE CHALLENGER: ITS BACKGROUND AND HISTORY

The Challenger was part of a space shuttle fleet whose roots reach back to the 1960s. An advisory committee to President Lyndon Johnson made clear

111

in 1967 that a reusable vehicle would be of great economic value to the space program. By March of 1972, the present design of the space shuttle was established (Presidential Commission, 1986).

In general, the shuttle worked for NASA. The shuttle proved itself capable of a number of tasks—retrieving and repairing satellites, delivering diverse payloads, and acting as an orbiting laboratory, to name a few (Begley, 1983a). The craft became NASA's work horse. By using the shuttle, NASA was able to do work not only for itself, but for the Department of Defense and for commercial interests (Presidential Commission, 1986). In addition, the media, the general public, and government officials viewed the program favorably.

Looking back, however, the space shuttle program operated under paradoxical conditions. Throughout its development, testing, and 24 successful flights, the program met with great successes, but also with some rather embarrassing failures that usually took the form of costly delays. The shuttle became a symbol for the can-do spirit of Americans—however, a symbol whose tiles might fall off at any given minute. Nevertheless, the shuttle appeared more and more in everyday life. It took the form of children's (and adult's) toys, it became a logo for MTV, and it represented the quality of engineering for Ford Motor Company ("Ford Pulls," 1986).

Early shuttle flights received a great deal of attention. There was also continued interest in "firsts" performed by shuttle craft, and Challenger had its share of these accomplishments. The first space walk from a shuttle, for example, was performed on Challenger's maiden mission (Presidential Commission, 1986).

Perhaps Challenger's most intense media coverage came on its second flight. Mission Specialist Sally Ride became the first American woman to travel into space. Her exuberant depiction of the flight—calling it an E-ticket ride at Disneyland—marked a point when the culture of NASA, with its macho, right stuff astronauts, was being tempered by a new breed of space explorer (Adler, 1983; Begley, 1983b; Begley, 1983c).

For the most part, the shuttle had captured the public's imagination, and people wanted to participate. The shuttle made space seem accessible to everyone (Carey, 1983). The flights were safe; they were routine. The shuttle worked (Toufexis, 1983).

Yet, in some ways, the shuttle worked too well. As the flights went more or less "like clockwork," attention to the risky nature of the program waned (Wilford, 1986). Delays became more annoying and seemingly trivial, while the potential for disaster appeared more remote. In a 1985 article that now seems eerily mistitled, "Challenger's Agony and Ecstasy: A Shuttle Mission that Began in Near Disaster Ends in Triumph," *Time* noted almost in passing, "Yet a few gremlins still lurk. Three times in the past year, the launch procedures have resulted in near disaster" (Angier, 1985, p. 59). The mystique of the can-do image of NASA had developed to the point where tragedies dwelled in the land of imagination.

These views affected NASA's culture. NASA had been the agency of heroes, of risk taking. It was becoming the agency of the "space truck" (Begley, 1983a). The spirit of adventure that had marked the first shuttle flights had given way to a routine of delayed successes. With each and every flight, NASA personnel seemed more confident, yet also more complacent (Wellborn, 1986a). They faced conflicting purposes: to maintain the public's interest and support, to uphold a tradition of cockiness and risk taking, and to keep the flights as routine and predictable as possible. This jumble of cultural inputs no doubt contributed to the consequences of the final Challenger launch.

NASA attempted to maintain interest in the shuttle program in several ways. For example, some interest was raised by the staging of the first night launch, which was performed by Challenger (Begley, 1983d). However, NASA developed its closest ties to the public through the Citizen in Space Program. T-shirts emblazoned with an "I want to go" motto superimposed over an image of the space shuttle were purchased by the thousands (Large & McGinley, 1986). Rumors swirled that newscaster Walter Cronkite, an avid supporter of the space program, would be the first journalist in space. He would simultaneously become the oldest astronaut ("Cronkite: Space Cadet," 1986). Having the right stuff had been reduced to being in adequate physical condition.

Before that choice was made, however, the first teacher in space was selected to fly. Although she had been preceded by congressmen, Christa McAuliffe was to be the first "ordinary" American to fly in a space craft. She fit into NASA's culture well: "She had the effervescence of a teenager and the zeal of a missionary . . . [she] thought of the shuttle ride as 'the ultimate field trip' " ("A Special Breed," 1986, p. 29). McAuliffe approached the trip with a sense of adventure coupled with the notion of turning in a day's work. Further, her presence on the flight touched a nerve with many Americans, especially in the nation's school systems. NASA appeared to have made a wise decision (Broyles, 1986).

The Citizen in Space Program seemed a logical next step in space travel. In over 2 decades of successful space missions, NASA had compiled an enviable safety record. The 24 shuttle flights capped this achievement. However, the self-confidence that emerged from these triumphs may have been evolving into a sense of invulnerability. The agency's officials down-played the risks involved; like the public, these decision makers may have viewed failure as improbable, if not impossible (Greenberg, 1986). Thus, when delays began to plague mission 51-L of the Challenger, these setbacks may have been seen more as an irritation than a risk.

The launch of the craft was delayed three times. The first postponement was due to delays in a prior mission. Weather conditions forced the second delay. The third postponement was perhaps the most frustrating for NASA's personnel. The shuttle, "the most visible symbol of American leadership in space technology," was rooted to the ground by a balky hatch handle (Wilford, 1986, p. 38; Presidential Commission, 1986).

The press may have added to NASA's troubles. While there was favorable coverage of McAuliffe, the rest of the crew was generally ignored. Further, the press consistently reported the delays as though they were an inevitable part of the shuttle launching ritual. The launch was deemed so routine that only one network, Ted Turner's Cable News Network, planned to carry the launch live ("Disaster Puts," 1986).

In short, the events leading to the shuttle launch may have worked to create an atmosphere of confident, almost arrogant, complacency among NASA's membership. Also, the public and the press seemed less intrigued by NASA's mystique. Delays were viewed as inconveniences, not as necessary safety measures, and consequently they became less tolerated. More efficient launch successes were needed to keep the public involved and interested in the space program and to enhance NASA's image.

These factors undoubtedly influenced NASA's decision to launch on January 28. Extremely cold weather and ice accumulation existed at the launch site. However, a final inspection was made, and all the decision makers involved waived the weather restriction and gave the go ahead for launch rather than waiting through another delay. "The final flight of the Challenger began at 11:38:00.010 A.M., Eastern Standard Time, January 28, 1986" (Presidential Commission, 1986, p. 17).

THE IMMEDIATE REACTION

Less than 2 minutes later, Challenger was destroyed in a spectacular fireball. The event was so unexpected that for a brief time Mission Control maintained normal procedures before announcing that there had been "a major malfunction" ("The Craft," 1986). When the realization sank in, "large numbers of people fell into true mourning" (Garment, 1986, p. 20). NASA's culture and image had changed through a critical event (Pettigrew, 1979).

Initial reactions to the accident were mixed. The dangerous aspects of space travel were highlighted, and the necessity of taking risks to achieve progress was emphasized. Some were quick to point out that in terms of sheer numbers, the Challenger accident represented less loss of life than the crash of a jumbo jetliner. Many messages eulogized the members of the flight crew with special emphasis on the civilian, McAuliffe, and offered solace to a grieving public (Morrow, 1986). President Ronald Reagan's State of the Union Address was rescheduled so that he could deliver a memorial speech to the nation (Magnuson, Ajemian, Hannifen, & Jackson, 1986).

In the immediate aftermath of the explosion, the public was still generally in favor of NASA and its policies. A *Newsweek* poll conducted on January 29 and 30 revealed that "Americans clearly believe that the United States must maintain a program of manned space missions—including civilians" ("The Public's View," 1986). School children from across the country began sending NASA pennies, nickles, and dimes to build a replacement shuttle (Magnuson, Ajemian, Hannifen, & Jackson, 1986). Supporters of NASA were also quick to point out that $2\frac{1}{2}$ years after the last NASA tragedy (in which the three Apollo 1 astronauts were killed in a launch pad fire), NASA landed a craft on the moon (Cate & Jackson, 1986).

In recognition of the accident, many corporations pulled their shuttle-related advertisements and promotionals off the air. However, MTV kept running their promotionals while adding the following announcement: "We express our sympathy to the families of the Challenger's crew and in tribute to the shuttle crew, MTV honors the spirit of exploration" ("Space-Related Ads," 1986, p. 70).

Clearly, Americans were deeply affected by the loss of the shuttle. *Time* correspondent Lance Morrow (1986) wrote of its loss:

> It inflicted upon Americans the purest pain that they have collectively felt in years. It was a pain uncontaminated by the anger and hatred and hungering for revenge that came in the aftermath of terrorist killings, for example. It was pain uncomplicated by the divisions, political, racial, moral, that beset American tragedies (Viet Nam and Watergate, to name two). The shuttle crew, spectacularly democratic (male, female, black, white, Japanese American, Catholic, Jewish, Protestant) was the best of us, Americans thought, doing the best of things Americans do. The mission seemed symbolically immaculate, the farthest reach of a perfectly American ambition to cross frontiers. And it simply vanished in the air. (p. 23)

Parts of NASA's image began to vanish as well. The ordinary citizen's role in space travel had lasted only a little more than 70 seconds. NASA and its publics would no longer take space flight for granted ("We Will Not," 1986). Moreover, even as the tributes were being spoken, questions were being raised by a public suddenly more aware of and concerned about the safety of space flight. Why had the craft exploded? Why man spacecrafts to perform routine tasks? More specifically, why include civilians on dangerous missions? Questions such as these marked a shift from a somewhat accepting approval of NASA's culture, mystique, and policies to a steely quest for accountability (Begley, 1986; Wolfe, 1986).

NASA aggravated the situation by initially isolating itself from the general public and the press. When the news media, which originally treated Challenger's launch as passé, descended upon the site, they found that the space agency's officials had retreated into a kind of "Fortress NASA" (Martz, 1986).

NASA had always been aware of risks—the early broadcasts from the Mercury capsules had a 60-second delay built in to prevent the live broadcast of a disaster (Moffett & McGinley, 1986). Moreover, NASA officials, with their wealth of experience in promoting the agency, were cognizant of the damage to their image and credibility that would inevitably result from delays in disclosure. As such, the agency had a clearly detailed emergency plan that called for some sort of announcement within 20 minutes of an accident's occurrence. NASA's claims that its obligations were met by announcing that the craft had exploded notwithstanding, almost 5 hours elapsed before NASA held its first news conference (Moffett & McGinley, 1986). Through these actions, previously complacent NASA personnel confirmed that they were truly caught off guard by the accident. The utterly unexpected annihiliation of their dependable space truck left NASA's membership in disarray.

NASA further alienated news organizations by impounding the press film from still cameras located around the launch area. This action, coupled with the limited official disclosures, implied that the agency had something to hide (Zoglin, Gauger, & McCarroll, 1986). Rumors and speculation—about everything from pilot error, to a collision with a derrick, to terrorist activity—abounded about the cause of the disaster (Marbach, 1986a). Still, NASA remained relatively silent, and in its organizational environment, that silence cost NASA in terms of credibility, prestige, and support.

In brief, in the immediate wake of the disaster, NASA projected conflicting images. On one hand, the image of NASA as the right-stuff organization built on the notion that progress is achieved through risk was reconfirmed. On the other hand, NASA's self-isolation fostered the image of an overly confident organization that had been shocked into inaction when the unexpected occurred. Before the launch, NASA's culture centered around a ritual, a routine, that had partially contradicted NASA's nurtured right-stuff image. Now the routine was gone, and the organization faced further controversy.

THE INVESTIGATION PERIOD

As the shock of the explosion wore off, NASA found itself under scrutiny from a number of sources—the general public, Congress, the White House, the media, its contractors, its astronaut corps, and so on (Wellborn, 1986b). Further, NASA seemed to be having difficulty launching anything; it was experiencing a series of unmanned rocket failures (Marbach, 1986b).

In order to address the Challenger issue specifically, President Reagan appointed a blue-ribbon panel to investigate the incident. Many critics accused Reagan of engineering a public-relations ploy to restore NASA's credibility (McGinley, 1986). After all, critics reasoned, the panel, which included Neil Armstrong, Sally Ride, and Chuck Yeager among its members, seemed to have more name recognition than investigative experience. However, this panel, chaired by William P. Rogers, dug deeply into the events surrounding the Challenger launch and found that the overconfident can-do culture of NASA may have had fatal implications.

The physical causes of the explosion were obvious. An O-ring pressure seal had been affected by the extremely cold weather on the launch day and had failed to respond properly. This failure had created a leak in the right solid rocket motor, which in turn led to the explosion (Presidential Commission, 1986).

During the course of the investigation, however, it became apparent that more than technology had failed on January 28. For example, NASA had clearly been warned of the risks involved with that particular type of O-ring as early as 1982 (Wellborn, 1986b). Further, precedent had been established for delaying a launch due to cold weather. A year earlier, the launch of shuttle 51-C had been postponed for 24 hours when the temperature had dropped to 19 degrees and heavy ice was in the area. Even with this delay, the O-rings had shown evidence of having been damaged ("A Growing Thicket," 1986).

Moreover, it was becoming increasingly apparent that the final launch was attempted despite warnings voiced by project engineers from two major contractors (Magnuson, 1986). The Rogers Commission faced the task of determining why, in the face of the evidence against launching, NASA let the Challenger proceed. The Commission discovered a variety of causes contributing to the explosion, some of which resulted as much from NASA's culture as anything else.

The Commission found a decision-making procedure that was circuitous at best. Who made the final decisions was difficult to determine. The warnings that were raised against the launch travelled a winding path that neither reached those individuals with actual launch responsibility nor the flight crew (Magnuson, 1986; Presidential Commission, 1986). It seemed as though NASA's decision procedures were arranged so that no one person could be held responsible in the event of an accident (Martz, 1986).

Apparently, the decision to launch rested somewhere in NASA's middle management where the can-do culture overrode the potential hazards. These decision makers had asked the engineers to prove that the system would fail; if they could not, the launch would go ahead. The following exchange during the testimony of Roger Boisjoly (Seal Task Force, Morton Thiokol Company) to the Rogers Commission, highlighted this problem:

MR. BOISJOLY: . . . I felt personally that management was under a lot of pressure to launch and that they made a very tough decision, but I didn't agree with it.

One of my colleagues that was in the meeting summed it up best. This was a meeting where the determination was to launch, and it was up to us to prove beyond a shadow of a doubt that it was not safe to do so. This is in total reverse to what the position is in a preflight conversation or a flight readiness review. It is usually exactly opposite that.

DR. WALKER: Do you know the source of the pressure on management that you alluded to?

MR. BOISJOLY: Well, the comments made over the net is what I felt, I can't speak for them, but I felt it—I felt the tone of the meeting exactly as I summed up, that we were being put in a position to prove that we should not launch rather than being put in the position and prove that we had enough data to launch.

DR. WALKER: These were the comments from the NASA people at Marshall and at KSC [Kennedy Space Center]?

MR. BOISJOLY: Yes.

MR. FEYNMAN: I take it you were trying, you were asked to prove that the seal would fail?

MR. BOISJOLY: Yes.

MR. FEYNMAN: And of course, you couldn't because as a matter of fact it didn't. That is five of them didn't and only one did, and if you had proved that they all would have failed, you would have found yourself incorrect and under criticism because five of them didn't fail.

MR. BOISJOLY: That is right (Presidential Commission, 1986, pp. 793–794).

In the context of NASA's culture, the decision to launch had already been made. NASA had begun to see itself as an agency that could do no wrong, and that attitude may have led to overconfidence in their ability to carry out a successful mission. Another delay was neither necessary nor desirable in this culture.

Thus, NASA's confident managers created an impossible "prove us wrong" dilemma for the engineers. The engineers had no way of establishing that the O-rings would fail. The O-rings had never been tested at temperatures below 53°F; therefore, no data existed for launches below that temperature. Nevertheless, the Challenger was launched at 36°F (Presidential Commission, 1986).

In addition, the can-do culture of NASA's management was persuasive. Graphic evidence of its influence was given during the testimony of Robert Lund (vice-president of engineering, Morton Thiokol Company). Lund originally opposed the launch of Challenger. However, during the preflight management caucus, he altered his stance when he was asked "to take off his engineering hat and put on his management hat" (Presidential Commission, p. 94).

CHAIRMAN ROGERS: How do you explain the fact that you seemed to change your mind when you changed your hat?

MR. LUND: I guess we have to go back a little further in the conversation than that. We have dealt with Marshall for a long time and have always been in the position of defending our position to make sure that we were ready to fly, and I guess I didn't realize until after that meeting and after several days that we had absolutely changed our position from what we had been before. But that evening I guess I never had those kinds of things come from the people at Marshall that we had to prove to them that we weren't ready. . . . And so we got ourselves in the thought processes that we were trying to find some way to prove to them it wouldn't work, and we were unable to do that. We couldn't prove absolutely that the motor wouldn't work (Presidential Commission, 1986, p. 811).

As such, when this engineering contractor was asked "to put on his management hat," that is, to buy into NASA's culture, he did—as did others. The thought of failure was apparently less important than the thought of another delay. A delay would cost not only in terms of money, but in terms of prestige and saving "face" as well. After all, the flights were seen as a matter of safe routine.

With these thoughts prevalent during critical prelaunch decision meetings, NASA's managers dared others to prove them wrong. When outsiders found this to be impossible, those involved in initial discussions refrained from raising doubts or warnings to those who would make the final launch determination.

In brief, the Rogers Commission found that clear indications of potential problems had become mired in the middle levels of NASA's decision-making processes. A contributing factor to this flawed decision occurred because NASA's managers and project engineers put themselves in an impossible situation of proving that the technology would not work. This position quite possibly evolved from the attitudes of infallibility that NASA's members possessed toward their space truck. In the context of NASA's culture, those with the right stuff had made the wrong decision.

THE FUTURE OF THE CHALLENGER IN NASA'S CULTURE

Challenger has remained important in NASA's culture. Thirty-two months after the accident over a million spectators converged at the Kennedy Space

Center and millions of others watched on television as Discovery, the space shuttle following Challenger, was launched. The image of Challenger haunted the scene. Leon Jaroff (1988), correspondent for *Time* magazine, noted that initially the crowd was hesitant to celebrate the launch. He wrote,

> Again, visions of Challenger arose. . . . "Go at throttle up," Houston called at around the 70-second mark, and more than a few stomachs knotted. That was the last command heard by the crew of Challenger, which exploded seconds later. . . .
>
> Discovery commander Rick Hauck promptly answered with a laconic "Roger go," bringing a smattering of applause and cheers that grew into a chorus near the 2-minute mark when the spacecraft successfully jettisoned its two spent solid rocket boosters. (pp. 20–21)

Further, on the final full day of Discovery's mission, its crew held a memorial service for the seven Challenger astronauts (Cowley, 1988).

The linking of Challenger and Discovery helped rid NASA of some of its doubts and questions and helped restore some of its prestige and reputation. However, the final fate of Challenger—as a positive symbol, such as the Alamo or Pearl Harbor, or as a negative symbol, such as Watergate or the Bay of Pigs—has yet to be established.

Currently, these are indications that Challenger will become a positive symbol. As a result of the explosion and subsequent investigations, the cavalier attitudes toward shuttle flights exhibited by NASA and its publics have been replaced by a more cautious approach.

For example, NASA has spent more than 2 billion dollars redesigning the shuttle. These changes include the incorporation of a variety of safety measures into the design (Jaroff, 1988). The process of testing these changes contributed to several delays. Discovery's launch was moved a number of times from the initial date in February 1988 to the launch in late September of 1988.

In addition, as a result of the recommendations made by the Rogers Commission, NASA has implemented programs to help unravel their web of decision making. Efforts were taken to insure that prelaunch decisions leaned more in favor of caution than risk (Report to the President, 1986).

For example, 2 weeks before Discovery was launched, NASA held a 2-day readiness review for over 200 individuals involved in the mission. The conference was organized so that anyone involved in the mission could ask a question at any time. In addition, before the conference ended, 25 group leaders were polled concerning launch readiness. All had to answer in the affirmative before the launch could take place (Adler, 1988).

Further, NASA, partly through choice and partly through necessity, has become more self-contained and self-reliant. Astronauts have more input into policies (Marbach, 1986c). Crews have been selected with the danger of space flight in mind (Adler, 1988). In general, the steps NASA has taken in the recent history of the shuttle have been slower, and presumably safer.

Perhaps most important in terms of Challenger's future meaning, NASA still has support. Many still feel that accidents of this nature are an inevitable part of progress (Royster, 1986). Even when most Americans felt that safety was sacrificed for the Challenger flight, a two-to-one majority still endorsed further shuttle missions ("A Growing Thicket," 1986). Business and industry leaders maintained support for the program, and shuttle-linked advertisements and promotionals have returned in the media (Forkan, 1986; "The Challenge," 1986).

The government also has evidenced support for the program. In promising a renewal of the shuttle program, plans were set to build a new orbiter (Smith, 1986; Waldrop, 1986). In addition, though almost lost in the wake of the Rogers Commission findings, a presidential commission released goals for the space program in the 21st century. These goals included the establishment of permanent bases on the moon and on Mars. As former Apollo astronaut Alan Bean noted, "The thing that would really capture the imagination would be going to Mars—going somewhere we've never been before" (Marbach, 1986d, p. 64). By focusing on these efforts, Challenger should ultimately be seen as a tragic, yet heroic step on the road of exploration.

In conclusion, the Challenger accident was affected by and has affected NASA's culture. Before the launch, NASA displayed a complacent can-do spirit toward the emerging shuttle routine of delayed successes. After the accident, NASA had to cope with the totally unanticipated event and then with later revelations that their own confident, right-stuff culture played an important part in the flawed launch decision. Presently, NASA is at a crossroads. Evidence suggests that NASA's personnel will build from the Challenger accident slowly as they retarget their immediate and long-range goals.

Acknowledgment. The author wishes gratefully to acknowledge the Honorable Jim Chapman from the First Congressional District of Texas for his help in the completion of this project.

KEY TERMS

crisis communication	organizational culture
critical event	organizational environment
decision making	organizational symbol

DISCUSSION QUESTIONS

1. In what way did NASA's history shape its culture?

2. What role did culture play in the decision to launch Challenger?

3. What might NASA's administration have done to respond more effectively immediately after the accident?

4. How was NASA's culture changed by the Challenger explosion?

5. What is likely to be the symbolic role of Challenger in NASA's future?

6. What future developments are likely to have the most impact on NASA's culture?

REFERENCES

A growing thicket of theories: Shuttle disaster. (1986, March 17). *US News and World Report*, p. 8.

A special breed, a lust to soar. (1986, February 10). *Newsweek*, p. 29.

Adler, J. (1983, June 13). Sally Ride: Ready for liftoff: America's first space-bound woman has already left the rest of the world behind. *Newsweek*, pp. 36–51.

Adler, J. (1988, October 10). After the Challenger. *Newsweek*, pp. 28–36.

Angier, N. (1985, August 19). Challenger's agony and ecstasy: A shuttle mission that began in near disaster ends in triumph. *Time*, p. 59.

Begley, S. (1983a, June 13). The mission of Challenger. *Newsweek*, pp. 37–39.

Begley, S. (1983b, June 27). Challenger: Ride, Sally Ride. *Newsweek*, pp. 20–21.

Begley, S. (1983c, July 4). Challenger's happy landing: The space shuttle ends a nearly perfect mission and makes Sally Ride a star. *Newsweek*, pp. 68–70.

Begley, S. (1983d, September 5). NASA's nighttime spectacular. *Newsweek*, p. 69.

Begley, S. (1986, February 10). New life for a debate: To man or not to man? *Newsweek*, pp. 40–41.

Broyles, W. (1986, February 10). It is like a death in the family. *U.S. News and World Report*, p. 25.

Carey, J. (1983, June 13). No joy riding allowed. *Newsweek*, p. 40.

Cate, B. W., & Jackson, J. O. (1986, February 10). It was not the first time. *Time*, p. 45.

Cowley, G. (1988, October 10). Liftoff, liftoff. *Newsweek*, pp. 22–27.

Cronkite: Space cadet. (1986, January 20). *Newsweek*, p. 5.

Disaster puts media coverage in overdrive. (1986, February 10). *Advertising Age*, p. 74.

Ford pulls ads comparing van, space shuttle shapes. (1986, January 29). *Wall Street Journal*, p. 20.

Forkan, J. P. (1986, February 3). Shuttle-tied promos expected to survive. *Advertising Age*, p. 70.

Garment, S. (1986, January 31). Under the grief, our will persists to touch a star. *Wall Street Journal*, p. 20.

Greenberg, J. (1986, May 10). The white coveralls of overconfidence. *Science News*, p. 293.

Jaroff, L. (1988, October 10). The magic is back. *Time*, pp. 20–25.

Large, A. J., & McGinley, L. (1986, January 31). For private citizens, Challenger disaster may put dreams of space flight on hold. *Wall Street Journal*, p. 2.

Magnuson, E. (1986, March 10). A serious deficiency: The Rogers Commission faults NASA's "flawed" decision-making process. *Time*, pp. 38–42.

Magnuson, E., Ajemian, R., Hannifen, J., & Jackson, D. S. (1986, February 10). They have slipped the surly bonds of earth to touch the face of God. *Time*, pp. 24–31.

Marbach, W. D. (1986a, February 10). What went wrong? *Newsweek*, pp. 32–34.

Marbach, W. D. (1986b, May 19). 1986: A space odyssey. *Newsweek*, pp. 62–63.

Marbach, W. D. (1986c, June 23). Astronauts get into the loop. *Newsweek*, pp. 66–68.

Marbach, W. D. (1986d, June 16). An agency without a mission: After the Rogers report, NASA has to set new goals. *Newsweek*, p. 64.

Martz, L. (1986, March 3). A fatal "error of judgment": Whatever caused Challenger to blow up, warning flags were raised and ignored. The implication was disturbing: The astronauts didn't have to die. *Newsweek*, pp. 14–20.

McGinley, L. (1986, February 12). Panel probing explosion of Challenger is pressed to prove autonomy in face of strong NASA ties. *Wall Street Journal*, p. 62.

Moffett, M., & McGinley, L. (1986, February 14). NASA, once a master of publicity, fumbles in handling shuttle crisis. *Wall Street Journal*, p. 23.

Morrow, L. (1986, February 10). A nation mourns. *Time*, pp. 20–23.

Pacanowsky, M. E., & O'Donnell-Trujillo, N. (1983). Organizational communication as cultural performance. *Communication Monographs, 50*, 126–147.

Pettigrew, A. M. (1979). On studying organizational cultures. *Administrative Science Quarterly, 24*, 570–581.

Presidential Commission on the Space Shuttle Challenger Accident. (1986). *Report of the presidential commission on the space shuttle Challenger accident*. (Vols. 1–5). Washington, DC: Author.

Report to the president: Actions to implement the recommendations of the presidential commission on the space shuttle Challenger accident. (1986). Washington, DC: National Aeronautics and Space Administration.

Royster, V. (1986, February 6). Tragedy after triumphs. *Wall Street Journal*, p. 28.

Smith, R. J. (1986, May 9). Fletcher promises rebirth of shuttle program. *Science*, p. 706.

Space-related ads pulled after tragedy. (1986, February 3). *Advertising Age*, p. 70.

The challenge of Challenger. (1986, February 10). *Advertising Age*, p. 17.

The craft has exploded. (1986, February 10). *Newsweek*, p. 28.

The public's view. (1986, February 10). *Newsweek*, p. 37.

Toufexis, A. (1983, August 29). NASA readies a nighttime dazzler. *Time*, p. 62.

Waldrop, M. M. (1986, May 9). White House group recommends a new shuttle. *Science*, pp. 706–707.

We will not disappoint them. (1986, February 10). *US News and World Report*, p. 14.

Wellborn, S. N. (1986a, February 10). Out of Challenger's ashes—full speed ahead: First U.S. space disaster stuns nation. *US News and World Report*, pp. 16–20.

Wellborn, S. N. (1986b, March 10). NASA falls from grace. *US News and World Report*, p. 20–22.

Wilford, J. N. (1986, March 16). America's future in space after the Challenger. *New York Times Magazine*, p. 39.

Wolfe, T. (1986, February 10). Everyman vs. astropower. *Newsweek*, pp. 40–41.

Zoglin, R., Gauger, M., & McCarroll, T. (1986, February 10). Covering the awful unexpected. *Time*, pp. 42–45.

PART III

Issues of Power and Ethics

CHAPTER 6

Stalking Tiger Brown: Racial Undertones of an Ethical Dilemma

PAUL PRATHER
University of Kentucky

Andrea was flattered and excited when State Editor Bob Kenton called her into the conference room to ask if she would work on the Tiger Brown story. Tiger Brown was the biggest story the Midcity *Daily News* had uncovered all year. Brown, the state's first black lieutenant governor—and one of the first in the country—had garnered national attention by winning office 2 years ago. The *Daily News* had endorsed his candidacy.

But almost immediately after Brown took office, unsavory rumors about him had surfaced in the halls of state government. Normally reliable legislators began buttonholing reporters and telling them, off the record, of course, that Brown was taking illegal kickbacks from businesses, that he was using state funds for improvements on his house, and that he had hired a woman believed to be his mistress as his "special assistant."

The *Daily News*, one of the state's two largest newspapers, had been quietly looking into those allegations for months, without success. Until the previous week.

Brown had supposedly been in Atlanta, at state expense, attending a national conference of lieutenant governors. But, during that same week, Brown stepped out of a hotel room in Miami with his "special assistant" on his arm—and bumped into a vacationing *Daily News* copy editor. Brown did not know the editor. The editor recognized Brown, though, and ran to the nearest telephone to call the paper.

Not wanting to tip Brown off, and not being able to say for certain that he had done anything wrong, the *Daily News* began discretely searching for

Brown's travel records. Reporters tried to determine whether Brown had simply left the conference for a day, at his own expense, and flown to Miami—or whether the Atlanta conference was only a cover for a Florida vacation with his mistress at state expense.

The problem was that Brown's trip, like other situations he was involved in, turned out to be murky. He seemed to be an expert at covering his tracks. The reporters got nowhere. Even the other lieutenant governors at the conference were of no help.

But today, a reporter at the state capitol had heard that Brown's long-time secretary, an elderly black woman named Ruby Radcliff, was fed up with Brown's waywardness. And she was responsible for making all of Brown's travel arrangements.

"We think that if we play it right, Ruby Radcliff will talk," Bob Kenton said to Andrea. "We want you to interview her. She could make this story."

Andrea's adrenalin was pumping. A "lifestyles" writer, she was not usually called out on big, breaking stories such as this one. She nodded eagerly.

"Sure," she said. "Thanks."

"Well," Bob said, "you've got a great advantage that no one on the investigative team has. You're black. You can probably get Radcliff to talk to you." Andrea was stunned.

"I don't even know her. Why would she talk to me any more than she would talk to another reporter?" Bob stood up and walked to the conference room door. He winked.

"Can you get up to the state capitol tonight? Go to her house, catch her away from her office." Andrea had begun to feel strange. But she was still excited—this was the kind of story that could win the paper, and reporters, important prizes. As she and Bob walked out of the conference room, Andrea said, "Do you have Ruby Radcliff's address?"

Bob nodded toward Donna Taylor, a white reporter who was a member of the paper's elite investigative team. "Donna's got the address. I forgot to mention it, but she's going with you. She'll take notes and write the story. You just get Ruby talking." He tapped Andrea's shoulder good-naturedly. "Hey, we've got to have the first team on this one, you know?"

Andrea just stood there. Somebody was being wronged, she thought. Maybe she was. Maybe Ruby Radcliff was. She did not know.

This case, based on an actual incident, demonstrates how complex and subtle racism can be. If Bob Kenton were asked whether he had insulted Andrea, he would probably be stunned. If Andrea were asked, she might say Bob was a bigot.

Bob could view the situation like this: Because Ruby Radcliff can make or break this important story, Bob wants her at ease when she is interviewed, and people tend to feel more comfortable with others who are like them. Also, Ruby might be less likely to think that Andrea is out to persecute Tiger Brown simply because he is black. Similarly, if Bob needed a story from some guy in rural Appalachia, he would likely send one of his good ol' boy reporters, perhaps Billy Roy Stamper. And if Ruby were a devout Jew, he might send Joe Steinberg, a reporter who is Jewish. The fact that Andrea is black is not the issue to Bob. The issue, to him, is that her being black may give the paper an extra edge.

As for not letting Andrea write the article once she has successfully completed her interview, well, again, Bob might say that has nothing to do with Andrea's color. The problem is that she is one of those artsy lifestyles writers. Hard-news reporters and editors hold lifestyles writers in a certain disdain—they're not "real" reporters.

And when it comes to the other ethical question—whether Bob is setting up Ruby—why should he worry about that, Bob might ask? He is under great pressure. He will leave that kind of problem for philosophers. Bob has an important job to do.

Except that, as Bob may have forgotten, in his "important" job he is dealing with flesh-and-blood humans, people no less important than the story he wants to publish. And in the case of minorities, especially blacks, he is dealing with people who have a long history of being treated as second-class humans, or worse. Andrea is likely to read Bob's actions as a slam against her race. And she may be right, despite all of Bob's possible pro-testations to the contrary.

Bob, despite his pressures, needs to rethink things.

KEY TERMS

ethics
culture
interethnic communication

DISCUSSION QUESTIONS

1. What are the ethical implications of trying to encourage Brown's long-time secretary to turn on him?

2. What are the assumptions Andrea's editor makes about Andrea and Ruby? Are those assumptions fair to Andrea? To Ruby?

3. Why does Andrea's editor assume that Donna Taylor should actually write the story?

SUGGESTED READINGS

Cressey, D. R., & C. A. Moore (1983). Managerial values and corporate codes of ethics. *California Management Review, 25,* 53–77.

Ewing, D. W. (1983). *Do it my way—or you're fired!* New York: Wiley.

Gellerman, S. W. (1986). Why "good managers" make bad ethical choices." *Harvard Business Review, 4,* 85–90.

Mathews, M. C. (1988). *Strategic intervention in organizations: Resolving ethical dilemmas.* Newbury Park, CA: Sage.

CHAPTER 7

Power and Sex Roles
in the Workplace

Shereen G. Bingham
University of Nebraska at Omaha

Rhonda Dean[1] entered the workforce for the same reason many other married woman her age did in the 1970s: economic need. After her three children started school, Rhonda's major obstacle to starting a career outside the home had been her husband. "No wife of mine will get a job," he had bellowed. His attitude changed remarkably, though, when his trucking company approached bankruptcy. A year later Rhonda was selling homes for Rockfield Realty.

Rhonda worked for Rockfield for almost 5 years—more than enough time to discover that real estate was her forte. She gained a reputation for her hard work, persistence, and an unmatched ability to listen to customers and give them what they needed. Mike Rockfield recognized Rhonda's ambition and natural ability and offered her the opportunity to advance her career with a position in commercial real estate. He taught her the basics of leasing commercial property, paid her to take college courses, and even helped her financially as she earned her broker's license. Rhonda was forced to give up her career with Rockfield, however, when her husband took a position in another city.

In 1984 Rhonda was hired as a leasing director with the commercial real estate division of Nason's Department Stores, Inc. Among its numerous properties, Nason's owned 19 shopping centers in the western United States. Rhonda's primary responsibilities as leasing director were to bring successful stores into these malls, to monitor and renew store leases, and to manage tenant–landlord relations. Her education, experience, and skills prepared Rhonda well for the position, and she had reason to expect a long, prosperous, and fulfilling career with Nason's. As she became acculturated into the organization, however, Rhonda learned a bitter lesson about the power of sexual harassment to belittle women and prevent their success.[2]

One of the first things Rhonda learned about the organizational culture at Nason's was that traditional sex roles strongly governed relations between employees. Traditional sex-role attitudes and expectations concerning appropriate behavior for women and men were evident in every aspect of organizational life. Jobs within the organization were highly sex segregated, with men dominating positions at the top and middle levels of the hierarchy, and women concentrated in jobs at the bottom. This structural feature of the organization reinforced traditional stereotypes of women as submissive, subserviant, and dependent, and men as dominant, masterful, and independent. All secretarial positions were held by women, who were referred to by their male superiors as "girls," and who were expected to tend to personal matters for their bosses (such as running errands and buying gifts), in addition to secretarial duties. Women were considered incapable of demonstrating the leadership and decision-making abilities necessary for management-level positions and rarely were given opportunities to prove otherwise. For example, no women were included in the long-range planning group that charted future directions for the company, and women generally were not included in networks involving influential organizational figures. As a result, women were not provided key information concerning matters such as expectations and opportunities for advancement and were not members of the groups and networks in which they could demonstrate their expertise and competence. The few women who were able to advance were viewed as anomalies, and their success was usually attributed to luck or sexual exchanges rather than personal competence. These women were also paid substantially less than men holding similar positions.

Perhaps the culture that evolved within the organization can be partly traced back to the philosophy of its founder, Edward Nason. Edward viewed himself as a cold, tough, aggressive, businessman. He started a business with the purchase of a single department store and built it into a multimillion dollar corporation through ingenuity and ruthless competitiveness. Edward had become something of a legend among Nason's employees. His philosophy of business could be captured by a phrase he had been fond of repeating at meetings and addresses to the organization and that had become Nason's slogan: "Success is to the tough, failure to the timid."

The sex-role traditionalism that pervaded Nason's culture became evident to Rhonda during her first day of work. She arrived at Northway Shopping Center where she was to meet George Parks, Nason's West Coast vice president. George would be Rhonda's immediate superior, and she was expected to keep him informed of her progress on the job through written reports and weekly luncheon meetings. "I've been instructed to keep a close eye on you," George said, winking at Rhonda when they met. "The men upstairs want to see just how well a woman can do."

George was a bright, articulate, outspoken man, with a domineering manner and a hearty sense of humor. He had been instrumental in Nason's decision to hire Rhonda and had a stake in seeing her succeed. Rhonda felt a bit overwhelmed by George's friendly, controlling style, but she appreciated the interest he seemed to take in her and believed she could learn a great deal from him if she earned his respect.

George put his arm around Rhonda's shoulders as they walked through the shopping center, calling her attention to empty store areas that he felt should be her first leasing priorities. He escorted her to her office on the east wing of the Northway Center and introduced her to the employees who would share her office. Rhonda was immediately uncomfortable with Ben Daniels, the manager of the shopping center. Ben was a loud, arrogant man in his late 40s. Although he was Rhonda's equal within Nason's organizational hierarchy, his behavior conveyed presumed superiority. When George introduced Rhonda to Ben, Ben scanned Rhonda's body and commented snidely, "If I'd known you had a shape like that, I might have hired you myself!"

Rhonda thanked Ben for his "compliment" but regretted doing so the moment she spoke. His remark could have been intended as a compliment, but Rhonda felt degraded by it. As she thought more about the comment, she realized why it was humiliating. In one simple statement, Ben had assumed the right to comment on her body, had implied that her "shape" was the reason for her being hired, and had suggested that she might easily have been working for him.

Ben's initial greeting was only one of many times that he undermined Rhonda's competence and status through his communication with her. His verbal and nonverbal messages functioned to make her gender more salient than her role as an organizational employee. When she arrived at the office in the morning, for example, Ben frequently insisted on greeting her with a hug and kiss. Likewise, in the evenings, he regularly asked her if she would come home with him "for drinks and a little fun." Rhonda tolerated these rituals even though she disliked them. She did not want to make trouble with Ben, and she knew that if she complained he would insist he was just being friendly.

Rhonda's tolerance for Ben's behavior deteriorated as weeks passed. He continued to impose stereotypical feminine characteristics on her, especially in the presence of other men. A male audience seemed to call forth in him an especially sexist demeanor. He frequently asked Rhonda to make coffee and take notes at meetings, spoke to her primarily about sexual and family-related topics, and accused her of being too emotional whenever she disagreed with him on decisions concerning the shopping center. On one occasion he called Rhonda into his office while he was meeting with two male city officials. When she walked into the office Ben announced, grinning at the two men, "This is one of my fringe benefits!" Embarrassed, angry, and speechless, Rhonda returned to her own office.

As Ben's behavior became more degrading and offensive, Rhonda decided she would have to take action to deal with it. She wondered why he was behaving as he was. Was she intimidating this man or inviting his behavior by projecting an unprofessional image? Perhaps she should ask for his opinions more often or wear drabber clothing to the office. Regardless of the reasons for Ben's behavior, Rhonda knew she would have to do something about it soon because it was beginning to affect her ability to concentrate on work. Ignoring and joking about his behavior certainly were not helping the situation. Should she confront him directly? If so, what strategy should she use? Should she assertively tell him to stop, politely ask him to change his behavior, threaten to file a formal grievance against him, or what?

Rhonda also considered confiding in George about Ben's behavior, but she was hesitant for two reasons. First, she did not want George to lose confidence in her. She worried that George might view her problem with Ben as an indication that she could not handle her position. Second, George was not entirely unlike Ben in his behavior. Although George did not intentionally humiliate Rhonda, he did frequently cause her discomfort with sexual remarks and inappropriate touching. For example, when she successfully negotiated her first lease for the Northway Center with a large furniture store owner, George gave her a big congratulatory kiss on the lips. He also put his arm around her during their weekly luncheon meetings and frequently commented on her sexual attractiveness.

Whenever George engaged in lewd talk or inappropriate nonverbal behavior, Rhonda tried to ignore or joke about it. Sometimes she changed the subject by mentioning her husband or by asking George about his wife and children. She never told George directly that his behavior made her uncomfortable. Although she was sure he would alter his behavior if she told him she disliked it, she worried that doing so would damage their rapport. She did not want to lose George's support and friendship, damage his affiliation with her, or hurt his feelings. Rhonda liked George and enjoyed interacting with him when his behavior was not lewd or offensive. Moreover, she was convinced that George did not realize that his behavior was unwanted and inappropriate. Sometimes Rhonda even wondered whether she was being overly sensitive. She had seen George behave similarly toward other women at the office and noted that they did not seem offended.

Finally, Rhonda thought of an approach that might alleviate her problem with Ben and send George a message about his own behavior at the same time. She decided to confide in George about Ben's behavior and elicit his support. During her next luncheon meeting with George, Rhonda described Ben's conduct and explained how it was affecting her self-confidence and ability to work. She revealed that Ben's behavior was affecting her motivation on the job, that he humiliated her in front of others, and was undermining her professional image.

George reacted to Rhonda's disclosure with sympathy, support, and indignation. He condemned Ben as a "sexist pig" and provided Rhonda with information that helped her understand Ben's conduct in a new light. According to George, Ben was interested in shifting his career focus from shopping center management to lease negotiations. In fact, Ben had applied for Rhonda's leasing director position himself, but the application had been rejected. Ben then had raised a controversy on the issue among organizational executives, arguing that Nason's hiring decision constituted reverse sex discrimination. George assured Rhonda that Ben was wrong; she had been hired because she was the more qualified applicant. However, he admitted that he had been unable to persuade everyone in the upper ranks to disagree with Ben. Several others at Nason's were doubtful that a woman was capable of doing a competent job as leasing director. Still, George encouraged Rhonda to confront Ben about his behavior and urged her to report back to him immediately if the behavior did not change.

Although Rhonda appreciated George's verbal support and understanding, she was amazed by his apparent inability to see similarities between Ben's behavior and his own. Even as he condemned Ben, George patted Rhonda's thigh and commented on how much he enjoyed working with women. Rhonda's talk with George also worried her. She had not realized previously how unstable her position was with Nason's or the extent to which she was indebted to George for taking her side in the hiring decision. Now more than ever she was reluctant to complain to George about his behavior. He clearly viewed Ben's actions as sexist and inappropriate, while considering his own conduct to be acceptable. George would be offended and disgruntled if she told him she viewed his behavior as similar to Ben's. At this point in her career, Rhonda did not want to risk alienating George and losing his support.

The next day George called Rhonda to tell her he had a perfect solution to her problem with Ben. "You need to get away from the office," he insisted. George explained that he would be flying to Texas that weekend to attend a national conference for owners and managers of commercial real estate. "It will be a wonderful opportunity for you," he argued. "You'll learn a lot, make contacts with important people, relax, and have some fun for a change."

Rhonda agreed to attend the conference and thanked George for the opportunity. As she hung up the telephone, however, she felt danger pangs

in the pit of her stomach. She worried that attending an out-of-town conference with George could escalate his sexual behavior toward her. Resolved
to prevent such a catastrophe, however, Rhonda disregarded her feelings
and began to plan for the trip. She reasoned that she could not miss an
opportunity to advance her career because of fears about how George might
behave.

Approximately 250 men and 10 women attended the conference. A
substantial portion of the conference was spent socializing in the lounge of
the convention center. At first Rhonda mingled about on her own, but soon
she discovered it was in her best interest to stay at George's side. On her
own, she found, the men she met did not take her seriously as a professional.
The first man she spoke to asked if she were attending the conference with
her husband. Several other men engaged her momentarily in polite conversation and then asked her to join them for dinner or a cocktail in the
nearby bar. After a number of such interactions, Rhonda began to recognize
the conversational pattern that would end in a date request. The man would
ask her about the nature of her work, brag about the large office buildings he
owned, comment that he needed someone like her to lease the buildings,
mention that he was unhappily married, and finally ask her to join him for
dinner. When Rhonda refused the dinner invitation, the man never spoke to
her again. She quickly learned to divert the progression of such conversations before they concluded.

In contrast, Rhonda's experience was rewarding and productive when
she mingled with George. George introduced her to important people in the
field and always presented her as a competent, intelligent professional. She
was impressed by George's social astuteness and grace and was grateful for
his support. She was pleased with herself for having come to the convention
with George and for squelching her doubts about his professionalism.

On the final night of the conference, a large cocktail party was held in a
grand room of the convention center. Those who attended were visibly tired
from the conference but clearly ready to enjoy themselves. George had
consumed several drinks by the end of the party and was in an especially
good humor. When Rhonda said she was tired and would be turning in for
the night, George offered to walk her back to her hotel room for protection.
Rhonda accepted his offer because it was late and because she wanted the
opportunity to thank George for bringing her to the conference and being
supportive of her. When they arrived at her hotel room Rhonda expressed
her thanks to George and kissed him lightly on the cheek. She unlocked the
door to her room, looked back at George, and was startled to find him
standing very close to her. All at once, he grabbed her and began to kiss her
while pushing her into the room.

"Now, George," Rhonda said struggling and pushing George away.
"You've had too much to drink. Let go of me! Let's not do something we will

regret." George staggered back, looked out the door to see if they had been seen, and left, closing the door behind him. Rhonda locked the door with trembling hands and stared in disbelief at her reflection in the mirror. What had happened? Did she mislead him somehow? Could she have prevented his attack? Should she have refused his offer to walk her to her room? What should she do now?

The next day George acted as though nothing had happened the night before, and Rhonda played along. All night she had anguished over the moment she would have to talk to George about what happened, and his pretense came as a relief. On the plane home George hardly spoke, saying he was tired, worn out, and hung over. Rhonda considered the possibility that George did not remember what had happened. Perhaps he had been drinking more heavily than she had realized. Rhonda preferred that possibility to its alternative: that George knew exactly what he had done but was too ashamed, embarrassed, or angry to discuss it.

When Rhonda returned to work, it became evident that George remembered the hotel incident only too clearly. His contact with her dropped off sharply. He lost interest in her work and began to cancel their luncheon meetings. Even when they did meet, George was unenthusiastic and distracted. His manner became polite, aloof, but never hostile.

Six months later Rhonda was fired. She was told that Nason's had eliminated her position because it was determined to be superfluous; the managers of Nason's shopping centers would acquire her previous responsibilities. That is, instead of having one leasing director for several shopping centers, the manager of each shopping center would negotiate leases as necessary. Ben Daniels received a sizable raise and promotion for taking on Rhonda's responsibilities at the Northway Center.

Although Rhonda suspected that the hotel incident with George contributed to the elimination of her position, she chose not to pursue the situation legally. Without documentation or witnesses, Rhonda believed that her case was hopeless.

NOTES

1. The incidents of this case are based upon actual experiences informally reported to the author by professional women. The author conducts research on communication strategies for managing sexual harassment in organizations.

2. In 1980, the Equal Employment Opportunity Commission issued guidelines that defined sexual harassment as "unwelcome sexual advances, requests for sexual favors, and other verbal or physical conduct of a sexual nature" that are connected to employment decisions, or that create an intimidating, hostile, or offensive working environment.

KEY TERMS

false assumptions   sex roles
organizational culture   sex-role traditionalism
power   sexual harassment
self-disclosure

DISCUSSION QUESTIONS

1. Would you describe Ben's behavior toward Rhonda as sexual harassment? Would you describe George's behavior as sexual harassment? Why or why not?

2. How realistic was Rhonda's behavior? Why do you think she behaved the way she did? What other strategies would you suggest for deflecting sexual harassment?

3. What presumably false assumptions did Rhonda and George each make that contributed to the problem of sexual harassment?

4. How does a founder contribute to the development of an organization's culture?

5. Do you think the organizational culture at Nason's encouraged behavior like Ben's and George's? If so, how?

6. How are sexual harassment and organizational power related?

SUGGESTED READINGS

Backhouse, C., & Cohen, L. (1981). *Sexual harassment on the job: How to avoid the working woman's nightmare*. Englewood Cliffs, NJ: Prentice-Hall

Bingham, S. G. (1988). *Interpersonal responses to sexual harassment*. Unpublished doctoral dissertation, Purdue University, West Lafayette, IN.

Booth-Butterfield, M. (1986). Recognizing and communicating in harassment-prone organizational climates. *Women's Studies in Communication, 9*, 42–51.

Equal Employment Opportunity Commission (1980). Discrimination because of sex under Title VII of the Civil Rights Act of 1964, as amended: Adoption of final interpretive guidelines. *Federal Register, 45*, 74676–74677.

Farley, L. (1978). *Sexual shakedown: The sexual harassment of women on the job*. New York: McGraw-Hill.

Hemphill, M. R., & Pfeiffer, A. L. (1986). Sexual spillover in the workplace: Testing the appropriateness of male–female interaction. *Women's Studies in Communication, 9*, 52–66.

Gutek, B. A. (1985). *Sex and the workplace*. San Francisco: Jossey-Bass.

Jones, T. S. (1983). Sexual harassment in the organization. In J. Pilotta (Ed.), *Women in organizations: Barriers and breakthroughs* (pp. 23–37). Prospect Heights, IL: Waveland.

Livingston, J. A. (1982). Responses to sexual harassment on the job: Legal, organizational, and individual actions. *Journal of Social Issues, 38,* 5–22.

Remland, M. S., & Jones, T. S. (1985). Sex differences, communication consistency, and judgments of sexual harassment in a performance appraisal interview. *The Southern Speech Communication Journal, 50,* 156–176.

Wood, J.T., & Conrad, C. (1983). Paradoxes in the experiences of professional women. *Western Journal of Speech Communication, 47,* 305–322.

CHAPTER 8

Communicators Spanning the Boundaries: A Story of Power, Loyalties, and Stress

MYRIA WATKINS ALLEN
Louisiana State University

JOY HART SEIBERT
The University of Tulsa

THE ORGANIZATION

InfoNet[1] appears to be a product of today's information age, however, it was founded early in this century by a man with a vision for better communication between government and industry. He created an informational headquarters through which business people, policy makers, and governmental officials could access and share needed information. During the decades following its formation, InfoNet grew and played an increasingly important part in business, state, and regional policy decisions.

Periodically, through the years, InfoNet has faced environmental pressures that have forced management to redefine the organization's missions, and either to increase or decrease staff size dramatically. Turnover has always been moderately high due to work pressures, funding problems, and job mobility opportunities. In the late 1980s, the organization is again growing, and its missions and culture are once again changing.

The organization is structured as three divisions based on its three missions: general information collection and dissemination, specific research and information for clients, and policy and strategy analysis (see Figure 8.1). The information division responds to a wide range of requests for information, conducts research, and publishes a variety of resource documents. The client services division plans meetings and conventions, provides information on request, conducts research, and publishes newsletters for client

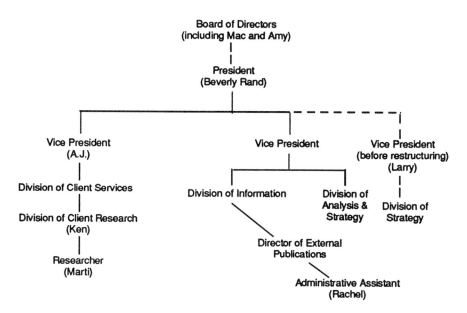

FIGURE 8.1. An organizational chart of InfoNet after restructuring.

organizations across the country. The policy and strategy area is responsible for policy analysis, trend tracking, and strategic planning recommendations for clients, as well as for InfoNet.

At InfoNet, telephone calls may go out to and come in from anywhere in the northern section of this hemisphere. The issues discussed change continually, and it is important to be abreast of the latest developments. Staying ahead in the information race is crucial.

Most of the 98 staff members are highly educated. Many pride themselves on their ability to keep track of the most recent developments in their area, since this enhances their ability to improve the quality and circulation of information entering and leaving InfoNet. About a third are boundary spanners who have most of their work-related contact with people in other organizations. Boundary spanners spend most of their time managing the flow of information and resources into the organization and/or from the organization to outside groups. Being a boundary spanner means you spend a lot of time on the phone or on the road travelling to meetings. Marti is a boundary spanner who works in the client services division. She is InfoNet's liaison to five client groups. Because Marti spends so much of her time working with outside groups, often she does not feel she is really part of InfoNet and its informal communication network. This case focuses on the intraorganizational problems and opportunities Marti faces as a boundary spanner.

THE SITUATION

Marti hesitated before opening her office door as she wondered what mess was waiting on the desk for her this time. June was one of her busiest months. Last June, she had spent 15 working days out of the office, and it looked as if this June would be no different. After every trip, it took at least 2 hours to sort through the chaos on her desk—hours that she desperately needed to devote to working on reports and publications, planning meetings, or researching client questions.

Squaring her shoulders and taking a deep breath, Marti pushed open the door. Sure enough, chaos reigned. She would have to sort through all the mail, messages, and memos (it seemed that this organization ran on long, detailed memos), before she could finish the report that she needed to telefax to San Francisco by 10:30 A.M.

Skimming quickly through the material on her desk, one memo seemed especially important. A meeting was planned for 1 P.M. at the InfoNet headquarters office to discuss organizational restructuring and redirection, which was supposed to last for 1 1/2 hours. Like most of the 43 people she worked with in the company's shabby downtown annex, Marti actually had very little interest in events at headquarters. Most of her work, work-related friends, and funding came from her clients. Ordinarily she would not go to a headquarters meeting because she felt isolated from the headquarters staff and operations, but the changes mentioned in the memo worried her, so she decided to go.

She knew that the meetings were partially designed to build cohesion between the different facets of the organization. Due to the large number of boundary spanners in the organization, such meetings were often the only time people had to meet individuals working in other areas, learn of progress across divisions, and become familiar with "new hires." Still, generally Marti felt her time could be better spent interacting with her clients.

At 10 A.M., when Marti was rushing frantically to finish the report, there was a heavy rap on her door and Ken, her supervisor, strolled into her office.

KEN: Hi Marti. Did you have a nice trip to Louisiana?

MARTI: It went pretty well. I think our environmental lobbying group down there is beginning to get some things done.

KEN: Great. Say, I need you to fly up to Oregon next week and speak at the national meeting of NAEPAE. They could really use our services, and you're just the woman to sell them on the idea. Also, how are you coming on the report about environmental lobbying efforts involving acid rain? Don't forget—you've got to get that off to our clients by Friday. Oh, by the way, I think A.J. is going to ask you to speak to the local Rotary Club about what a good corporate citizen InfoNet is. You'd better try and fit his request in. I know headquarters doesn't pay much of our salaries but it wouldn't do us any good to get a V.P. down on us. You going to the meeting at headquarters later?

MARTI: Yeah, I'm curious what the changes will mean to us, but I kind of hate to leave my office. I have so much work to do, even without what you just gave me.

KEN: Oh, you can handle it. Well, stop by and see me if you have any questions after the meeting.

At 12:30 Marti rode to the meeting with Rachel, an administrative assistant to the director of external publishing. Beginning as secretaries together 5 years earlier, they had remained friends as Marti was promoted to researcher while Rachel became an administrative assistant. Although they both spent most of their time dealing with external groups, Rachel rarely spoke to the same group twice and her work mainly involved planning meetings for her boss and selling publications. On the other hand, Marti worked closely and regularly with "her" clients who, she felt, had come to respect her opinions and depend on her competence and friendship. She certainly had received every indication that this was their view. In fact, many clients frequently complimented her both on her ability to get the job done and on her ability to do it right.

MARTI: Gosh, I feel I haven't seen you or anyone at the office in a long time. When I walk down the hall there are so many new faces. What's been going on around here? Anything interesting?

RACHEL: Mostly the same old things. But there have been some interesting rumors about what this reorganization will mean in terms of how much funding headquarters will be giving to the researchers in our units.

MARTI: Don't forget to fill me in on the rumors, but first I have got to get something off my chest—and I know I can trust you. One thing that causes me conflict is that I've got all these bosses. I have to answer to Ken and A.J. and my clients and ultimately I have to answer to Beverly [the company president]. I get all kinds of different pressures. Beverly or A.J. could call the annex and tell me I have to do a project and meanwhile I'm swamped here with things I have to get out for my clients. It happens two or three times a week. Ken constantly gives me something else to do. He knows I want to see our department grow and he doesn't hesitate too often to give me the assignment to go out to get new groups. But there's a limit to what I can do.

Fortunately, everybody is flexible enough, so it's not an impossible situation. But InfoNet has its priorities and its bureaucratic demands, and the organizations I work for and that support me financially have theirs . . . It's an inherently schizophrenic kind of job.

RACHEL: I know. I know. But admit it, you really enjoy what you do, despite all pressures.

MARTI: Sure I do. One of the plusses is the people I have met in positions with lots of importance. It's really fun to me that I've got friends across the U.S. My relationship with those folks is very rewarding and I'm committed to giving them 110%.

But still, I frequently don't feel that headquarters gives me any support. Sometimes I feel like the bastard child of InfoNet. What's the point here? We're the people out there actually having contact with clients. Headquarters needs to give something back to me like a decent carpet, better office space, a computer that works. It's a terrible environment to put people in—especially under the pressures here and the deadlines. I think it's an underlying respect problem. I don't feel very respected, very useful here. I don't feel that our division is either—by the hierarchy, that is. Well, there, I've had my say. Now, what's this gossip you've heard?

RACHEL: I've heard quite a lot. You're gone so much lately I guess you've missed it. Where to begin . . . Talk is that divisions are being reevaluated and that some will be merged and others disbanded. Rumor also has it that some folks will lose their jobs. I've heard Larry [the former vice-president of strategy before the restructuring] will get the ax, but nothing's confirmed yet. There are just so many stories. Looks like some will get promotions and increased power from this as well. I don't know—it just seems like a lot of confusion. Most people in our area are worried. I've heard a lot of complaints lately.

And I'll tell you what—I've got some complaints too. You know the folklore here is that no matter what else happens it is not possible to be bored because we deal with exciting people and what we talk about and what we do is exciting and one can't experience boredom in this environment. But there are periods of time, particularly when we're getting ready for meetings, when I have to handle a million logistical things and I find it can be very boring. It's not the same as really getting into a single issue and spending a lot of time with it. I really don't have that luxury. I get assigned a new topic and I become an instant expert. It's not the same as really understanding and spending time with something. These aren't very positive comments, but it's my sense of what it's like to be a boundary spanner.

Each wanted to continue sharing her frustrations, but they had reached headquarters. Rachel whipped her Chevette into a parking spot in the back lot of InfoNet. Together they walked into the modern brick building, through the elegantly furnished reception area, and into the mahogany-paneled conference room. As she sat down, Marti noticed that very few of her coworkers from downtown were at the meeting.

Later, back in her office, Marti began to fume. Bits and pieces of what she had learned at the meeting and what Rachel had said began to come together. The reorganization meant there would be two vice-presidents instead of four as there had been before the Division of Strategy and the Division of Analysis merged and when each division head was a vice president. Management hoped that would bring the different parts of the organization together, but Marti could not help thinking that it might also widen the division between researchers like herself and the rest of the organization.

The gap was already wide, partially because of how the divisions were funded. The strategy and analysis divisions received money from appropriations made to the organization by its members. These appropriations were relatively stable. Employees in the research division generated most of their own funding through grants and contracts. Such money never seemed to stretch far enough. The pressure from InfoNet headquarters was always toward bringing in new funding sources. That pressure was familiar, but difficult these days with all the travel and additional responsibilities.

Marti knew that there were on-going battles between some client services researchers and employees in the other divisions. Several times she had heard her coworkers telling others, "Well, you're on hard money [organizational allocations], and you can do that. But if I do this for you, who's going to pay for it?" Yes, indeed, funding differences led to real intraorganizational battles.

Rumors were already spreading that headquarters would stop providing retainers for speaking to the public on behalf of InfoNet and for occasionally writing brief magazine articles for InfoNet's major publication. The rumors suggested that management might even begin to charge the researchers for previously free supplies and services. Marti was reasonably sure InfoNet management would continue to ask her to write and speak promoting the organization, even if these changes occurred.

Marti decided she should tell some of her key clients about the restructuring, rumored funding changes, and possible new promotion policies. Also, she thought she might ask them to speak to Ken about her raise. Before she had left on this last trip, Ken had offered her a much smaller raise than she felt she deserved. She decided to call her clients Mac and Amy about these issues. They both served on InfoNet's board of directors and the groups they represented provided substantial funding to support InfoNet's activities.

Following her conversations with Mac and Amy, Marti went back to work determined to do battle with management for the interests of her client groups every chance she got. She was sure that other researchers were making similar calls to their primary clients. Since the work of at least half the organization, especially the client services researchers and their support staff, was almost entirely funded by grants and contracts, Marti assumed the rumored funding plans would be slightly modified over the next several days.

At 2:15 P.M. the next day, Ken called Marti and asked her to come to his office. Marti had been trying to work on the acid rain issue all day but had been interrupted at least 20 times with calls from clients across the country wanting to get information or publications, or to confirm a meeting detail. Her day had been so fragmented that she saw her meeting with Ken as another intrusion.. Frustrated and slightly angry, Marti arrived at Ken's office only to be kept waiting 10 minutes while he was on the phone. Once in his office the following conversation took place:

KEN: Marti, the reason I asked you to come see me was that Beverly and A. J. are upset because they both got calls from Mac, Amy, and at least three other clients I don't know, about some kind of rumored funding changes. The odd thing is that Amy called me early this morning to discuss a raise for you. Can you tell me what is going on here?

MARTI: I must admit that I called Mac and Amy to tell them InfoNet might be withdrawing my retainer funds and begin charging clients for basic supplies and services. Those changes are going to cause economic problems for some of our smaller clients. I was just trying to look out for the interests of my groups. You can't fault me for that. After all, they are the ones who pay our salaries.

KEN: No, I don't fault you for that, but your calls put this organization in an awkward position. Headquarters feels that our division is living beyond the means of the total organization. InfoNet is having some funding problems. Grants are down. All the members aren't paying their dues. Management just feels that it is fair for the clients to pay for the services they get. Your phone calls created a stir. If this keeps up, we'll have to renegotiate with each client separately, which will make it hard to be fair across the board.

Now, as for your raise, why in the world did you bring your clients into this?

MARTI: Ken, the stories are legion of how staff members go around the structure to get things done. You were not swayed by my arguments so I thought it might help if I had my clients' support.

KEN: You're making it hard for me to do my job. I don't know about the raise and I'm not too happy with the phone calls you made. Is this just a power play? But you are an excellent researcher, you're an expert on the environment, and your clients seem to like you, so I'll give your request some more thought.

MARTI: I hope you do and while you're at it, consider how to decrease the impact of any funding changes on my clients. If you can't work out something, I'm worried that some of them may feel they can get the services provided through InfoNet more cheaply somewhere else. They've asked me to leave InfoNet if it comes to that and work for them at another location. You know this organization needs the fees my groups pay. I'd hate to see us pull away, but we will. Personally, I'm tired of the lack of support I get here and all the pressures that are being placed on me. Contrary to popular opinion, not everyone who works here is my boss and I can't do everything. You've got to step in and help me.

KEN: I hadn't realized things were getting so serious. I'll see what I can do but I can make no promises. You know that it's hard to get management to recognize the problems that individuals face in this division. But I'll see what I can do. Just give me a couple of days.

Marti left the interview shaken by what she had said. Although she had spoken to Mac and Amy about finding another organization to service them if charges became too high, she was not sure that their groups would actually support such a move. Still she knew of several other cases where client organizations had pulled away when their needs were no longer satisfied in one way or another. She also knew that as "their" researcher she could certainly influence whether or not they decided to move.

Only last month Bruce had told her why Andy, a highly competent researcher for PRONET, had left the organization. He had provided services to the southern divisions for quite a while. The pressures at headquarters became so great that he simply went to work with one of his clients, making a whole lot more money and not working in an organization having the type of conflict existing at InfoNet. The conflict stemmed from what was perceived as management's attitude: "You're our employee, you will do what we say." Andy just said, "My loyalty is to my clients. They're paying my bills." And he left.

Marti returned to her work on the acid rain issue determined to confront Ken, and maybe even A.J., if the rumored funding changes occurred unmodified. Still, Marti knew she must proceed with care. A common expression heard around InfoNet was that InfoNet, and others' perception of it, was more important than any individual. But still the organization's structure and funding differences created an environment ripe with potential conflicts. Marti realized that top management must continually try to maintain the balance within the organization. She feared that these new changes might tip the fragile balance between the needs of InfoNet and the resources of staff members in client management services.

NOTES

1. Events and perceptions described in this case are based on extensive observations of and interviews with organizational members. For the purposes of simplicity and clarity here, composite characters are often used. Therefore, individual and organizational names have been changed.

KEY TERMS

boundary spanners
communication network
role conflict
job stress
organizational story

DISCUSSION QUESTIONS

1. What are the problems here from management's point of view? From Marti's? From Ken's?

2. How should management deal with the influence attempts exerted by Marti and her coworkers. What are special considerations in dealing with these?

3. What kind of power resources does Marti have? Are all boundary spanners equally powerful? What factors would make some more powerful than others?

4. What should management do to keep the separation between the organizational divisions from widening?

5. What problems do boundary spanners experience? What impact might their role conflict have on the organization and the individual?

6. What can be done to integrate the boundary spanners into the internal communication network and thus reduce their isolation from the rest of the organization?

7. How can the organization-wide meeting be used more effectively? What other type(s) of internal communication might be more effective at building cohesiveness between divisions?

8. What role do stories play in keeping organizational members informed? How would managers view these stories?

9. What types of stress is Marti experiencing? Why?

SUGGESTED READINGS

Adams, J. S. (1976). The structure and dynamics of behavior in organizational boundary roles. In M. D. Dunnette (Ed.), *Handbook of industrial and organizational psychology* (pp. 1175–1199). Chicago: Rand McNally.

Albrecht, T. L., & Adelman, M. B. (1984). Social support and life stress: New directions for communication research. *Human Communication Research, 11,* 3–32.

Brown, M. H. (1985). That reminds me of a story: Speech action in organizational socialization. *Western Journal of Speech Communication, 49,* 27–42.

Beyer, J. M., & Trice, H. M. (1987). How an organization's rites reveal its culture. *Organizational Dynamics, 15,* 5–24.

CHAPTER 9

Assessing the Ties that Bind: Social Support versus Isolation in Communication Networks

Eileen Berlin Ray
Cleveland State University

Bryan Elementary School had been known as one of the most innovative and high quality schools in the community. Many people chose to buy houses in the area so that their children could attend Bryan. Much of the credit for its reputation was due to its founding principal, Stuart Cranfill. During his 20-year tenure, teacher satisfaction and stability were high and the school could count on strong positive community support. When Cranfill retired, the community and school jointly threw a huge, day-long retirement party in his honor.

The new principal, Dave Maxwell, had been the assistant principal at a neighboring school. He had impressed the school board with his articulate answers during his interview. However, the word among the teachers at Bryan from their friends at his previous school was that he was very autocratic, unsympathetic to teachers' needs, and primarily interested in using the position to establish contacts for future political endeavors. When several teachers expressed their concerns to School Board President Hal Richards, he replied, "Now, you just do your job and let us do ours. You don't have any hard evidence to support what you're saying. We like Dave and that's what matters." So when Dave arrived at Bryan Elementary, he was greeted cautiously by the teachers. They were very concerned that their world as they knew it under Stuart Cranfill was about to end.

THE TEACHERS

When Suzanne Levitt was in the seventh grade, she had a teacher who made a significant impact on her life. It was then that Suzanne also decided to

150

become a teacher and help other students as she had been helped. After receiving her B.A. at State University, she was thrilled to be hired to teach fourth grade at Bryan Elementary School. She knew she could make a difference in the kids' lives. Her enthusiasm was high as she looked forward to beginning her teaching career.

Donna Jensen had switched majors in college several times before finally deciding on teaching elementary school. The thought of working did not thrill her but she liked the idea of having her summers free. She planned to teach until she got married and then quit to raise a family. She had been at Bryan for 3 years.

Marla Donovan had been teaching at Bryan for 14 years. She had seen the school become an innovative, exciting place to work but she had also seen a change in students' and parents' attitudes. She felt the students were less inclined to work hard and parents increasingly expected the teachers to do much of the disciplining. While she still enjoyed teaching, she was concerned about these changes and the implications for the school and the teachers.

Steve Markham had always loved kids and knew as soon as he took his first elementary education class at college that teaching was for him. He had been at Bryan for 2 years and felt it was a good place to work. While the salary was not great, he could make extra money teaching summer school. And he felt like he could make a difference in the kids' lives. He did not mind being one of only two male teachers at Bryan. He had recently married and was looking forward to starting a family.

Jennifer Reynolds had been teaching sixth grade at Bryan for 2 years. She viewed her job as supplemental income to her husband's executive job and looked forward to quitting to raise a family. While she did not mind teaching, she refused to do any work related to it once she left the building for the day. So she graded all her papers during her free period and had a reputation among students of providing minimal and vague comments to justify her notoriously average-to-low grades.

Louise Alberts had been the vice-principal for the last 6 of her 15 years at Bryan. She was recently widowed and had two high school age children and one in junior high. She assumed she would retain her position regardless of who the new principal was since her evaluations had always been excellent.

Alan Schmidt had been teaching at Bryan for 8 years. It was his first and only teaching job. In addition to teaching the third grade, he coached the coed softball team. Alan had tried to get other teaching jobs during the past years but had not been successful. He had become cynical and liked to talk about how great Bryan used to be. He was married and had three young children.

Rhonda Barkley had started out as a substitute teacher at Bryan. Eventually she was hired full time and had been teaching special education for the past 4 years. Although her college training was not in this area of elementary education, she had attended numerous workshops and read a great deal on working with special-ed. kids.

Lesley DuVal had taught second grade at a neighboring school for 6 years when she was hired at Bryan. She had now been at Bryan 4 years and was considered one of its best teachers. She was the faculty advisor to several student clubs and spent much of her free time working with students or on school-related activities.

Ellen Carpenter had taught virtually every grade in her 20 years at Bryan. She was the first teacher hired by Stuart Cranfill and had played a major role in the growth of the school. Ellen was a very social person and the daily banter and interaction she had with the other teachers was very important to her. She especially looked forward to lunch each day, when the teachers would share their views about life in general and about Bryan, as well as have some laughs. She was extremely loyal to Bryan and known throughout the community. Realtors referred Ellen to parents new to the area to tout Bryan's excellence.

Ruth Leggiere and Susan Frank had each been teaching at Bryan for 5 years. They had both had their first child the same year and had taken a year's maternity leave at that time. Their friendship had strengthened over the years, and they often helped each other out with child-care needs.

Roger Taylor had taught first grade at Bryan for 3 years before becoming a guidance counselor. He had a reputation as an excellent teacher and was doing a good job as counselor but he also missed teaching. He was trying to figure out a way to do both.

Carolyn Erskine was beginning her first year at Bryan. Fresh out of State University, she was anxious about performing well in her first job. Her social life revolved around her friends from the university and while she was polite to the other teachers, she shied away from discussing the problems at Bryan with them. The other teachers felt she seemed "nice enough" but no one really knew her because she kept to herself.

Jerry Bartlett had been the guidance counselor at Dave Maxwell's previous school for 4 years. Before that, he had taught fourth grade. He was a likable person but not a strong leader. He was more content to follow the directives of his principal than initiate action on his own, a characteristic Maxwell viewed favorably.

MAXWELL'S INTRODUCTION

One of the first things Maxwell did as principal was hold a faculty meeting to announce that he was replacing the current vice-principal, Louise Alberts, with Jerry Bartlett. The teachers were very upset for several reasons. Louise

had always done an excellent job, and they took some solace in knowing they
had at least one friend still in a supportive administrative position. They
were also upset because it had taken a long time to get a woman to an
upper-level administrative position. The teachers had hoped Louise would
get Cranfill's job. When she did not, they at least felt comfortable knowing
they had an adminstrator they knew and trusted. Now Maxwell was
recommending that she return to teaching the fifth grade. The teachers
were feeling increasingly uncertain about how their school was going to
change.

Several teachers mentioned that they had heard a rumor that a neighboring school might be closed the following year and Bryan would receive
most of the students with no upgrade in facilities and only adding two or
three new teachers. The result would be significant overcrowding. Maxwell
said he had also heard the rumor but he had no definite information yet. One
of the teachers asked if he would keep them informed if there were any
changes. "Only if I feel it would affect you. Otherwise, you don't need to be
bothered about it," Maxwell said. There was an uneasy silence in the room.
They were used to Cranfill giving them complete information on anything
that might affect them. That way they felt like they had some degree of
control over what happened at Bryan.

Maxwell presented other changes at the faculty meeting. Merit pay
would be based on quantifiable outcomes. Teachers had to keep records
of how many papers they graded, the length of time from when papers
were collected until they were returned, and the amount of time spent interacting with students and parents outside of class time. Lesson plans had
to be submitted to Maxwell monthly for his approval and were expected to be substantially updated annually. The teachers were shocked by
these new rules and it was against this backdrop that the new school year
began.

THE REACTION

Maxwell had timed his news well. The day after the meeting, school started,
so teachers were extremely busy getting their classrooms and lessons prepared. As a result, they had little time to touch base with each other. They
knew that once school started, their time would be even more limited,
especially with the new rules. While they all ate lunch together in the main
lunchroom, each was responsible for his or her own class during this time so
their meals were usually hurried. Unless people were willing to stay after
school, they only saw the other teachers who shared the same planning
period. With all the new paperwork to do, that would leave little time to
relax and chat during their one break of the day. Ellen Carpenter had a

feeling that Maxwell had planned it that way. He wanted to make all the decisions and not have to deal with the teachers. If they never had a chance to talk or organize, he could do what he wanted. She knew she could not be the only one who was upset. This year she shared her planning period with Donna, Steve, and Marla. She sought their opinions.

"You know," she told them, "we've always been an innovative school and that's because we shared a lot of ideas and were willing to try different ways of doing things. Stuart fostered that in us. Now here's Maxwell treating this place like it's boot camp. All he cares about is that we're 'accountable' so he'll look good. He could care less about the kids and he could care less about us. We've got to do something. I've been here too long to take this stuff."

Steve had never seen Ellen so upset. He was concerned too but he did not let it get to him. He tried to keep to himself when he was at work. When he was done at Bryan, he went home, spent time with his family, and forgot about the school. "Well, Ellen, I know you're upset but try not to let it get you down. Maxwell's just trying to act tough because he's new. He'll simmer down after a while, especially if he thinks we support him."

"Steve has a point, Ellen," replied Marla. "But I'm not sure we should be so passive. He needs to know that we're not willing to be treated this way. There are more of us than there are of him. I'm giving him until the winter break. If things haven't changed by then, I'll be looking very hard for a new job for next year."

"What do you think, Donna?" asked Ellen.

"Well, to tell you the truth," she answered, "I have so much work to do to get prepared and stay on top of things I haven't given it much thought. I'm feeling an incredible amount of pressure to get everything done."

By now school had been in session for several weeks and teachers had only heard from Maxwell by memo. Ellen had been appalled by the lack of concern shown by the others. She decided to talk to them. Later that week, she stopped by Roger's office. They had been friends for several years but did not have a chance to talk much any more. After she expressed her opinions to him, he replied, "I know what you mean, Ellen," he said. "But I'm in a sticky spot. I like counseling and want to keep doing it. Some day I want to become a principal. I need this experience. If I go against Maxwell, you know, he'll have me back teaching before I can blink. But I'm a teacher first and I'm very upset about what I see happening here. I've never seen morale so low and the kids are definitely picking up on it. I've lost a lot of sleep over this and I still don't know what to do. I feel like I'm selling out. And on top of it, I have several parent conferences coming up, four reports to get written, two discipline cases, and several meetings this week. I'm being pulled in every direction."

Rhonda, Suzanne, and Lesley shared the third planning period. Ellen wanted to talk with them but there was no one available to cover her room if she left it. This meant any talking had to be done between classes or at lunch. Finally, she had a chance to talk with them briefly before class started. After she expressed her concerns with Maxwell, she asked for their opinions.

"I don't like his approach at all," said Lesley. "At first I was really mad about it. Now I just ignore it. I come in, I do my job, I leave and try to forget about it. I know my teaching isn't as good as it used to be but I just don't care. The only way we'll get any merit pay is by filling out forms. That has nothing to do with teaching. It's not why I went into teaching but it may be why I'll get out of it. It's just not worth it to make it a big deal. I'm exhausted, physically and mentally."

"It's just one more thing," noted Rhonda. "I had a kid throw a desk through a window yesterday morning. When I called his parents to tell them, his mother wanted to know what I had done to provoke her child. I was so mad. So I want to Maxwell and told him about it and he said, 'Well what did you do?' I came very close to quitting but I need the money too much. I can't believe his lack of support for us. Jerry saw me leave Maxwell's office and asked what was wrong. He seemed very concerned but, let's face it, he's not going to do anything against Maxwell."

Suzanne agreed. "It never used to be like this. I always liked coming to work. We had a good time. We could always come up with creative ways to deal with the problem kids and their problem parents. Since school started, I've had at least five parents call me at home at night. One called me at 11:30. Scared me to death. He said his daughter wasn't bringing home any homework and he was worried that she was lying about it. Why couldn't he have sent me a note or called me during the day? They think we live, eat, and breathe their kids' lives. Between them calling, kids acting up in class, trying to get papers graded and returned quickly, barely having a planning period left with all these forms we have to fill out for Maxwell, and trying to keep my own family going, it's just too much."

Rhonda often carpooled with Jennifer, and they usually talked about the changes at Bryan since Maxwell had become principal. Over the past couple of months, Jennifer found herself feeling lethargic and could not concentrate very well. She and Rhonda often stopped off for a couple of beers on their way home and she felt that helped calm her down so she could cope with her own two children better. Her husband was concerned that she was sick and insisted she see her doctor. The doctor performed a complete physical and found nothing physically wrong, but prescribed Valium to help her relax. Jennifer knew what was really wrong; she was sick of work. She never felt like she had any free time. Her kids were going in a million different directions. They never even had dinner together any more. "But that's O.K.," she thought, "I never even cook any more. My mother would die. She would think I was awful." And to top all this, she had not been to aerobics in weeks. She was feeling like a total failure.

Rhonda also played tennis frequently with Alan. After voicing her displeasure, she asked Alan about his perceptions of life at Bryan since Maxwell's arrival. Alan was somewhat surprised. "As you know, I don't talk to people very much during the day but I haven't noticed many changes. The extra paperwork isn't thrilling, but it's no big deal. I think if you look for trouble you're going to find it. I've overheard some of you talking about how rotten things are now. But a lot of you thought that Cranfill could do no wrong so I don't think you'd be happy with anyone new. Maxwell doesn't hassle me, and I just do my job like I always have. I don't know where some of you find the time to sit around and gossip so much anyway."

Louise and Ellen had been friends for years and often sat next to each other at lunch. Louise was still upset at being removed as vice-principal. Ellen, still angry over the way Maxwell was running the school, was a very sympathetic and supportive friend. She encouraged Louise to vent her frustration and rehash her feelings repeatedly. Several teachers had walked by Louise's classroom to hear her berating and threatening students. She had told Ellen she was really feeling down—embarrassed, humiliated, and angry because she was not named vice-principal—and how embarrassing to her friends outside the school. At least everyone at Bryan knew how the system worked. Just the other day the director of the Girl Scouts had asked her to come speak to Troop #17 about life as a school administrator. "What was I supposed to tell them?" she asked, "that I wasn't one any more?" No wonder she was short tempered and feeling out of control these days. Ellen was extremely concerned and after discussing it with several other teachers decided to approach Maxwell with it. She was hoping he would talk to Louise and recommend personal counseling. Instead, she found him less than empathic. "Well, I'll certainly talk to her. If she doesn't shape up, she'll be shipped out," he said.

Ruth and Susan were seldom seen by the other teachers. They often rode to school together and their classrooms were next door to each other. By reputation, both were considered excellent teachers. The other teachers, however, did not know them very well. They tended to keep to themselves and spent their planning periods in their own rooms rather than in the lounge.

Carolyn had kept her promise to herself to be friendly enough to the other teachers but to not get involved in school politics. She rarely interacted beyond saying hello and worked very hard at her job. By all accounts, she was doing a very good job. Maxwell especially liked her because her paperwork was always done ahead of schedule. So far, she was very pleased with her first year at Bryan. Since she had never worked for anyone other than Maxwell, she had no comparison and did not understand why so many of the teachers were always talking about how lousy things were. She usually spent her planning period in her classroom so she could ignore them and get her work done.

Jerry Bartlett had been hearing rumors about disgruntled teachers for months. He had noticed an increase in the number of students being sent to his office for discipline and several parents had asked him if there were problems at the school. Their children did not enjoy school as much as they used to and said the teachers were yelling at them more. Bartlett reassured the parents but did not pass the information on to Maxwell. Instead he went to see Ellen. "Ellen," he asked, "What's going on around here? Students are complaining, parents are complaining. I hear rumblings but I don't know the details. Would you fill me in? I'd like to help."

Ellen proceeded to tell Jerry the teachers' concerns. When she finished, he seemed surprised. "I had no idea people were this upset. I could talk to Maxwell, if you want," Jerry suggested.

"No," said Ellen. "You know that would only make things worse. He'd probably say if we don't like it here we can leave. I've got news for him. That may be exactly what happens."

Jerry promised that he would say nothing to Maxwell. He was not sure what he would say anyway. Ellen and her buddies seemed pretty down on Maxwell. She said she talked to Louise, Donna, Marla, and Steve about it almost constantly. He was not sure what Rhonda thought but knew she would certainly have a handle on how Jennifer, Alan, Lesley, and Suzanne felt. They were a pretty close-knit group. As for Ruth and Susan, probably no one knew how they felt. They rarely complained anyway. There were always too busy to get caught up in the school grapevine. He knew for a fact that Carolyn thought Maxwell was a great principal; she had told him that just the other day. She had a positive attitude about everything. She was going to be a great addition to Bryan, Bartlett thought.

THE ACTION

As the school year went on, teachers continued to hear from Maxwell primarily through memos. Faculty meetings were rarely held and when they were Maxwell spent most of the time telling them what they were doing well and what they were doing poorly. At each meeting, someone brought up the possible closing of the neighboring school and each time Maxwell replied, "It doesn't concern you at this point in time." However, the rumors continued and some teachers had heard that two schools would be closing and Bryan would get all the overflow students and no new teachers to help out. No one could get confirmation or denial from Maxwell. Jerry took over the role of information provider. Whenever teachers had questions, they went to him and he would find out the answers for them. They came to like him, although they knew he would never cross Maxwell.

In December, Jennifer took a medical leave of absence for the rest of the year. By the middle of the spring, Rhonda, Donna, and Louise announced that they were leaving Bryan at the end of the school year. Rhonda and Donna had teaching jobs at other schools in the city. Louise was going to quit teaching altogether.

When parents heard about the number of teachers leaving, they were alarmed. Several went to talk to Maxwell about it and found him arrogant and unsympathetic. They decided to then go to the school board and at the next meeting voiced their concerns. The board was upset by the news, too, and Hal Richards, its president, scheduled a meeting with Maxwell for the next day.

THE MEETINGS

Richards arrived early for his 8:30 A.M. meeting with Maxwell. He had spent much of the previous night thinking about his approach to Maxwell. If what the parents were saying were true, Bryan was in bad shape and getting worse. He would not tolerate unhappy parents or students, and he could not believe Maxwell was not aware of the problems he had heard about at the board meeting. However, it quickly became clear early in their meeting that Maxwell had no idea there were any problems.

"Dave," said Hal, "Last night several parents came to our school-board meeting and complained about things here at Bryan. They said students were routinely being sent to see Jerry for any discipline problems; the kids were telling them that teachers were yelling at them all the time; and the teachers are so unhappy that several of them are leaving at the end of the year. You know, Bryan has always been a model school and the only time we've ever had parents come to our meetings has been to praise it. Needless to say, we're very upset and that's why I wanted to see you first thing this morning. What do you know about all this?"

"Well, to tell you the truth, Hal, I haven't been worried about things here," replied Dave. "Sure, a couple of teachers are leaving but you always have to expect some turnover. Teachers are getting their paperwork done on time and their lesson plans look good. I don't know of any increase in students being sent to see Jerry. As far as the teachers yelling more, well, you know how parents can be overly sensitive. I do think some of the teachers may be a little touchy since they have more work to do, with the extra paperwork I get from them. But it sounds to me like things are being exaggerated."

Hal left Dave's office unconvinced. He decided to spend the next several days interviewing the teachers. What he heard was a general consensus that Maxwell was not doing a good job as principal and that the teachers were extremely disgruntled. The teachers who were leaving directly blamed Maxwell for their departure. Only Alan and Carolyn did not feel that things were that bad.

Hal then had a long meeting with Jerry. "Jerry," he said, "I don't understand how these problems could be going on all year without Dave knowing about them. Did you know what was going on?"

"I didn't at first but then some of the teachers told me." Jerry replied. "I wanted to tell Dave but he gets defensive pretty easily and the teachers didn't want me to tell him they were upset. They were afraid he'd just tell them to find other jobs. So I tried to handle it myself."

"Well, it's clear that Dave had no idea of the magnitude of the problems," said Hal. "This used to be such a high-spirited school, especially the teachers. You couldn't find a more enthusiastic bunch of teachers anywhere in the city. Now they're all talking about leaving—not just Bryan but teaching altogether. They don't like Maxwell, they don't like the parents, they don't like the kids. There isn't anything they do like. I've never seen morale so low. I only wish we could have kept it from getting this bad in the first place."

Jerry nodded. "It is hard to believe that things have gotten this bad and Dave never noticed. It started out with some little things and it kept escalating. But you know, Hal," Jerry said, "I've been here the whole time and I'm not sure I know exactly what happened and why."

NOTES

1. This case is a composite of schools and teachers based on the author's research and consulting experience. The names of the school and the teachers are fictitious.

KEY TERMS

individual stressors	perceived control
role stress	uncertainty reduction
burnout	social support
informal networks	supervisor support
network roles	

DISCUSSION QUESTIONS

1. What are the individual, group, and organizational stressors at Bryan Elementary and how did they come about?

2. What role does the formal and informal organizational communication play in exacerbating or mediating the stressors?

3. What changes need to be made at Bryan to reduce the negative effects of the teachers' stress and burnout?

4. What are the positive and negative effects of being an isolate?

SUGGESTED READINGS

Beehr, T. A. (1985). The role of social support in coping with organizational stress. In T. A. Beehr & R. S. Bhagat (Eds.), *Human stress and cognition in organizations: An integrated perspective* (pp. 373–398). New York: Wiley.

House, J. S. (1981). *Work stress and social support.* Reading, MA: Addison-Wesley.

Maslach, C. (1982). *Burnout: The cost of caring.* Englewood Cliffs, NJ: Prentice-Hall.

McLean, A. A. (1985). *Work stress.* Reading, MA: Addison-Wesley.

Miller, K. I., Stiff, J. B., & Ellis, B. H. (1988). Communication and empathy as precursors to burnout among human service workers. *Communication Monographs, 55,* 250–265.

Pines, A., & Aronson, E. (1988). *Career burnout: Causes and cures.* New York: Free Press.

Ray, E. B. (1986). *Communication network roles as mediators of job stress and burnout: Case studies of two organizations.* Paper presented at the annual meeting of the Speech Communication Association, Chicago.

Ray, E. B. (1987). Support relationships and occupational stress in the workplace. In T. L. Albrecht & M. B. Adelman (Eds.), *Communicating social support* (pp. 172–191), Newbury Park, CA: Sage.

Ray, E. B., & Miller, K. I. (1990). Communication in health-care organizations. In E. B. Ray & L. Donohew (Eds.), *Communication and health: Systems and applications* (pp. 92–107). Hillsdale, NJ: Erlbaum.

PART IV

Managerial Communication

Management Communication Issues in Family Businesses: The Case of Oak Ridge Trucking Company

DAVID R. SEIBOLD
University of Illinois, Urbana–Champaign

Although organizations have undergone unparalleled economic, design, and technological changes during this century, the *family* remains a vital force underlying modern work organizations. Two-thirds of the nation's 15 million enterprises are small or privately held firms that employ 44 million people and generate 40% of the gross national product (Beckhard & Dyer, 1983). More than 90% of all corporations are either owned or controlled by families (Galagan, 1985).

Family businesses are those in which one or more family units exert appreciable influence on the firm's policy and direction. This influence may be exercised through ownership, and, in fewer cases, through family members' formal roles in managing the firm. As Davis (1983) notes, it is the interplay between both social systems, business and family, that determines the basic character of the family business and defines its uniqueness. It is estimated that more than 1 million privately owned U.S. companies are actually run by families.

Oak Ridge Trucking (ORT) Company is one such small, privately held, family-run business. Located near a major coastal city, this for-hire freight transport firm leases tractor-trailer rigs and drivers to major corporations whose own trucking operations cannot meet seasonal or competition-spurred needs for increased product distribution throughout the United States and Canada. Some 40–60 persons (mostly drivers and mechanics) may be employed at any time to handle ORT's fleet of 40 diesel truck tractors and 70 semitrailers. Despite its small size (especially when compared with large interregional general commodity carriers), the company consistently has had gross revenues of more than $1 million. Its proprietors are quick to highlight this as an accomplishment in a sector of the economy made particularly competitive following the Motor Carrier Act of 1980, which significantly constrained the Interstate Commerce Commission's regulatory authority in the truck transportation area (Williamson, Singer, & Peterson, 1983). The owners attribute the firm's success to its acknowledged service orientation to clients, economies of scale, willingness of nonunion employees to assume more responsibilities than Teamster counterparts in competitors, and financial independence associated with the fact that ORT is family owned and managed.

ORT and other small trucking firms display a variety of problems not normally found in business organizations. These include spatiotemporal difficulties associated with mobile and round-the-clock employees' needs to communicate with managers and dispatchers working on a more limited and fixed schedule; coordination problems inherent in ORT's and leasees' efforts to monitor and control equipment; technological changes that appear to have given large motor carrier firms an advantage over smaller competitors like ORT (Friedlander & Chiang, 1983); patterns of communication and decision-making unique to autonomous frontline employees; the less formal nature of planning in small businesses (Rice, 1983); role strain experienced by ORT drivers after they have been leased to other companies for an extended period of time; and drug use motivated by occupational, not recreational, demands of long-distance hauling (Guinn, 1983).

However, it is the dynamics associated with the overlap of two major social systems—the business and the family—and their impact on the *management* of ORT that will be the focus here. The owners/managers' personal characteristics and interpersonal orientations, their relations and interactions with each other as family and as management members, and the dynamics emanating from nonfamily ORT employees' difficulties integrating with the management "in-group" have fostered an organizational structure and climate that is simultaneously successful and problematic. In order to examine these dynamics, it will be helpful to trace three key periods in the firm's history: (1) the years prior to 1980, during which both family and business were forming but existed separately for the most part, (2) the period between 1980 and 1985 in which family and business were blended but still managed by the owner/founder, and (3) the emergence of a group of younger family managers during the years since 1985.

As a result of efforts to cope with changing environmental, internal, and family pressures during these times, three distinct organizational designs evolved. In turn, these designs were associated with social, pyschological, and organizational problems all caused by, and the cause of, group and organizational dynamics. At root, the problems stemmed from the leader's efforts to produce and maintain a joint family business system operating according to rules derived from the needs of family members and the firm as separate parts, but adapted to the needs of the whole. Sketches of each of these stages in the organization's development will reveal much about three critical subsystems inherent in any family-firm system: (1) the business as an entity, (2) the family as an entity, and (3) the founder as an entity (Beckhard & Dyer, 1983).

PRE-1980: THE FORMATIVE YEARS

Oak Ridge Trucking Company was founded in the early 1960s. As a young man, its president and sole owner, Matt, left his father's dairy business, taking his brother-in-law Vic and two trucks. Like many entrepreneurs who leave a family business to start their own (Collins, Moore, & Unwalla, 1964), Matt had had an uneasy relationship with his father. He relished the opportunity to escape the elder's authority and pursue greater success. In the first years, Matt and Vic sometimes worked around the clock, doing whatever was needed to provide reliable service to clients whose freight they hauled. The company philosophy that emerged from their early success survives today: "Whatever the customer needs."

As they won new contracts, more trucks were added to the fleet, and Matt selected drivers for their willingness to work as hard as he and Vic did. He was quick to terminate anyone whose performance did not measure up to his demanding standards. Within a few years, he had built a larger firm, and a workforce of loyal, trusted drivers. Their commitment grew from their respect for his transportation skills, determination, "savvy," and generosity (e.g., Matt might provide a no-interest loan to assist an employee with a mortgage down payment).

Five years after he had begun ORT, Matt stopped driving and established a small office with a truck terminal and a garage for servicing the vehicles. He hired a staff at ORT headquarters, or "command center," as he jokingly referred to it: Ben was the mechanic, Kathryn handled payroll and clerical work, former driver Kenny became the dispatcher, and brother-in-law Vic determined rates and handled billing, while Matt sought clients and managed the firm. This group was to be ORT's "management" team for the next 15 years (see Figure 10.1). During that time Kathryn's role evolved into office manager as more secretaries were hired. Ben became the manager of fleet maintenance when additional mechanics joined the firm. Kenny's span of control increased to supervision of more than 25 drivers by 1980.

Matt had not only been central in creating ORT's "corporate culture" (Schein, 1983) but, as is frequently the case with small businesses, ORT

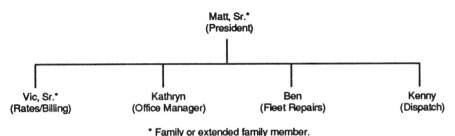

FIGURE 10.1. ORT management structure pre-1980.

reflected its founder's personality (Levinson, 1971). Matt trusted employees whose values were similar to his own, and had "special" ones whom he favored. Authority was highly centralized. None of the managers had budgetary discretion; Matt made all decisions regarding the company's direction, policy, and operations. When he was on business trips, managers were reluctant to make decisions without his approval. Successful practices from the past became institutionalized procedures, and Matt rarely permitted deviation from them. "It's my way or the highway" was his not-so-veiled threat. Those who disagreed with him were free to leave and "push a rig over the road for a living" as he had. The firm was tightly controlled by Matt, and he would never consider sharing ownership of ORT with his brother-in-law or his "lieutenant," Vic, much less with stockholders.

As long as Matt had financial, formal, and operational control of ORT, he could be sensitive to employees. Recognizing his drivers' need to blow off steam, Matt's door was always open to them after long road trips. He acknowledged them as his "eyes and ears on the road," and paid attention to their ideas about trucking equipment and client needs. Of course, any suggestions adopted were implemented in his characteristically autocratic style. Matt's tendency to supervise every detail of his business personally made ORT the epitome of the "closely managed" firm. As long as employees at all levels could abide this control, they were amply rewarded. While salaries were on scale with those of competitors, benefits and "perks" (e.g., profit sharing, bonus incentives, opportunities to purchase equipment from ORT to become "owner–operator drivers," excellent medical plan, and Matt's responsiveness to employees in times of need) were strong inducements for employees to remain with ORT.

During ORT's formative years, Matt was also forming a family. By the late 1970s, he had three boys and three girls ranging in age from mid-20s (his oldest daughter) to 10 (his youngest son). Rosenblatt (1985) suggests that analysts of family businesses should look for the influence of (adult) family members who are *not* on the organizational chart. In this case, Matt's wife,

Helen, affected ORT indirectly. She was ambivalent about "the business" largely because her pleasure at its success was offset by the fact that it was a trucking firm, with less status than her own family's professional occupations; about Matt's lack of higher education (compared with her college degree); and about the long hours he spent at the firm. Her attitude, combined with Matt's own gender bias against having his "little girl" work in the firm, discouraged their oldest daughter from working at ORT. On the other hand, Helen's efforts to encourage the next two children (Matt Jr. and Quint) to go to college merely drove them toward the company, much to Matt Sr.'s delight. They had been around the trucks from the time they were young boys, and became drivers immediately after high school—just like their cousins, Vic Jr. and Cobb (Vic Sr.'s sons).

By 1980 Katie and Karen, Helen and Matt's twin daughters, had graduated from college but also entered the firm in office roles. They found that entry-level positions elsewhere did not afford all the privileges (company car, extra vacation time, etc.) of working for their father. Matt's gender bias had moderated in the years between his older and younger daughters' college educations. Now he had less difficulty with their involvement in ORT, afterall it was only office work. However, he did not believe either of the twins were as capable as Matt Jr. or Quint, or as suitable as the boys for succeeding him at the helm of ORT.

During their formative years, family firms benefit from the "institutional overlap" of family and business (Lansberg, 1983). ORT was no exception. Matt's immediate and extended family members provided a steady stream of trustworthy labor. Family employees' unquestioning loyalty to the founder during the early years proved invaluable. Informal familial relations that were carried into the firm also fostered commitment to the founder's dream. In turn, the successes of the firm were brought home and solidified the fabric of the family. Still, Matt faced a difficult dilemma—how to make room in the *management* of the firm for two sons, two daughters, and perhaps two nephews without displacing any of the three nonfamily employees already in those positions. His subsequent effort to blend family and firm led to a second period in the firm's development.

1980–1985: BLENDING FAMILY AND FIRM

In 1980 Matt acquired Barker County Motors (BCM), a truck dealership located just 5 miles from ORT. The tax benefits, available parts inventory, opportunity to buy trucks for the ORT fleet at dealer's cost, and the value of the new business and property made the purchase an attractive investment. More importantly, BCM offered Matt a resolution to his personnel dilemma.

There was now a new set of management positions for members of his immediate and extended family. Under Matt's direction, family members could be trained to replace or supplement managers in the newly acquired truck dealership, without loss of long-term managers at ORT.

Under the new management structure (see Figure 10.2), Matt Sr. managed both companies as owner and CEO. Matt Jr., president of BCM for tax purposes, in reality served as general manager of the dealership, administratively assisted by younger sister Karen. Her twin, Katie, was moved from the office at ORT to supervise billing, payroll, benefits, and to act as office manager at BCM. The BCM service manager (Harry) and sales manager (Charlie) were the only top-level staff retained.

Meanwhile, Vic Sr., Kathryn, and Ben continued in their respective managerial roles at ORT. Matt's nephew Vic Jr. was promoted to replace as fleet dispatcher the aging Kenny. Kenny sought retirement rather than deal with the new responsibilities he would have to assume after the BCM acquisition. His other son Quint was moved into a newly created management position with line report to Matt Sr., but shared responsibility with Vic Sr. (so the latter could "teach Quint the ropes" setting rates). Only Matt's nephew Cobb remained in a nonmanagerial function, largely because he enjoyed the relative freedom of being a driver "on the road."

The purchase of BCM solved Matt's immediate personnel problems, but the acquisition also proved to be a "trigger event" (Beckhard & Dyer, 1983)—an event that destabilized the firm because of the organizational, administrative, and family problems it created. First a host of organizational difficulties were apparent in the first 2 years. Despite Matt Sr.'s well-

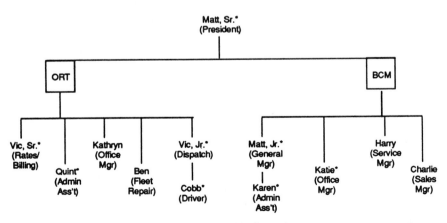

FIGURE 10.2. ORT/BCM management structure 1980–1985.

meaning intentions and hit-or-miss assistance, it was painfully clear these young employees were not ready for the managerial responsibilities they had been given.

The positions they occupied suffered from their lack of expertise, managerial ability, and interpersonal skills. In turn, others in the organization who depended on and interacted with them were adversely affected. As a result, the firm was characterized by weak horizontal integration. Productivity, coordination, and communication problems abounded at BCM, and even in Vic Jr.'s dispatch function at ORT. Imitating his father's style, Matt Jr. tended to overmanage, and his weak interpersonal skills led to outright conflicts with the older and more experienced service and sales managers whose jobs he tried to supervise. An unhealthy competition evolved between ORT and what employees there termed their "weak sister," BCM.

Outright role conflicts and power struggles also occurred between managers and employees in comparable positions in the two firms (e.g., Ben versus Harry as heads of fleet and dealership truck maintenance respectively). There was a "technology gap" in the hardware and software needed to handle payroll, billing, inventory, benefits, and marketing. An in-group–out-group dynamic that followed family lines led to polarization and lack of cooperation among managers that was felt at lower levels of BCM.

The organizational problems were compounded by administrative ones. Matt Sr.'s overly centralized decision-making style now also left BCM incapacitated during the times he was "down the road" at ORT. His failure to share information undermined his children's ability to do their jobs. His informal and unwritten planning style—characteristic of owners of small companies (Thurston, 1983)—was inadequate to the complexity of managing two firms and the inexperience of the new managers. He sometimes failed to pass on details he managed intuitively, but that family members had no way of knowing. Matt's overly rigid conception of "how things should be done" led to substantive conflicts with long-term employees at BCM and with Matt Jr. who sought to prove himself by doing things his own way.

Matt Sr.'s administrative difficulties were evident in other areas, too. Sociologists and psychologists recognize that family-business dysfunctions derive from the functional differences between family and business institutions in our society (Galagan, 1985; Kepner, 1983). Families exist to serve the needs of their members for care and nurturance, whereas businesses exist to produce products or services profitably with less concern for their members. These differences became blurred at ORT and BCM.

Matt Sr. had to reconcile incongruous norms that regulated giving and getting in the family versus in the business. Exchanges in families are guided by affective principles that focus attention on others' needs, but reward systems in firms are tied to economic principles concerning the market value of goods and services. It is not surprising that the compensation system that emerged was an amalgam of both family and business criteria. Because commitment to the firm was expected of family members and because paying family members with above-market salaries would be perceived as favoritism by nonfamily employees, salaries for family members were actually lower than for others—an *under*-reward system fairly common in family businesses (Lansberg, 1983).

On the other hand, Matt's desire to meet the developmental needs of his children led him to *over*compensate in the areas of release time for education and frequent additional benefits. These were practices that met a father's need for fairness to his children but violated conceptions of fairness to all employees. This inequity was exacerbated by nonfamily employees' realization that no matter how long their tenure and no matter how great their contributions, their advancement possibilities would never be commensurate with those of "the kids." Drivers' departures from the firm increased between 1980 and 1985 when they realized that there was no room for them at the top, as there had been for former drivers like Kenny. As one said, "All the 'kids' have the office [managers'] jobs."

The blurring of family and business distinctions were not limited to Matt Sr. For some family managers, the company became equivalent to the family. Negative feedback from nonfamily employees was perceived as criticism of the family as a whole. At home the dinner table became a battleground, as Matt's children vented frustration at their father's reluctant granting of power to them and quick retrieval of it whenever he disagreed with their actions. Matt Sr. and Matt Jr. fought over policy and practices, much as the elder had done with his father. Matt's daughters attacked him for placing them in second-class roles at work, the same position they felt they had in the family compared with their brothers.

At the same time, the BCM workplace became an arena for longstanding sibling conflict between Matt Jr. and Karen (whom Matt Sr. had deliberately paired because "that way they *have* to learn to work together"). "Secondary tension" (Fisher, 1980)—deep-seated interpersonal conflicts among group members—even surfaced between Matt Sr. and Vic Sr., when the latter realized that his son was consigned to a "second-place career" behind Matt Jr., just as he had been behind Matt Sr.

The locus of all these pressures fell on Matt Sr., who experienced "role conflict" (Shaw, 1981) in attempting to reconcile incongruous principles guiding him as "father" and "boss." Psychological pressures that came from the conflicting demands of being head of the family and head of the business were magnified by Matt's self-imposed pressure of trying to manage both companies. The physical demands on him became great as his span of control doubled and he constantly felt the need to be in two places at once. His tendency to retract authority from his children when they did not act as he anticipated only heightened their dependence on him and increased the pressure he felt. Perhaps as a result of these internal and external pressures, Matt Sr. began to experience the pervading sense of loneliness common among entrepreneurs and small-business owners (Gumpert & Boyd, 1984). He was trapped in a destructive cycle of increasing, internalized pressure, with no one to confide in about it. Realizing that his problems and those of his companies demanded attention and resolution, he entered a period of reflection and self-absorption. As a result of insights developed during this time and ensuing actions, ORT moved into a third phase of development.

POST-1985: CONSOLIDATION OF THE FAMILY BUSINESS

Matt Sr. recognized many of the organizational problems noted above: insufficient technology, intergroup competition, poor coordination and inadequate horizontal integration, role conflicts, tense communication climate, and in-group–out-group dynamics between family and nonfamily employees. He was painfully aware of the pressures and tensions within the family as members struggled with him and in their jobs to achieve managerial competence. He realized that he had erred in assuming he could teach them the skills needed to do those jobs, and that he may have fostered their dependency on him by frequently doing things for them.

Matt Sr. also recognized a series of strengths in his family that had contributed to the firm's continued financial success. Most analysts' discussions of family businesses have focused on weaknesses in those firms stemming from dysfunctional influences of family subsystem on organizational subsystem (Davis, 1983). These typically include the father/founder's entrepreneurial personality, disturbances in the father–son relationship, nepotism, and the influence of internal family dynamics on organizational decisions (Kepner, 1983). But these firms also evidence strengths that insure their survival—at least during the founder's life.

ORT was no different, Matt Sr. reasoned. Its strengths included its ability to adapt previous successful practices to new clients, his great experience and acquired knowledge, family members' willingness to work long hours whenever necessary, its success at introducing cost-cutting measures, his zeal for efficiency, a trustworthy and committed workforce that included many long-term employees, and attention to detail ("It's small things that count" was one of his favorite sayings). And Matt mused that, despite their difficult introduction to management roles, all of his children and nephews *had* improved year by year. In particular, he acknowledged that "the girls'" performance had exceeded his expectations. He grudgingly admitted to himself that one of the twins, Katie, showed more promise for running the firm than either Matt Jr. or Quint—but only time would tell. This recognition corresponded with what experts identify as a weakening of traditional gender bias against women in family-run businesses, leading to more equal access to the business and invitations to take high-level positions in the firm (Galagan, 1983). More generally, it parallels a trend in female ascendance in American businesses: The U.S. House of Representatives' Small Business Committee reported that women ran 2.5 million companies in 1985, up 33.4% from 1977 (Timberlake, 1985).

Still, Matt Sr. had a spate of organizational and family problems to resolve, not to mention the pressures he had been experiencing from trying to manage both firms. He, too, had to think about the future. After all, he was in his mid-50s. How long could he keep up this pace? How long should he try? When could the children be counted on to run the business so that he might enjoy "other pursuits?"

As in the firm's past, it was an economic opportunity that precipitated real change and made some of the restructuring Matt Sr. had been mulling over possible. In 1985, he got an opportunity to sell the BCM facility—not the dealership itself but the property and building where it was located. After some tough bargaining (one of Matt's strengths), he sold the facility for much more than he had paid, but he retained the dealership, its customers, service department, and inventory. The infusion of new capital made it possible to do something Matt had been considering for a while: enlarge the original ORT facility and consolidate ORT and BCM under one roof. Consolidation would enable the firm to eliminate redundancy (one manager could be used for both fleet and dealership mechanics), to achieve economies of scale (mechanics could be used to work on both fleet and customers' trucks as needed), to bring the parts inventory of both firms under the same roof, to move surviving employees to one location so that he could more easily supervise them (including Matt Jr., Katie, and Karen), and to eliminate the competition between the two companies. The renovations to the ORT terminal would also improve its value tremendously, since it was situated in what had now become a desirable location. In the future, Matt reflected, he could retain ownership of the property and lease it to his children so they could run the business that he was slowly turning over to them (in title—for tax purposes—if not operationally yet).

There were more pressing problems in the present, however, not the least of these was encouraging Kathryn to take early retirement so that his daughter Katie could assume her responsibilities as office manager in the consolidated firm. Also, like many family-firm owners, Matt found himself in the extremely difficult position of having to release a family member (Vic Sr.) no longer well-suited to the company, and thereby jeopardize his relationship with that part of the family (Lansberg, 1983). After some anguishing conversations, Vic Sr. agreed to move into a staff/advisory function so that his responsibilities could be integrated into Katie's operation. Ben would handle both his own and Harry's duties as manager of the down-sized crew of mechanics. Quint would take a true managerial role by replacing the terminated Charlie as sales manager. And Matt Jr. could utilize the knowledge he acquired as ORT driver and part-time truck mechanic (before he had been "dropped into BCM" as he called it), to integrate both firms' extensive parts inventory. Karen would assist him in that capacity (recall "They *still* have to learn to work together"). She would be a liaison with Ben's department through a computerized inventory control and fleet maintenance record system that she would implement. In the end, Matt Sr. had created a new management team that, with one exception (Ben), was comprised entirely of family members (see Figure 10.3).

Other changes were made to complement the restructuring of ORT–BCM management. Each of the managers was provided with extensive training and development. Quint and Matt Jr. benefitted from dealer and manufacture "schools" for sales and parts managers. Katie and Karen continued taking evening courses toward second baccalaureate degrees in business and computer science respectively. Both attended computer companies' training programs for utilizing the new equipment ORT purchased (this time a *joint* decision of Matt Sr. and the twins). Computer-assisted procedures were introduced by Katie to handle sales/service records, taxes, payroll, and billing. All the children and nephews were sent to management development training courses, and a consultant was brought to the firm to "coach" them in their interpersonal and managerial skills.

All of the managers—including Matt Sr.—initiated systematic efforts to master an array of data bases that had been developed to keep informed about legislation, economic trends, and new technology in the trucking industry. A "company retreat" was held in which managers voiced some frustrations with Matt Sr.'s centralized decision-making practices and asked

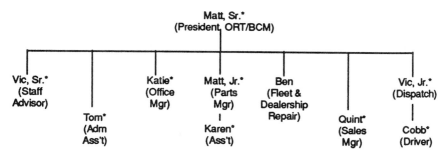

*Family or extended family member.

FIGURE 10.3. ORT/BCM management post-1985.

for department budgets or at least a comptroller. Little came of the suggestions, except for more frequent staff meetings so that Matt Sr. could keep managers up to date. Helen observed that there was far less rancor at home than in the past about "business matters." But she noted disagreements about a different class of issues: the extent to which profits should be reinvested into the firm or distributed among family members, and the extent of entitlement of the children's spouses who were not working in the firm.

CONCLUSION

Today, Matt Sr. points with pride to the fact that gross revenues are still increasing each year and that ORT received a transportation service award from a regional association of manufacturers whose members ORT has long served. Matt's business friends tell him he is a fortunate man to have his children in the business. On days when things are going well, he agrees with them. But when "we're up to our ears in alligators," he voices a series of concerns. "Can *any* of them really run this business?" So far, he has resisted suggestions to develop a succession plan. Other times he says, "I should just give it to them, retire, and let them swim with it or sink."

Occasionally he wonders, "Maybe I should sell it outright to a competitor and let us live the good life." But each day he continues to go to the office, as he has done for the just over 20 years since he "stopped pushing a gearshift." Still, he is troubled when he reads in periodicals that the average life span of a family-owned business is only 24 years. Roughly seven out of 10 family firms are sold, go public, or fold before being passed to a second generation. He ponders this carefully: 70% of family-owned businesses do not survive beyond the tenure of their founder (Galagan, 1985).

KEY TERMS

affective versus economic exchange	institutional overlap
autocratic style	limited human resources
centralized decision making	retention problems
corporate culture	role conflict
entrepreneurial personality	role strain
family-run firm	secondary tension
father–son rivalry	sibling power struggle
founder loneliness	technology gap
gender bias	trigger event
horizontal integration	underreward/overcompensation
in-group–out-group dynamics	inequities

DISCUSSION QUESTIONS

1. In what ways did Matt Sr.'s personality, attitudes, and management style contribute to the strengths *and* weaknesses of ORT/BCM?

2. What alternative cost-effective methods could Matt Sr. have used to "blend" his children and nephews into the management of ORT/BCM?

3. What strategies could Matt's children (Matt Jr., Quint, Katie, and Karen) have used to deal with their father and their new jobs more successfully?

4. What can be done to reduce "in-group–out-group dynamics" that occur in family firms like ORT between family members and nonfamily employees?

5. What problems will ORT face in the future?

REFERENCES

Beckhard, R., & Dyer, W. G., Jr. (1983). Managing continuity in the family-owned business. *Organizational Dynamics, 12*, 5–12.

Collins, O., Moore, D., & Unwalla, D. (1964). *The enterprising man*. East Lansing, MI: Michigan State University Bureau of Business Research.

Davis, P. (1983). Realizing the potential of the family business. *Organizational Dynamics, 12*, 47–56.

Fisher, B. A. (1980). *Small group decision making: Communication and group process* (2nd ed.). New York: McGraw-Hill.

Friedlander, A., & Chiang, S. (1983). Productivity growth in the regulated trucking industry. *Research in Transportation Economics, 1*, 149–184.

Galagan, P. (1985). Between family and firm. *Training & Development Journal, 39*, 68–71.

Guinn, B. (1983). Job satisfaction, counterproductive behavior and circumstantial drug use among long-distance truckers. *Journal of Psychoactive Drugs, 15*, 185–188.

Gumpert, D., & Boyd, D. (1984). The loneliness of the small business owner. *Harvard Business Review, 62*, 18–24.

Kepner, E. (1983). The family and the firm: A coevolutionary perspective. *Organizational Dynamics, 12*, 57–70.

Lansberg, I. (1983). Managing human resources in family firms: The problem of institutional overlap. *Organizational Dynamics, 12*, 39–46.

Levinson, H. (1971). Conflicts that plague family businesses. *Harvard Business Review, 49*, 90–98.

Rice, G., Jr. (1983). Strategic decision making in small businesses. *Journal of General Management, 9*, 58–65.

Rosenblatt, P. (1985). *The family in business*. San Francisco: Jossey-Bass.

Schein, E. (1983). The role of the founder in creating organizational culture. *Organizational Dynamics, 12*, 13–28.

Shaw, M. E. (1981). *Group dynamics: The psychology of small group behavior* (3rd ed.). New York: McGraw-Hill.

Thurston, P. (1983). Should smaller companies make formal plans? *Harvard Business Review, 61,* 162–188.

Timberlake, C. (1985, May 30). Daughters find way into family businesses. *Champaign-Urbana News Gazette,* p. B-7.

Williamson, K., Singer, M., & Peterson, R. (1983). The impact of regulatory reform on U.S. for-hire freight transportation: The users' perspective. *Transportation Journal, 22,* 27–54.

CHAPTER 11

Shootout at Midwest Manufacturing: When Supervisors and Staff Clash

Anita C. James

Sue DeWine
Ohio University

Often, communication consultants are asked to "fix" an individual's style of communicating with others. The belief that a change in a person's style will solve interpersonal relationship problems is pervasive. The following case study is based on an actual intervention by the first author, and an assessment of that intervention and development of points by the second author. The association between the consultant and the client lasted for 3 years and involved training programs, data collection for needs analysis, and one-on-one consulting with several of the employees.

Ed Denning, vice president for administration at Midwest Manufacturing, Inc. (MMI), began one June day with a phone call to Alexis Davenport, a faculty member in the Communication Department at a midwestern university.

ED: Good morning. I'm Ed Denning with Midwest Manufacturing in Bigtown. John Kramer gave me your name.

ALEXIS: Good morning, Mr. Denning.

ED: I need an external person to come into MMI and work on a staff communication problem. John has worked on other projects for us, but he's not a communication consultant, so he recommended that I talk with you. I've known John for years and trust his judgment so I'm calling to see if you're interested in working with us at our manufacturing plant in Smalltown. I know that you have a busy schedule at the university, but I'd like to arrange a meeting with you at our corporate offices in Bigtown as soon as possible.

ALEXIS: I appreciate your call. I don't know if I can live up to John's advance billing but I'm interested in talking with you. What kind of problem are you having?

ED: Well, it's fairly involved and of long standing. It's a personnel matter; interpersonal conflict is what I'd call it. I really think it would be much easier to explain if you could meet with me at the corporate offices.

ALEXIS: If I were able to meet with you, would there be anyone else at the meeting?

ED: There would be three of us: you; Jerry Hammel, the vice president for operations; and me. Jerry is responsible for the line operations—the short- and long-term business plans and the day-to-day operations at our manufacturing plant. I am in charge of the administrative staff end of things including personnel, finance, sales, and training and development. Jerry and I both report to Peter Foreman, the company president.

ALEXIS: What do you want to accomplish at this meeting?

ED: We would brief you on the company, the background of the problem, and the employees involved. I would like two things to result from the meeting: your agreement to help Midwest with its problem and a general discussion of a written proposal to follow the meeting.

ALEXIS: Let me look at my calendar. O.K., I will meet with you. My schedule is pretty tight for the next 2 weeks. How does July 3 look for you?

ED: As far as I know July 3 is fine. I'll have to cross-check with Jerry's calendar, then I can confirm the date and time with you.

ALEXIS: How long do you think we'll need?

ED: I imagine an hour to an hour and a half will be sufficient. What time could you be here?

ALEXIS: I can be there at 10 o'clock.

ED: Fine. Jerry and I will expect to see you in Bigtown at 10 A.M. on July 3. If Jerry can't make it, I'll get back to you. I look forward to meeting you in person. John had many good things to say about you.

ALEXIS: Thank you for the call, Mr. Denning. I look forward to meeting you.

In the weeks before the July 3 meeting Alexis tried to learn about her potential client. MMI was not a major corporation so the university library did not have any copies of its annual reports. The company was listed in one of the manufacturing directories, but it only gave information about the locations of its offices and manufacturing plant.

She asked John Kramer, an assistant vice-president at the university in charge of personnel and development, for any information he had. Alexis learned that the company was family owned; the current president was the son of one of the founders. It had a small, but respectable 5% share of the market for custom steel shelving and cabinets. The manufacturing plant was still housed in its original building in Smalltown.

On July 3, Alexis was at the corporate offices in Bigtown for the meeting.

RECEPTIONIST: May I help you?

ALEXIS: Yes, my name is Dr. Alexis Davenport. I have a 10:00 appointment with Ed Denning and Jerry Hammel.

RECEPTIONIST: Just a moment while I let Mr. Denning know you're here. Please have a seat.

Alexis chose to wander around the lobby instead of sitting down so soon after the drive to Bigtown.

RECEPTIONIST: Dr. Davenport, Mr. Denning will be with you in just a moment.

ED: Dr. Davenport? I'm Ed Denning. It's nice to meet you. This is Jerry Hammel.

ALEXIS: Ed, how do you do? Please call me Alexis. Jerry, it's nice to meet you. I was just looking at that old photograph on the wall. Is that this location or the manufacturing plant in Smalltown?

ED: It's the facility in Smalltown. That photograph was taken more than 25 years ago, for the company's 25th anniversary!

ALEXIS: Well, it seems to me that the company respects its history. Where are we meeting?

JERRY: We're back in the executive conference room.

AN OVERVIEW OF THE COMPANY

Once in the conference room, the discussion turned to the reason for the meeting.

ED: Let me give you an overview of Midwest Manufacturing, Inc., so you understand what we are and what we do. I've been with the company for 14 years. Jerry was hired to help us restructure our approaches to problems—about 2 years ago, wasn't it, Jerry?

JERRY: Yes, I came on board in late October 2 years ago.

ALEXIS: It's my understanding that MMI is a family operation and that the son of one of the founders is the president now. Is that correct?

ED: Yes. Midwest Manufacturing was founded in 1935 by two men, Carl Foreman and Gerhard Gerbner. It was, and still is, a family-owned operation. Both Foreman and Gerbner are now dead and Foreman's son,

Peter, is the company president. No one from Gerbner's family is involved in the company any more. The company was established in Smalltown. Up until 6 years ago the corporate offices were also in Smalltown, right next door to the manufacturing plant.

ALEXIS: What made the company move its offices away from the manufacturing facility?

ED: The move to Bigtown, which was not well received by the employees, came at the end of a 17-week strike by the union. As you might expect, ill feelings resulted from the strike. In addition, Peter wanted MMI's offices closer to other companies who were potential customers. The two circumstances combined to force the move. Now there are 50 employees in Bigtown, including the corporate office staff and the warehouse staff.

ALEXIS: Isn't it rather awkward for a small company to have the plant in one location and the offices in another? There must be some coordination problems that have resulted from the move.

THE WORK FORCE

JERRY: There have been a number of problems, particularly communication problems. But Mr. Foreman didn't want to pull the plant out of Smalltown, and it was a good idea to move the company offices.

ED: That's right. MMI has been a major employer in Smalltown since its founding. It's not unusual for three generations of the same family to work in the plant.

ALEXIS: What can you tell me about these workers, Ed?

ED: Their average age is 50 and the average number of years on the job is 28. The plant operates one shift, 5 days a week. There are 60 workers in the plant, all members of the United Steel Workers union, and all male. Relations between the union and management are fairly typical; no major problems, but no love lost either.

ALEXIS: You said all of the workers are male. Are there any women at the plant?

ED: Just two, the secretary/office manager and the traffic manager.

ALEXIS: What's the population of Smalltown and what are the major employers?

JERRY: Smalltown has about 8,000 people. There used to be three large manufacturing operations there—two of them were heavy steel, including MMI, and the other was a clothing manufacturer. That's changing now.

The other steel-based manufacturing company is closing its doors at the end of the year. The clothing company is doing O.K. because one of its other plants closed and transferred its work to the Smalltown plant. About 8 years ago, a food processing plant moved into the area and is doing all right now.

ALEXIS: What are the job options for the employees from the plant that's shutting down? It doesn't sound as if there's much for them in town.

JERRY: There isn't. Ten or fifteen years ago we could have hired some of the guys. That's when the plant was running two shifts and had 110 people on the payroll. Now, there's not much for those other laid-off guys to do unless they want to learn to use a sewing machine.

ALEXIS: How have the changes in the community affected the men at your plant?

ED: The environment of the plant and the size of the town makes creating change difficult. The union workers live literally next door to management. They've all gone to school together, their children play together, they're on the same sports teams. When they quit work each day, they are all part of the same community. The community is being put to the test in coping with these problems. It seems to be pulling through, though.

There's a strong union mentality dating from the early days of working in the coal fields. Folks are used to pulling together to get things done without managers interfering. At the same time, there's a deep sense that the union actually runs things; that management's superfluous. This is as evident in the general community as at MMI.

ALEXIS: Okay. What about the management personnel, Jerry? What can you tell me about them?

THE SUPERVISORS

JERRY: If you look at this organizational chart of the plant you can see some of what I'll be talking about. It's a flat organization (see Figure 11.1). The supervisors came up through the union ranks and sometimes find it difficult to separate themselves from their former coworkers. If you remember Ed saying that it's a small town and everyone knows everyone else, well, you can see how a supervisor giving orders to a union employee who may be his next door neighbor can feel some ambiguity. These are not real sophisticated guys. I've overheard one or the other of them say things like, "Joe knows what he's supposed to be doing. I don't have to tell him his job." Or "Buck's been welding for 25 years. Where do I get off trying to tell him how to do his job?"

The supervisor with the *least* seniority has been on the job for 11 years. The supervisor with the most time in the position has 20 years.

Some of the difficulty with encouraging leadership and strong supervision among the supervisors is the history of management in the plant, their own lack of academic preparation, and what I see as a lack of self-confidence. Three of the five supervisors are high school graduates, one did not graduate from high school, and one (the newest supervisor) has a college degree. He's

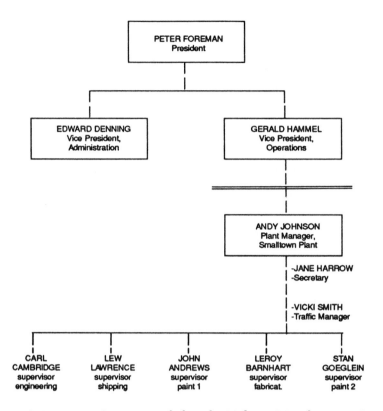

FIGURE 11.1. Organizational chart for Midwest Manufacturing, Inc.

the exception; none of the other supervisors has ever worked anywhere else but MMI.

The supervisors are good, honest men, but they're uncomfortable with the role of supervising their friends and former coworkers. Until Hank took over the job of plant manager, his predecessors had made all the decisions and told the supervisors what to do. There was no job training, job development, or job enrichment—being a supervisor was a change in status but not in responsibility or accountability for what happened. Supervisors were not encouraged to think or act on their own. The plant manager let them know what was necessary for them to know. One result of this is a history in the plant of the workers going *around* the supervisors to get information and answers.

ALEXIS: It isn't clear to me how you can have five supervisors who don't supervise and 60 workers who don't need supervision.

JERRY: Well, it is partly the result of the experience level of the workers. They're a mature workforce and they think they know how to run the plant as well as, or better than, the supervisors. Compounding the problem is the interrelationship between union employees and management staff. For instance, the union committee president is the brother of one of the supervisors. The plant manager has two brothers who are union members in the plant, one of whom is on the union committee. One of the supervisors is also the plant manager's father. Neither Ed nor I happen to be related to anyone in the plant, but that's because we were brought in from outside the area.

ALEXIS: Does Mr. Foreman have relatives working in the plant?

ED: No.

JERRY: As I said earlier, I think there's also a problem among the supervisors of low self-confidence and low self-esteem. The plant has a strong union and a relatively weak management. In the last 18 months I've been trying to upgrade the supervisors' skills so they can form a first line of effective leadership. However, it hasn't been easy. I've seen some progress with one or two of them, but it's not enough. The company has even sent them to training programs offered by the American Management Association (AMA), an university, as well as professional manufacturing associations.

The experience with the AMA program is a case in point about the role of the union in running the plant. While the supervisors were away from the plant for a 3-hour period *every Friday* morning for 4 months, not a single call was made to any supervisor and there was absolutely no change in the output of the plant during that period! In other words, the plant operated *without the supervisors exactly as it did with them!* You could say that's a good sign. The union says it proves that the supervisors aren't needed, that the union can do everything itself. This puts the supervisors in a difficult position.

ALEXIS: That's a good overview of the company. I appreciate the information since it helps me begin to understand the culture of the plant. I worked with a fiberglass plant in this area, so I have a general feeling for what you've described.

Let me summarize what you've told me so far. (1) MMI is a family-owned company that's been in Smalltown for more than 50 years; (2) what must have been a bitter strike 6 years ago resulted in the move of the corporate offices to Bigtown; (3) over the years, the number of employees has dropped from about 110 to the figure of 60 today. How long ago did the plant have 110 employees?

ED: That was in the years immediately after World War II.

ALEXIS: So, (4) the plant has a relatively flat hierarchical structure with a fairly large span of control for each supervisor; (5) the workforce is mature, with high job knowledge and competence; (6) the supervisors were promoted from the union ranks and have had minimal formal training and little company support, until recently, for doing anything that resembles supervising the workers. In fact, they were seen as obstacles by the former plant manager and the union; and (7) the community is suffering the loss of jobs, thereby reducing the options for young and old employees alike.

I think it's time, gentlemen, to find out what the problem is that brought us together today.

THE CONFLICT PROBLEM

JERRY: It's conflict. As we've explained, five supervisors and the plant manager form the management and first-line leadership for the plant. No females or union employees are in the group. One of the supervisors is often in conflict with members of the union, and we want this conflict to stop.

ALEXIS: I need some clarification, Ed. What do you mean by "conflict?"

ED: It may be easiest for me to define "conflict" in this instance by giving you examples of it. Lew sees a worker smoking a cigarette on the loading dock, a part of the area he supervises. He says, "Hey, Andy, it's not break time. Get back to work." Andy responds with, "That's a bunch of bull. I'm taking my break now." Lew counters, "No, you're not. Get up and back to work now or I'll have to write you up." It escalates when Andy says, "Who do you think you are, Lew? You're just a dumb schmuck like the rest of us. You ain't gonna write anyone up. Get off my back!" Andy goes to his union steward; a grievance is filed against Lew.

ALEXIS: Who's Lew?

ED: He's the supervisor we have the problem with—Lew Lawrence.

ALEXIS: I have three questions for you, Jerry. What is the nature of the conflict? Why do you think it's occurring? And how do you think it can be stopped?

JERRY: The conflict manifests itself as grievances filed by the union against this particular supervisor. The grievances are filed three to four times a year. They are filed only against this one supervisor. That's why we believe the problem is with the supervisor. We think the problem will be stopped if the supervisor's communication style is changed.

ALEXIS: How do you know the grievances are filed against the supervisor because of his "communication style?" Are there other possible contributory causes that are being overlooked?

JERRY: I don't think we've overlooked anything that's important. And, we know that Lew's communication style is at the root of the grievances because the union always cites his tone of voice, his words, or his attitude as the basis for the grievance. That's why he's got to be changed!"

ALEXIS: Wait a moment. What do you mean by "change?"

ED: Lew's been with MMI for decades. He has to be made to change how he communicates with the union employees in his sector. We want him to behave differently.

ALEXIS: I think I need some background on Lew. Tell me about him?

ED: Let me look at his file. Lew Lawrence has been with the company since 1943. He was born in 1924 in Smalltown. He's been a supervisor for the last 15 years. He's now in his 60s, but he's not interested in retiring and there's no mandatory company retirement policy. The company doesn't want to fire him because he's a valuable employee when he's not bogged down with grievances. He supervises the removal of the steel shelves and cabinet parts from the paint line. He's also responsible for getting the parts packed according to the customer order and loaded into either the company trucks (for transshipment to the Bigtown warehouse) or the customers' trucks. He's rarely ill, works hard, does his best, and is loyal to MMI.

ALEXIS: He certainly does sound like a valued employee. What's the problem with his subordinates?

JERRY: Lew is the supervisor who is least likely to compromise on anything. He seems to have a very strong need for discipline. His workers seem to like to bait him and he rises for the hook every time. The problem has been developing for years. The result is a series of one-on-one grievances filed by the union approximately every 3 months.

ALEXIS: Let me see if I understand what you're telling me. Lew has been employed by Midwest Manufacturing for more than 40 years. He's in his 60s but not likely to retire or be fired. He has been a supervisor for about 15 years. Lew likes discipline, but apparently communicates that desire for discipline in a manner deemed inappropriate by the union. Consequently, grievances are filed against Lew on a regular basis; in fact, in 3-month cycles. You want me to change Lew's behavior so no more grievances will be filed.

JERRY: We're not idealistic enough to believe that no more grievances will ever be filed against Lew. But we would like you to work with him to diminish the number and frequency of grievances against him.

ALEXIS: Can you give me another example of the kind of conflict situation Lew gets into with his men?

JERRY: The union contract guarantees the employees a 15-minute break in the morning and another one in the afternoon. Over the years the men have stretched the 15 minutes into a 20- or 25-minute break. The other supervisors don't care much about the length of the break as long as the work is getting done. Lew, on the other hand, starts to time his men when they leave their work stations. At the end of 15 minutes he might go to them and tell them to get back on the job, or he'll report them. He adds words like "goofing off" and "bagging it" when he confronts them.

ALEXIS: It sounds to me as if Lew is trying to keep to the letter of the contract. Usually, numbers and lengths of breaks are specified in the contract. What happens to the grievances after they're filed?

JERRY: Most of them are settled amicably. The union committee meets with the management team (Ed, Andy, and me), we all talk, and it usually ends with Lew being asked to shake hands with the offended party in the grievance.

ALEXIS: How would you describe the problem that results from these grievances?

JERRY: It's the hassle of it all. Lew is placed on the defensive after a grievance is filed. There's time lost on the line when a grievance hearing is called because the union committee has members from all over the plant, not just from shipping. Although it seems as if everything is OK after the handshake, we all know it's going to happen again. It's almost like a game with them: bait—words—grieve—talk—shake hands. Time passes, and the sequence is repeated.

ALEXIS: I can see how that becomes psychologically tiring as well as costly to MMI. Is there anything else you can tell me about Lew?

ED: Lew seems to take everything personally that happens in his sector. He feels that others want his job, which isn't the case actually. In fact, the last time there was a supervisory opening, none of the union employees wanted the job. That's why we recruited Carl Cambridge 11 years ago.

ALEXIS: That is interesting. None of the union workers wanted to move into the management ranks. Certainly, there seems to be little cause for Lew to worry about his job being taken by someone else. There's no real need for Lew to play the hard-nosed rule enforcer to improve his image with the company, is there?

ED: No, but we don't seem to be able to get that across to him. That's why John Kramer recommended we talk with you. We don't think that packaged programs or seminars off-site are the answer either. We've tried those for other problems and there just doesn't seem to be enough application to the MMI situations. What we're looking for is a program tailored to the specific conflict problems between Lew and the union workers. That's why we'd like your help. How can we change Lew so we have fewer problems with the union?

ALEXIS: I don't know right now. It's obvious to me that I cannot change Lew's basic personality; it's had too many years to develop. If he's interested, it may be possible for him to learn ways to modify his behavior or communicate his wants and needs as a supervisor more effectively.

Have you thought about including the other supervisors in whatever program develops so Lew doesn't feel he's been singled out for some sort of punishment? If, as you say, none of the supervisors have much formal training, then they might learn something from a program designed for Lew.

I gather that the contract with the union prevents focusing on the union employees as the source of the problem. Are you sure that Lew is the problem and not his subordinates?

JERRY: Yes, we're convinced it's Lew. And no, we really haven't thought about including all of the supervisors. It might be worthwhile, though, to provide all of the supervisors with the same program. That could lead to reinforcement of the changed behaviors.

ED: That sounds like a good idea. Are you ready to take on the project?

ALEXIS: Well, it sounds like a real challenge. Yes, I'll tackle it.

ED: When can we see something in writing?

ALEXIS: I can have a proposal ready for you, Ed, within the next 3 weeks. I would like to know if you have any preconceived ideas about what you want to see in the proposal. What are my constraints?

JERRY: I don't have any preconceived ideas about the content. I think this is a communication problem, in general; a conflict problem, in particular. I'm assuming that the proposal would focus on communicative behaviors, but other than that, there's nothing I want. You have as much freedom as you need.

ED: Why don't you address the proposal to Jerry. He's the one who actually oversees plant operations and handles Lew and the problems now.

ALEXIS: All right. The proposal will be on your desk, Jerry, by July 25.

THE PROPOSAL

On July 25 Alexis Davenport's proposal was on Jerry Hammel's desk at Midwest Manufacturing, Inc. The proposal was in four parts; Alexis planned to (1) explore the background and value assumptions of the supervisors; (2) promote the modeling of appropriate communication behaviors and the development of the supervisors as change agents within the plant; (3) conduct short-term observation and feedback of the supervisors' communication; and (4) conduct long-term, periodic observation of their communication behavior.

The proposal was approved by both Jerry Hammel and Ed Denning. They then discussed it with Peter Foreman, the president of MMI. He accepted the proposal and authorized funding for the project.

During the background and value assumption discussions Alexis conducted, five issues surfaced as primary concerns:

1. There seemed to be some uncertainty about supervisors' responsibilities and accountability.
2. Plant supervisors felt that they did not have the support of the plant and upper management.
3. Relationships between supervisors and workers needed rehabilitation: There was some evidence of partiality and favoritism by some supervisors; a "get even" attitude permeated the plant; rules were not clearly defined or enforced; and the use of coercive power was the primary method of control.
4. Individuals reported that the communication and scheduling systems at the plant were dysfunctional, that feedback was often based on incomplete information.

5. There were also complaints that those in leadership roles were plagued with indecision and avoided making hard choices, and that top management was inefficient and not altogether trustworthy or honest.

6. Communication from supervisors was not considered open, honest, or timely; employees felt formal channels were not used enough.

KEY TERMS

credibility	accountability
perception	formal channels of communication
symptoms versus causes of problems	interpersonal conflict and conflict management
focus groups	power
one-on-one interviews	goal conflict
hierarchy	

DISCUSSION QUESTIONS

1. Often the problem as presented by the client is only a symptom of the underlying problem. A symptom is immediate evidence that something is wrong, such as a person being late for work. The problem is the *reason why* this behavior is occurring. People describe symptoms rather than causes when the following conditions exist: (1) when the client does not understand the problem well enough to describe its cause, (2) when the client purposefully hides the problem so that others will not have access to what is considered confidential information, (3) when the immediate symptoms are so stressful that they must be dealt with first, or (4) when other causes mask the basic, underlying problem.

    What questions might the consultant ask in the first contact with the client's representative(s) to help uncover the real problem? What was the problem as presented with Midwest Manufacturing, Inc.? What do you suspect are the underlying causes or problems?

2. What steps would you take next to begin the process of data collection? How would you design a proposal to meet the needs of MMI, Lew Lawrence, and the other supervisors?

3. Many types of data-collection techniques are available to individuals attempting to assess communication problems in organizations. Some of the most frequently used include survey instruments, interviews, communication audit procedures, self-report communication-style tools, focus groups, and observations. In this case the consultant selected interviews and focus groups. What were the advantages and the disadvantages of using these methods?

4. What areas might have been explored in greater depth using other methods of data collection?

5. A number of communication theories are readily applicable to the organizational setting, particularly when dealing with superior–subordinate relationships. Some of these include (a) general systems theory—examining the entire organization and observing how changes in one part effect changes in other parts; (b) exchange theory—every relationship has costs and rewards; we enter into a relationship because the rewards outweigh the costs. At Midwest Manufacturing, Inc., how would each of these theories help explain the problem and the solution?

6. Given what we know about good superior–subordinate relationships and communication satisfaction, what would you propose to solve the problems at Midwest Manufacturing, Inc.? Why?

SUGGESTED READINGS

Baum, E., & James, A. (1987). *How to P.R.A.I.S.E., T.R.A.I.N., or C.H.A.N.G.E. employee behaviors*. Unpublished manuscript, Athens, OH.

Blanchard, K., & Johnson, S. (1981). *The one-minute manager*. West Caldwell, NJ: Morrow.

Downs, C. (1988). *Communication audits*. Glenview, IL: Scott Foresman.

French, J., & Raven, B. (1959). *Studies in social power*. Ann Arbor, MI: Institute for Social Research.

Gibb, J. (1961). Defensive communication. *The Journal of Communication, 11*(3), 141–148.

Lewin, K. (1952). Group decision and social change. In G. Swanson, J. Newcomb, & E. Hartley (Eds.), *Readings in social psychology* (pp. 459–473). New York: Holt, Rinehart.

Lippitt, G., Langseth, P., & Mossop, J. (1985). *Implementing organizational change*. San Francisco: Jossey-Bass.

Littlejohn, S. (1988). *Theories of human communication* (3rd ed.). Belmont, CA: Wadsworth.

McGregor, D. (1960). *The human side of enterprise*. New York: McGraw-Hill.

Pfeffer, J. (1981). *Power in organizations*. Marshfield, MA: Pitman.

Phelps, L., & DeWine, S. (1976). *Interpersonal communication journal*. St. Paul, MN: West.

Schein, E. (1970). *Organizational psychology* (2nd ed.). Englewood Cliffs, NJ: Prentice-Hall.

Watson, G. (Ed.). (1966). *Concepts for social change*. Washington, DC: National Training Laboratories.

Zemke, R. (1984). *Figuring things out*. Reading, MA: Addison-Wesley.

CHAPTER 12

The Indictment:
A Superior–Subordinate
Confrontation

Cal W. Downs
University of Kansas

Frank Cochran, Ron O'Daniel, and Seth Wharton were the three assistants to John Bommarito, who had been city manager of Southwestern City for about 12 years. All three had graduated from the M.A. program in city management at the University of Kansas. Frank and Ron had gone through the program together and had just graduated the previous summer. They had taken a number of classes together, and while they were not close friends, they were comfortable with one another. Seth had graduated a year earlier, but he had known both of them. He was glad to have them join him on the staff because of their common educational background. For all three this was the first job. Seth had worked in the city manager's office for 18 months, and Frank and Ron had been there for about 6 months.

During their university experience, they had taken a graduate course in human relations, which focused a great deal on interpersonal relations, conflict, and conflict resolution. The course was designed to create situations so that the students could actually work as groups and analyze their own group processes. Direct confrontation was often the means that the groups used to solve problems. During these discussions, Frank emerged as the person the group respected most. He would often remain quiet and did not volunteer information or opinions until he had carefully thought through his position. In terms of communication style, he would be classified as a thinker—analytic and systematic. Ron, on the other hand, was much less introspective. His comments were much less analytic, and he often experienced a bit of frustration when analyzing situations. He would rather talk about what ought to be done than what had been done. In this sense, he was very solution oriented. Because he felt that Frank was more capable than

190

himself, he did not mind following Frank's lead. Seth had taken the same course a year earlier. He did not find the analysis particularly appealing, but he did enjoy group dynamics and was especially adept at reducing tensions during conflict. It was he who could tell a joke or make a remark that would help diffuse anger and frustration.

THE PROBLEM

It was 5:30 P.M. on a Friday evening in January, and many of Southwestern City's 600,000 citizens were hurrying home for the weekend. However, Frank had asked Ron to stay at the office and discuss a few matters of mutual concern.

During the 6 months they had been assistants, both had occasionally voiced some surprise at how the office was run, and they had encountered a number of frustrations. The situation had grown so worrisome for Frank that he felt something should be done. The dissatisfaction had begun to gnaw at him so much that he felt he was spending too much time thinking about it. That is why he wanted to talk to Ron. Trying to be fair and objective about the situation, he carefully pointed out that he did not know whether his frustrations were the product of the system or the individual behind this system. For over an hour they shared their concerns and finally concluded that the only thing to be done was to talk to Mr. Bommarito personally, point out some of the problems, and recommend a few changes in the operation.

The following Monday, Ron approached Mr. Bommarito requesting a conference later in the week to discuss the current office organization. Although Mr. Bommarito was somewhat surprised by the request, he set the time for the meeting at 5 P.M. on Thursday. He could not meet until then because he had scheduled himself out of the office for most of the week. Southwestern City was growing rapidly and was emerging as a cultural and economic force in the state. While he was proud of his contribution to the city, he found the demands to be almost unmanageable at times. This was one of those times.

THE PREPARATION

That Monday evening Frank and Ron met again to outline their presentation to the city manager. They wanted to be thoroughly prepared and to be exact in what they said. In their discussions that evening, they made two very deliberate decisions. First, they would not include Seth, the third assistant, in the matter. Seth had never voiced any dissatisfaction to them and, therefore, did not seem to share the same frustrations. He just seemed to take things as they were. Second, they decided to prepare a presentation outlining those areas in the current system tht seemed most critical and recommending ways to correct the apparent deficiencies of the system. When they had finished, they had prepared the document shown in Table 12.1. When they had finished writing their evaluation, both Frank and Ron wondered aloud about the possibility that they would need to look for new jobs soon. Nevertheless, they were glad that they had done it. They felt a kind of relief at finally getting their thoughts organized so well and down on paper. Ron commented, "I don't think that I could ever have done this alone."

THE CONFRONTATION

It was a long week as Frank and Ron waited to make their presentation. They were obviously preoccupied with what they were going to say, and they were glad that Mr. Bommarito was out of the office so they did not have to

TABLE 12.1. Organization: The System and the Individual

A. *Critical Areas of Concern*

1. Processing Requests

   Example: asphalt machine for public works.
   The request was received in August, and a reply was drafted by an assistant in September. Yet, the request is still pending.

2. Delegation of Responsibilities.

   Example: federal grant for police department.
   Delegation for preparation of an application was withheld until the original deadline had expired. Then it required special authorization to continue the grant application.

   Example: appointment of a building inspector.
   A new building inspector position was authorized and a person hired without notifying personnel for proper processing. Normally, the city manager delegates this responsibility to an assistant.

3. Communication.

   Example: work load organization.
   Projects and assignments are given to assistants without knowledge of their current work load. Can you tell us the projects for which we are responsible at the present time?

   Example: priorities and deadlines.
   Projects are not assigned priorities or reasonable deadlines.

4. Personal Relationships.

   Example: personal evaluations.
   Two months ago we were promised personal evaluations of our performance, and it still has not happened.

Example: failure to be punctual.
Scheduled staff meetings are changed, and assistants are forced to reschedule previous commitments.

B. *Recommendations*

1. Schedule daily work load.
2. Involve assistants with projects when they first come to the attention of the manager.
3. Organize assignments; set priorities; and honor deadlines.
4. Schedule staff meetings on a regular basis.
5. Take individual initiative to improve working relationships.

C. *Summary*

This presentation is the product of our frustrations and we feel that our frustrations are the product of the current organization of this office.

We have both considered the effects this evaluation may have on our personal relationships with the city manager as well as on our future careers here or in other cities. In preparing this evaluation, careful consideration has been given to each comment, and we strongly feel that we share the blame for not pointing out each of these indictments earlier. We now offer our complete cooperation to better the existing organization.

However, a final question centers on whether the existing problems are the product of the system or the individual. Regardless of the answer, we feel that the individual must now take the initiative.

---

interact with him. At lunch Thursday, Frank and Ron met again to review their evaluation. They decided that Frank would open the presentation by (1) explaining their purpose, (2) giving their reasons for not including Seth, and (3) listing the examples in the critical areas of concern. Ron would follow Frank's remarks with the recommendations and summary of the evaluation. They were as carefully rehearsed as they could be. Finally, Frank and Ron agreed to close the presentation with a statement that both assistants would submit their resignations in June if some effort was not made to correct apparent deficiencies in the existing organization.

In the meeting with Bommarito, they followed their plan exactly and ended their presentation by giving him a typed copy of the prepared document. Throughout the presentation, Mr. Bommarito had listened nervously, but had not said anything. It was a very tense situation. Even after the presentation ended, he remained silent while he wrote some notes on a pad. Finally, he looked straight at them and made the following comments: "First, let me say that I admire your gall. In the 5 years that I have been here, a lot has been said behind my back concerning the operations of this office, but no one has ever told me to my face just how they saw the present organization and the man behind it. I would like to spend some time going over your comments and then meet with you late tomorrow afternoon."

Nothing more was said as Mr. Bommarito got up and walked out. Frank and Ron stared at one another, uncertain about what they had accomplished and what was in store for them the next day. Anticipating that Mr. Bommarito would be more defensive, they were unprepared for his reaction.

Mr. Bommarito pointedly refrained from any contact with either Frank or Ron all day Friday. At precisely 4:45 P.M., however, he had his secretary call and summon them to his office. He asked them to take a seat; then he stood and began to talk.

"Gentlemen, I have carefully reviewed your evaluation. I would like to comment first on the format and content. Your evaluation does present constructive criticisms, justified by actual examples. However, it lacks any reference to the positive elements of this organization—both the system and the individual. In my experience, I have always believed in judging the good as well as the bad.

"As for the examples you used, there are explanations that justify some of my actions; however, the majority of the examples serve as good evidence of present deficiencies in office operations. I feel most disturbed about the personal indictment that is implied. It has been very hard for me to understand why you feel I have failed to display initiative in maintaining good working relationships. Since the time you two joined my staff, I have increased your salaries on two occasions. That ought to have let you know I appreciate you. My door has always been open to you to discuss matters affecting this organization. You could have come in on any one of these matters at any time Yet, you wait and submit a very negative judgment on me and my organization.

"As for your recommendations, it is impossible for me to schedule a daily work load. Things move too fast for that. There are simply too many interruptions. When I became city manager, I tried to establish a daily schedule, and it just didn't work.

"With respect to project assignments, I plan to implement your suggestion immediately. Staff meetings will be scheduled regularly, and I apologize for my previous neglect in this area.

"Finally, you can be most assured that I will make every effort to maintain good working relationships with my staff. However, this must be a two-way street. Any time you have a question or are frustrated by my actions, come in and talk. It is hard for me to read your minds or know what is bugging you if you don't tell me."

The meeting ended with a surprised Frank and Ron expressing appreciation for Mr. Bommarito's apparent interest and acceptance of their evaluation.

Immediately after the meeting with Bommarito, they took time to share their perceptions of what had happened. Interestingly enough, throughout all of their planning they had never suspected that he would be so reasonable and accepting; they had really expected him to be defensive and threatening. Now they reiterated their resolve to understand the city manager's situation and to cooperate more in improving office operations.

SUBSEQUENT EVENTS

Since their confrontation with Mr. Bommarito, both Frank and Ron had a rush of good feeling both about Bommarito and the organization. They changed their perceptions of the situation and were more tolerant. These changes in themselves were so surprising that periodically they would talk about what had happened. They concluded that their old frustrations were not so much the product of the system or the individual, but of a lack of communication within the organization. They now felt a greater tolerance for things that once would have frustrated them. Operations seemed much smoother, and they felt that working relationships improved greatly in the office. Both the city manager and his assistants tried to be more aware of what was happening and why. They never became close, but neither was there a deterioration in their relationship as a result of the incident.

No one else in the office ever learned about this incident. Seth never showed any sign of frustration and faithfully pursued his daily routine of flirting with the office secretary. Ron was able to settle into a routine and handle his assignments without much difficulty. Frank, on the other hand, outgrew his job. He never had any other major confrontations with Mr. Bommarito, but began to feel stifled and want something more stimulating. Whenever he talked with Ron about the office, he recognized that their points of view were not really alike any longer. Within a year he was looking for a new job opportunity and eventually took a foreign administrative post for a professional association.

KEY TERMS

communication style	effective communication
conflict	feedback
confrontation	perception
effective subordinancy	time management

DISCUSSION QUESTIONS

1. What were the real problems in this case? From whose perspective?
   a. Were they resolved well?
   b. Why did some people apparently not perceive a problem?

2. What principles of giving feedback were followed? What actions ran counter to principles of giving feedback?

3. How would you evaluate Mr. Bommarito's response? This case could have had an explosive ending. What prevented it?

4. What were the implications of having the feedback written (a) for Frank and Ron? (b) for Mr. Bommarito?

5. What were the communication styles of the participants?
   a. How did differences in styles affect the interaction?
   b. How does communication style affect people's perceptions of a situation?

6. Who was the most competent communicator in this case? Why?

7. What standards of "effectiveness" can be applied to the outcome of this case?

8. In what sense can Ron and Frank be said to be effective subordinates? How would they compare with Seth in effectiveness?

9. What might you have done differently if you were (a) a subordinate (b) the city manager?

SUGGESTED READINGS

Bednar, D. A. (1982). Relationships between communicator style and managerial performance in complex organizations: A field study. *Journal of Business Communication, 19*, 51–75.

Downs, C. W., Archer, J., McGrath, J., & Stafford, J. (1988). An analysis of communication style instrumentation. *Management Communication Quarterly, 1*, 543–571.

Downs, C. W, & Conrad, C. (1982). Effective subordinancy. *Journal of Business Communication, 19*, 27–38.

Downs, C. W., Johnson, K., & Barge, K. (1984). Communication feedback and task performance in organizations. *Organizational Communication Abstracts, 9*, 13–48.

Duran, R. L., & Kelly, L. (1985). An investigation into the cognitive domain of communication competence. *Communication Research Reports, 2*, 112–119.

Gabarro, J. (1979). Socialization at the top—how CEOs and their subordinates evolve interpersonal contacts. *Organizational Dynamics*.

Gabarro, J., & Kotter, J. P. (1979). Managing your boss. *Harvard Business Review, XX*, 92–100.

Infante, D. A., & Gorden, W. I. (1981). Similarities and differences in communicator styles of superiors and subordinates: Relations to subordinate satisfaction. *Communication Quarterly, 30*, 67–71.

Norton, R. W. (1983). *Communicator style: Theory, application, and measures*. Beverly Hills: Sage.

CHAPTER 13

Implementing Self-Management at Holiday Inn

THEODORE E. ZORN
University of North Carolina at Chapel Hill

Walking into the Holiday Inn Reservations Center in Raleigh, North Carolina, one is struck by something different about the way the place operates.[1] While some of the employees are dressed in clothes they might wear to a business meeting, others, apparently doing the same job, are dressed in jeans or even sweatsuits. Some people do needlepoint or knit as they perform their jobs; managers walk by and seem to take no notice. The director's office is easily accessible—there is no sign of a secretary to screen his visitors. In fact, one of these sweatsuited employees can often be found meeting with him—apparently not getting disciplined, but discussing such things as the company bowling league or his or her paycheck concerns. The human resources manager may be found helping an employee polish a resume, preparing her or him to get a better job somewhere else! The lounge area has a television, video games, and a quiet room with a sofa on which employees may rest or nap.

This reservations center obviously is not a typically managed organization. Neither is it an organization out of control. Rather, each of the features described above reflects a conscious set of decisions to encourage employee self-management.

HOLIDAY INN'S RESERVATIONS SERVICES

Since Kemmon Wilson founded Holiday Inn in the 1950s, it has become perhaps the world's most recognizable hotel chain. One of the reasons for its rapid growth was its use of centralized reservation services. We have all seen the advertisements that invite us to call 1-800-HOLIDAY; a call to this

197

number will connect the prospective hotel guest with an agent in a central reservations center. The agent can reserve a room in a Holiday Inn anywhere in the world.

According to Dave Milidonis, director of the reservation center in Raleigh, Holiday Inn was one of the first hotels to offer centralized reservation services to the public. As the result of its initial success, other hotel chains soon followed suit. Today, the establishment of centralized reservation centers is common practice. Milidonis claims,

> "We were the model to copy from. You can go to Omaha, Nebraska today and there's a reservation center *row;* there's a street in Omaha where you have a Marriott and a whole bunch of other reservation centers, all on the same street like they came out of cookie cutters. . . . "

One of Holiday Inn's chief selling points in getting franchise contracts in its early years was the reservation system. Through this service, Holiday Inn was able to guarantee a high percentage of occupancy at a set rate. No other hotel could make these guarantees in the early '60s. However, other hotels soon caught on. It was not long before others were offering similar services.

Through the '70s, Holiday Inn had two reservation centers—one in Memphis and one in Chicago. Management had for years considered creating a third—partly because the volume of calls justified this action, and partly to create the redundancy needed in case of a forced shutdown of one of the other centers—for example, because of natural disaster. A third reason was to give Holiday Inn back the competitive edge they had lost since other hotels had centralized their reservation services. Once the decision was made to create another reservation center, Holiday Inn decided that the new center had to be unique in its design if they were going to be competitive.

In April 1984, the vice president of reservations selected Dave Milidonis as the director of the new center, and gave him input in to its design. He told Dave, "I want you to come up with something that cannot be copied by our competitors, at least not without some major changes in philosophy and not without major risk."

Dave's background was in industrial engineering and human resources management. In a former position, he visited various Holiday Inns in the Chicago region to consult with them on problems they were having. He sometimes worked at the same hotel as Ron Washington, the current manager of human resources at the Raleigh reservation center. They agreed that management philosophy and organizational design were at the root of most problems they encountered. Ron explained;

> "Occasionally, we would meet at a hotel. Every time we'd come up with the same recommendation about correcting the situation. . . .

People were getting beat over the head—you could look in their personnel files (I'd be doing personnel audits) and find nothing but negativisms. And then you turn right around and ask the employees of that hotel to provide the utmost quality, cleanliness, and service while beating them over the head."

Dave continued,

"As soon as I got that job, that's when I called Ron, because Ron and I had a lot of work experience together in the Chicago area with the infancy of this whole concept. There was a period of time towards the end of our stay in the Chicago area when we were meeting, looking at trying [to implement more of a self-management system] at the individual hotel level. We always got blocked somewhere along the way and went our separate ways. So to us, designing this new reservation center was the opportunity of a lifetime."

In response to the instructions to create a reservation center that could not be copied, Dave said,

"I decided . . . the only thing that can't be copied was what's inside everybody's head. They can come in and copy the building. . . . but it didn't matter where we worked, as long as the environment we had was conducive to high productivity. The chief risk . . . [was] . . . to make a quantum leap from power-control management to *environmental* management. My feelings were, in the hotel industry anyway, in the business of reservations, that if we jumped on that one first it would be a while before anybody else would jump on that kind of a bandwagon, because they would want to see how this place worked."

Dave and Ron, like many of the employees interviewed, seemed energized by the feeling they were a part of something new and innovative. As they saw it, creating the center was a chance to try out what others had only theorized about. For example, Dave said,

"It was just a fledgling idea at first. Our own experience base was theory. It was just individual, short-term experiences and a lot of theory. You can go back to the OD books in the late '70s and they only devote the last chapter—every one of them—to what *could* be. And when you looked for actual experiences, well, nobody's ever tried it."

DESIGNING THE ENVIRONMENT

After hiring Ron, Dave hired two call service managers and two analysts in June 1984. The reservations center was yet to be constructed. The six of them met in a Holiday Inn hotel conference room in Raleigh to attempt to turn their ideas into a working plan for the reservations center. Their goal was, first, to articulate their values, and then to design the jobs and the work environment around these values. The result of these meetings was a document outlining their mission, philosophy, and plans, excerpts from which are shown in Table 13.1. This document was sent to the vice president of reservations for approval and was approved with no changes.

What they proposed was essentially a system in which goals were clearly laid out; reservations agents were given the training, information, and resources necessary to do their jobs without close supervision; and agents were given a system of incentives that encouraged them to take responsibility for managing themselves and to perform at a high level of productivity. A key selling point, as well as a major risk, was that the system required 50–70% *less management staff* than the traditional reservations center model.

Figures 13.1 and 13.2 show two organizational charts, one depicting the line organization of traditional reservations centers, and one depicting the Raleigh center. The traditional reservation center has general reservations agents and senior agents, who sit above them; these senior agents do the call-back tasks. That is, when an agent encounters a problem that he or she cannot handle, someone often has to call the guest back to address the problem. Agents and senior agents report to a supervisor, who in turn reports to an operations coordinator. There is usually one coordinator for every 25 or 35 agents. One or more operations administrators supervises the operations coordinators. Finally, there is the director.

The organizational structure of the Raleigh reservation center is quite different. There are basically three levels: general reservations agents (200–600 depending on the season), eight call-service managers, and the director. The traditional center has at least two organizational levels more than the Raleigh facility. How can eight call-service managers supervise the work of 600 agents? They do not; the agents essentially manage themselves.

Establishing a system of self-management requires training employees to perform their jobs competently, then creating an environment that encourages performance excellence. Dave Milidonis agrees,

> "What we wanted to do is kind of 'clone' as many people as possible that are basically self-employed—they're working because they want to, nobody's forcing them to—and give them the environment in which they can do that without any repercussions. We were going to hire people who don't need management because we don't see ourselves as needing management. I don't have to be told when to come to work and what to do when I come to work, and if I do have to be told, then obviously I'm not doing my job. . . . When I show up for work late,

TABLE 13.1. The Organizational Philosophy, Goals, and Strategies of the Raleigh Reservation Center

---

PHILOSOPHY

We will have an exciting and innovative environment in which individuals will share both responsibility and rewards for meeting *clear* organizational goals, as they relate to the reservations business.

We are an organization built on respect for: individual differences, initiatives, and successes; involvement in the decision-making process; purposeful change; and integrity in all relationships.

There are no limits to our potential—we are the leading edge of innovation.

MISSION

The Holiday Inn–Raleigh Reservation Center is in the business to sell roomnights for the Holiday Inn System in an accurate, cost-effective manner, leaving no unhappy guests, and as a result of achieving major breakthroughs in productivity through organization effectiveness.

ORGANIZATIONAL GOALS

· To handle the budgeted call volume.
· To handle the budgeted transactions.
· To operate the reservation center with fewer management levels.
· To create an environment that promotes innovative, purposeful changes in the overall reservations system.
· To organize a center that is insulated from unionization.
· To develop awards, benefits, and interpersonal communications systems that promote self-regulation of work patterns and behavior.

ORGANIZATIONAL STRATEGIES

· Open the center by October 29, 1984, with a minimum of 30 trained agents, reaching peak staff levels sufficient to handle 33% of U.S. call volume by June 1985.
· Train agents to handle all types of reservations, eliminating the senior agent level.
· Recruit and staff the center, skewed toward a professional, non-union-oriented workforce.
· Develop an interoffice means of interpersonal communication that is supportive of a participatory management environment.
· Decentralize responsibilities and accountability.
· Develop policies and procedures that promote honest support of organizational and group norms.

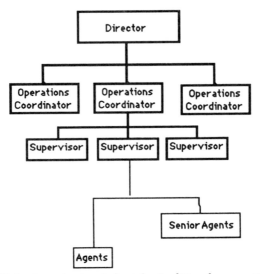

FIGURE 13.1. Organizational chart for traditional reservations center.

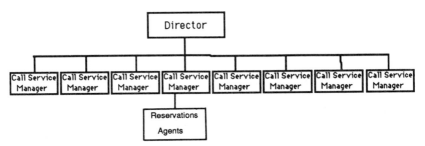

FIGURE 13.2. Organization chart for Holiday Inn Raleigh Reservations Center.

"I feel guilty. Nobody has to pull me aside and slap my hand and say, 'You were late.' I know I'm guilty, and I do a good job of disciplining myself. And we wanted our focus in this organization to come up with the same kind of feeling for everybody. We didn't want to put management in the position where they had to play watchdog. Our whole concept was to develop an organization where management's role was continually maintaining and creating an environment where people didn't need that."

Two features that stood out in making the organization work were the system of incentives and a supportive communication climate.

The System of Incentives

The centerpiece of the system is the "MAGIC" program of incentives. MAGIC is an acronym that stands for Meeting Achievable Goals through Individual Contributions. Its description in the employee guidebook is included in Table 13.2. The MAGIC program results in each agent earning a certain number of points, which are used to rank agents' performance. These rankings are used as the basis for distributing a host of rewards. Tracy Cashwell and Kathy Morris, two reservations agents who have worked at the center since it opened, were asked what motivates them to do a good job; they replied in unison, "the schedule." In other words, the scheduling preferences obtained by getting the MAGIC points is an important incentive for them. Kathy also mentioned the desire to be a "Mega Agent" as a big incentive. The top 20 rated agents at the end of the year are named Mega Agents; in 1987, they were treated to a 5-day trip to Disney World.

In addition to the MAGIC program, the other major incentive is the pay-for-performance system. All agents are paid a base wage of $4.50 per hour, and are expected to average at least eight transactions per hour. For every transaction over eight, they get an additional $.25 added to their hourly rate. The typical experienced agent averages approximately 20 transactions per hour, thereby doubling his or her base pay.

Other individual and group incentives are offered occasionally to meet new goals. Dave noted,

> "Right now we've got a push on for salesmanship, or what we call 'confirmation rate'—the number of sales against the number of calls handled. I've got a bet with the workforce right now. I bet them that if they get 51% for the month of June, every one of them gets $50 net added to their paycheck. There's also a challenge going on with the Chicago center. Whichever center has the better confirmation rate at the end of this month, the loser buys that center lunch."

The system seems to have had positive results with many of the agents. Tracy said, "They give you a lot of incentives to work toward, and if you put forth the effort, you get them. The points, the Mega Agent . . . last year if you were error free for the year, you got $500." Kathy agreed, "The incentive program here is good and I think that makes you strive to be a good employee—because they give you something back." Another reservations agent, who had worked at the center just over a year, hinted at the impact of the incentive program on his performance, as he was discussing his desire for feedback from a manager, "I basically wanted to know [from the manager] how I was coming across on the phone, because at this job . . . your pay is based on how quickly and efficiently you get the reservation done and you tend to rush. But you don't want the guest to know that you are rushing." Of

TABLE 13.2. The MAGIC Program

Our Holiday Corporation Raleigh Reservation Center believes in recognizing and rewarding employees for their individual contributions. The MAGIC program is designed as an incentive vehicle to encourage individual involvement in sharing both responsibility and rewards for meeting clear organizational goals as they relate to improving the productivity of our center.

Each quarter (3 months), agents will earn points for their individual achievements that will be used to select their shift, hours, and days off for the next quarter, and for any other job-related preferences. Recognition awards for Agents of the Month and Quarter will be selected on the same basis. The five key areas to be considered are:

- Performance (transactions per hour)
- Timeliness (no unexcused tardiness)
- Perfect attendance (no unauthorized absence from the workplace)
- Quality (maintaining error-free work)
- Confirmation rate (number of sells per calls handled)

Individual points will be accumulated and awards presented at year end. Agents will be enrolled into the very prestigious "Magic Mega Agent Club."

Additional points can be used to supplement the enrollment to the club. These additional points will come from the following:

- Safety (maintaining safe work habits)

You can do it! Let's see "the colors of your rainbow."

course, not every employee is happy with the system. Several newer employees expressed dissatisfaction with their schedules, and with what they had to do to get more favorable schedules.

A system that was just being implemented at the time of the interviews involved earning points that could be used to purchase merchandise. Two call-service managers, Brian Gossett and Anita Badon, created this system. The number of points agents earn are determined by their individual and team confirmation rate. Managers are also rewarded for performance. About 75% of their bonus is determined by the center's overall performance in meeting budgeted costs and budgeted room–night production. The other 25% is based on individual performance.

Recognition is also an important part of the system. Agents of the month are those who have the most MAGIC points for the month. Their names are announced and they are given special prizes, such as free dinners or weekends at the hotel of their choice. The six agents of the quarter, those who are the top ranked in terms of MAGIC points, are given special parking spaces with their names on them. In 1987, Tracy Cashwell was selected as a winner of the Chairman's Award for outstanding employees in the Holiday

Corporation; this award is given to eight employees annually out of over 30,000. Dave described her accomplishment:

"We started our heavy push on quality last year. Tracy handled in the neighborhood of 20,000–30,000 calls during the year. She sold around 20,000 rooms, which equates to well over $1 million in revenue for this company, without *one* mistake. She got a trip to Memphis . . . to meet with the board of directors. She set a standard that can never be beaten; it can only be matched. It was absolute perfection in what she did."

Regarding the award, Tracy said, "I was extremely excited." Kathy added, "She was in shock actually. She was like queen for the day; she had all these roses!"

SUPPORTIVE COMMUNICATION CLIMATE

The MAGIC system gives agents a clear indication of their goals and how to achieve rewards. However, Dave was quick to point out that a system of incentives alone is inadequate to make self-management work: "The *first* mechanism is the way you treat [employees]—openly and with a great degree of latitude and freedom." The climate of the center appears to be characterized by trust and supportiveness.

Trust is apparent in the freedom with which agents pursue activities throughout their workday. They are allowed to take breaks when they want, pursue hobbies such as knitting while they perform their jobs, and initiate programs such as a choir and bowling league for center employees. The employees' lounge is comfortably equipped. Dave explained his views on the freedom employees are allowed,

"The hardest job of the newly hired employee is learning how to grasp and deal with the concept that they're free to do as they please within the limits of our philosophy. Our job is to give them all the room to test those limits. . . . They get the message . . . that they are free to move anywhere in this organization as long as they are fulfilling the requirements of selling rooms for Holiday Inn. . . . That's a tremendous motivator in itself, to turn to somebody and say, 'Here's the job, here's the directions, now go for it.'

"The worst thing you can do to an employee is to train them 2–3 weeks on the job, give them every piece of knowledge you have and then walk out there when they're done with training and stand over them. It's kind of like, 'Wait a minute, why did you spend all this time training me? You don't trust me to do the job?' And that's the signal that things like that send. So our job is to go through the process of training and say 'There you go. Now you're on your own. Now here are the rewards and consequences of behavior. And all you have to do, when you do get into trouble or you have doubts, is stand up and ask a question. We will answer it.' . . . And it places you in the position of being a facilitator, a teacher, a counselor, instead of somebody who has to chew someone's rear end out."

Such freedom is made possible by the system of incentives. Managers can trust employees to use their time wisely, because it is in employees' best interest to do so. Dave explained,

> "If somebody doesn't show up for work, . . . they *know* that in order to earn a PPL [paid personal leave] day or in order to earn their MAGIC points for the month, they have to attend work according to their schedule. No questions asked. When someone's late, they say, 'I know. I've lost my day, I've lost my points. You don't have to say a word.' Well, I'm *not* going to say a word. What can we do to help prevent it in the future—*that's* where the focus of the discussion is. The manager and the agent sit down and discuss what they're going to do in the future. The punishment or reward is already there."

An obvious advantage of this system involves managing "shrinkage"— the situation in which an agent is on the clock but not on the phones. Agents become responsibile for managing shrinkage, and do so because it is in their interest. Dave explained,

> "One of the reasons you have a lot of supervisors and managers at other reservation centers is to make sure people are doing their job, getting them back on the phones. By telling people, 'You're not going to get paid but $4.50 an hour for shrinking,' I'm not going to be out there telling them to get back on the phones. They're hurting their own paychecks."

Similarly, managers do not spend time giving agents warnings regarding absences or tardiness. In the more traditionally structured reservations center, a significant portion of the manager's time is spent issuing warnings for these problems. Although Dave could not reveal the exact number of warnings per year in other centers, he said, "We're talking about four figures."

There are significant savings in the manager's time in not having to focus so much on shrinkage, absence, and tardiness issues. Perhaps even more significantly is that it changes the nature of manager–agent communication. Kathy explained,

"The managers work with you. They don't want you losing your [MAGIC] points. They want everyone doing the best they can do. They'll pull off the phones and say 'This is what I've found. There's this error that seems to happen a lot. Let's see what we're doing wrong and what we can do to fix it.' So they care. They really do."

This perception was supported by many interviews with other agents, as they described interactions with managers. Repeatedly, the agents recalled positive feedback provided by managers. And, even when agents described managers' criticisms, their perceptions generally were that the feedback was supportive. For example, an agent who had worked at the center only 3 months described criticisms from a manager, "She pointed out two mistakes that I had made that were pretty serious. But she was good about it. One mistake I had made . . . she wanted to be lenient and because it happened during training, she didn't take away my MAGIC points."

In addition to giving supportive task-related feedback, agents and managers are often observed casually conversing, laughing, or joking. This informal communication is even apparent in some task-related feedback sessions. Another 3-month employee demonstrated this as she described the following feedback from a manager, "Well, she just said that I was doing a good job—but we always joke, that's the main thing, we always joked in training. So she said, 'You are doing good, you are just boring!' She said she wanted to listen to someone who was having problems."

The supportive communication climate extends to helping agents prepare for life after the Holiday Inn Reservation Center. Ron explained one rather unusual way he helps agents:

"Just a couple of weeks ago I talked to my counterpart at a large corporation over at the Research Triangle Park and I told him that agents come into my office and say 'Would you critique my resume, kinda help me update it?' And I say, 'Of course,' as long as I have the time to do it. He said, 'You do that? They're going to go look for another job.' I said, 'What's wrong with that?' We know people aren't going to stay here forever. We'd like to maintain as many employees as we can. But if you don't do it for them, they're going to do it behind your back."

HOW THE SYSTEM PERFORMS

The philosophy and structure of the Raleigh reservations center are innovative—but what about results? What indications are there that the self-management system is working? Several indicators stood out.

Productivity and Cost Effectiveness

In its 4 years of operation, the center has been one of the highest producing and most cost-effective reservation centers in the world. Dave claimed,

> "Our productivity rates are much better than anything existing today—significantly better. If you would compare our costs [for running the center] to other reservation centers today, our costs are about what they were back in 1974 or '75. And you're talking about going through years of double digit inflation. And they have had to incur greater and greater costs through wage increases, labor increases with no productivity increases. . . . Our quality is as good or better than anyone else's. The retention is as good or better. The attrition is as good or better. The absences as good or better. And we're doing it with 50–70% less management than anything that exists today. Our savings are from less overhead in management and less labor costs because they are producing at a higher level of production."

Although he could not release the figures, Dave presented a report that indicated that in every quarter the Raleigh office costs significantly less per call than the other centers. He maintained that this was true "every week of the year for the last 4 years." Additionally, he suggested that the Raleigh center maintains those cost levels throughout the year as the workforce expands and retracts. For the other offices, he said, there is more variance. Again, he produced figures to support this.

Attractiveness in the Labor Market

Another indicator of the reservations center's success was that it was attracting new employees in a market that was short on unemployed workers and long on jobs. "You're dealing in this community with 2.3% unemployment," Dave explained. "We have hired close to 300–350 people since the beginning of the year, and they're still coming through the doors. . . . I would say in an area with 2–3% unemployment, that's a tremendous number of people. And they're coming in through referral, walk in, that kind of thing, saying, 'We've heard about this center.' "

Effects on Employees

Finally, management pointed to the effects on people—in terms of increased responsibility, maturity and growth—as an indicator that the self-management philosophy is working. Several specific incidents indicated the organization's success in developing responsibility in its members. Ron Washington remembered one such incident.

RON: A couple of years ago all the managers including Dave went to Arkansas for a team building thing. This center ran for a week . . .

DAVE: . . . with no managers . . .

RON: . . . *no* managers. We came back and everything was good. How many organizations can do that?

DAVE: Every department head in the building left. The only people running the place were agents and analysts, with no supervisory employees whatsoever. . . . We found out when we got back that very, very little happened. They got along fine without us.

RON: *(Laughs.)* In fact, when we got back they said, "You should have stayed out longer."

DAVE: We prepared them for that week by telling them, "We're going to take off for a week and we're going to leave you on your own. You guys have done well. We're taking off to get some work done on our own, and we want you to run the place." And they did. All 200 of them, at the time, took charge. The hardest part was getting the managers out. *(Laughs.)* The learning experience there was teaching the managers that you have to learn to let go.

Kathy and Tracy gave their version of what happened:

KATHY: We just did what we had to do. If we worked in callbacks, we had to make decisions on things that normally we wouldn't decide. We just picked up the ball and ran with it.

TRACY: I think we were able to run it and keep things going *because* we aren't constantly supervised.

KATHY: Yes, that's why it ran so smoothly. We don't have to have the manager. We know what we're expected to do and we do it.

Dave related another incident that happened more recently. In the spring of 1988, a fire in a telephone office wiped out all communications for the Chicago Holiday Inn reservations center. At that time, Raleigh and Chicago were each handling 50% of U.S. traffic. After the fire, Raleigh had to handle 100% of the calls for the next 2 weeks. Doubling the volume of calls handled obviously presented a challenge. Dave said,

"The entire office pulled together . . . and not only handled the traffic but ended up selling an equal amount of rooms that entire week that those two offices would have normally sold. [They] came in and they pulled together like a community would pull together if a tornado had hit this place. You didn't have to twist any arms or campaign."

Kathy described what happened,

"They called me Monday morning at 7:30 and asked if I could come in earlier than my schedule—I usually come in at 9:00—because there was this fire and we were getting hit with 100% of the calls. Of course, I don't live far from here, so I just got dressed real quick and came on in."

TRACY: We had to work very diligently those couple of weeks.
KATHY: It was a *lot* of work. We have a little red light on our phones that says "Call waiting" and that light *blared*. *(They both laugh.)* And then one day it went off, and we all said, "Oh, thank you!"

COMMUNICATION

One of the organizational strategies set forth in the original working plan for the center (see Table 13.1) was to "develop an interoffice means of interpersonal communication that is supportive of a participatory management environment." What this meant to management was giving agents access to the information that they needed to do their jobs, and encouraging them to solve their own problems. Management's efforts have been directed toward encouraging an on-going exchange of information between managers and agents and among agents. Several components to this communication system emerged: access to information, an open-door policy, participation in decision making, feedback, and encouragement of informal communication.

Dave and Ron admitted that they did not have a clear plan of action for creating a communication system for the center. As Dave explained,

"We really didn't know when we built this place what kind of communication avenues and policies and procedures we were going to have. . . . What we did was hold back and kinda let it happen. Let the agents work their routes and their paths through, and let the managers work their paths through, and as those became solid, that's what we set policies and procedures to. . . . For example, we learned right from the beginning that the one person everyone wanted immediate access to with no interference was me. So I said, 'Let it happen that way. . . .' So here I am sitting in this corner office and I'm the director of this huge organization. Most employees under a more traditional organization would visualize a secretary outside my office screening my calls, screening my appointments—but as you'll notice, it's a free flow.

"The system we started to play around with was one where any means of communication that would get the information across was one we would try. We're talking written, via the computer, oral, the grapevine, small meetings, large meetings. We knew as managers that one means or one vehicle of communication is never enough. You're going to reach part of the crowd but not all of them."

The reservations agents indicate that they get information from a variety of sources. When they log onto their computer terminal, an "agent briefing" provides them with information about special promotions or circumstances of which they need to be aware in booking rooms. For example, one message informed them that a flood had washed out a Holiday Inn in Roanoke, Virginia and no rooms were to be booked there. One experienced agent underscored the importance of the computer in getting the information he needs: "If I don't know something, I know exactly where to find it in the computer so I don't need to ask for any help or guidance from any [call-service manager]. . . ." The agents also get information from a bulletin board, from special training sessions, and from informal interaction with managers.

Having this information is essential to their job performance. Dave echoed the currently popular notion of "empowering the front line"—the idea that to provide quality service to customers, those who have contact with the customers need to be informed and able to make decisions. He said,

> "In this technology age, the ones who need the information most are the ones who are conversing with the guests up front. If a guest calls in to reserve a room, and that individual doesn't know this company inside and out, how can they sell it? That agent has to know more about this company than anybody else, because if they don't, they're not going to end up giving proper, good, quality sales service to our customers."

Open Access to Information

One value repeatedly espoused by Ron and Dave was that agents should have access to information:

> DAVE: If you go back to our philosophy, it's built on "respect and integrity in all relationships." One of the things we knew going in is that you couldn't limit access to information to any great degree. Otherwise, you'd send a signal of who you trust and who you do not trust. Everybody who came to work initially in this organization had to have access to every piece of information that came in: my operating statements, the general ledger, billing information, *salary* information . . .
>
> RON: . . . resumes . . .
>
> DAVE: . . . resumes, what is going on in the world. They had to have free and open access to information. . . . In this organization, there can be no secrets. If a person wants to move, let them know what they can move to. Give them that carrot to shoot for.

RON: The resume thing came about from agents walking in and saying, "What qualifications do I need to get so and so's job?" And after a while we said, "Let's come up with a resume book. Let's get the whole staff to put their resumes in a book." And then we could just say, "Here's the book."

Agents learn about this open communication policy beginning with the initial interview. The center's philosophy is explained to them along with its operating procedures and practices. Ron talks to them on their first day of training, and again explains the philosophy and the fact that they have access to any information in the building.

Another indicator of the value placed on open access to information was apparent in their description of one of the ways agents stay informed. Ron said, "Sometimes we have agents coming into our staff meetings. They're responsible for disseminating information. . . ." Dave added, "Not only that, but it's an open forum. The schedule for that meeting is published. Anybody who wants to come in and just sit down and listen can do it. It's a town meeting concept."

Open-Door Policy

Consistent with the open access to communication practice is an open-door policy. Dave explained,

"As you notice, the doors are wide open all the way through this building. One of the first things I did was, when managers were brought in from more traditional organizations, they would come in and close their doors. And I'd walk in right behind them with my master key and open them. And I'd say, 'This door stays open.' It was a teaching process.

"Unless I'm coping with a real tough case or an emergency, that door is never closed. And it doesn't matter what kind of meeting I'm in, anybody can walk in this office and say 'I've got this problem.' My job as the manager is to do everything I can to fix it. And I will drop everything. Our catch phrase is 'I will move with the speed of light and a high sense of urgency to make sure that one individual is taken care of.' If we do that, we're fulfilling this philosophy. . . . "

Ron gave two examples of the open-door policy in action:

"Just yesterday I was having a meeting with two people from a hotel here doing a presentation. We were in my office, and an agent walked in, and said, 'Ron, I hate to interrupt, but I've got a dilemma.' I said, 'Come on in.' We talked about it for 2 or 3 minutes, I gave her some direction, and she left. The two people I was meeting with said, 'You let this happen? You let an agent just walk in and interrupt?' I said, 'The door's open. If I didn't want her to come in I'd have closed the door.'

"I bet you thought that young lady who just walked in here was a secretary—because only the secretary can walk into the boss's office, right? No. She's an analyst, giving Dave some information."

Kathy confirmed that the open-door policy is more than just talk:

"We're all very good friends. The managers . . . we respect them as authority figures, but they're so open to you, even Dave. If you have a problem, his door is always open. I've worked several places in my life, but I've never worked in a place that had that much openness that you could go to the *director* if you have a problem and talk to him. Usually that was just taboo. And I think that's why it works here."

Agent Participation in Decision Making

Agents do not just sit in on staff meetings. They also make some important decisions and provide input in to other decisions. Managers often sit on committees as equal members rather than as leaders. Ron gave an example:

"The agent who interrupted my meeting yesterday was on a committee for handling '50% complimentary room requests.' Our agents have the opportunity to stay at other hotels at 50% off. Decisions concerning these requests are made by a committee this agent was on. She had a problem with a request and needed an answer right away."

This committee is made up entirely of agents, as are several other committees for social activities and special projects. Recently, for example, one agent wanted to start a choir composed of center employees. He got approval from Dave, who told him to get it organized. He did so on company time.

Agents also participate in suggesting and creating training and development opportunities. Although the center has designated trainers, agents also provide input in to the programs that are developed. For example, in the summer of 1987, a group of agents developed and implemented a refresher training program focusing on quality. They turned it into a game based on the popular board game, Trivial Pursuit, and called it "Quality Pursuit." The floor of the center was turned into a six-spoked Trivial Pursuit board. Each agent rolled dice and went to a specific station based on his or her roll. Then they had to answer trivia questions related to providing quality service—such as what promotions were currently offered. Like all training offered at the center, this program was conducted on company time.

Performance Feedback

Performance feedback is another important communication issue. Agents get feedback from multiple sources. For example, every 2 weeks their paychecks reflect the number of transactions handled. Each month, the MAGIC ratings are posted and agents find out how they are performing in relation to others. Also, new agents are monitored in their first month, and all agents are monitored by call-service managers at least once a quarter; the managers then provide oral feedback about how well they dealt with guests. At traditional reservations centers, agents are monitored much more frequently—as often as once a day at some centers. Obviously, this requires a larger management staff. More importantly, Dave believes, "The signal that sends is 'You don't trust me.' Our feeling was that if we got individuals who are responsible for themselves, we don't have to do that."

When agents are monitored, managers seem to emphasize praise and support. Managers are trained in leadership and communication skills, particularly the use of positive reinforcement. An overwhelming majority of the agents recalled managers' messages in these feedback sessions as involving praise and support, even when there were problems. For example, an employee who had worked at the center for 2 months recalled the manager's message in a feedback session:

> "You're doing much better than you did last time I monitored you. You're speaking more clearly, but you need to speak up a little bit more. And I like what you do when you get ready to hang up. I heard you say, 'Have a lovely day,' and it's the first time I ever heard anybody say [that]."

This agent, like most, responded favorably to the criticism she received. In recalling an earlier session in which she was told to slow down, she said: "What he was saying was basically true. The way he talked to me he didn't sound, you know, he makes you feel good and warm. You know, it doesn't feel like he's pushing you."

In the working plan (see Table 13.1), a concern expressed is that management–employee communications might be reduced since employees receive feedback from nonhuman sources. In fact, though, Dave and Ron both agree that this does not happen. Dave explained,

> "What often happens is the agent looks real hard at their paycheck and then seeks out their manager and asks, 'I worked my butt off this last time and I didn't make any more than the time before. Why?' . . . It forced the manager to be prepared for an onslaught every 2 weeks of agents asking why they weren't improving. Or, they come in all smiles and say, 'See what I've done. What you said last week worked.' Now,

every single payday, virtually every manager is here armed and ready to answer questions."

Encouraging Informal Communication

Another of management's central values is that informal communication should not only be encouraged, but should be the *responsibility* of every employee—agent and manager. Part of what this means is being responsible for finding the person with the information needed. Dave explained the importance of this approach and how agents learn it:

> "If you want feedback, be responsible and ask for it. That's the kind of people we were looking to hire in the development of the organization. In keeping with our philosophy, you *have* to be responsible for your own life. If you need information, you have the responsibility to stand up and ask. Our first job when agents come on board is to teach them how to ask when they need help. Because so often they've come on board and they've been force fed or they've come out of a work environment where their supervisor told them everything they needed, detail for detail. In this organization, we're the library and they're the ones searching out the resource information."

The process of learning to access needed information is encouraged by one group of agents referred to as "callbacks." The callbacks section is located in the middle of the reservation center's floor, and is manned by experienced, trained agents who volunteer to work in that section for a 2-month period. The purpose of callbacks is to answer guests' questions that cannot be answered by the agent who received the call. When an agent calls a callback agent to get a question answered, the callback agent is instructed not simply to give the agent the answer, but to tell him or her where to find it. Thus, agents are encouraged to seek out information on their own. They are further encouraged by the system of incentives; acquiring job-related information results in increased efficiency, which in turn results in higher pay and MAGIC points.

Management's goal is to rotate the entire workforce through the callbacks section. As Dave said:

> "The ultimate would be to have a workforce where I don't need a callback section, because everyone would have gained enough knowledge where they could handle that call right up front and answer everything. Obviously, that'll never happen as long as we're hiring and getting new trainees in. But the wider a base we have, the easier it becomes. Used to be we had 20 agents trained to do that. Today, I have close to 120. So now they don't even have to call callbacks to get an

answer. They can turn to their next door neighbor who has already been trained to get an answer. It creates a kind of teamwork that raises the performance of the entire workforce."

Informal communication is encouraged in the training process, according to Ron:

> "I talk about the fact that they are going to be working on their own and that they'll need to get information from others; it could be the person sitting next to them. They have to be able to open up, so we get into disclosure. We do interviewing, letting them interview each other. The point of this is to see how much you can 'open their window' and how willing you are to disclose. We try to get them comfortable with sharing information, helping each other in class."

Agents also receive this message as part of their socialization by peers. "The new people are often afraid to talk to the managers," Kathy explained. "When they need information one of the first persons they'll go back to is the trainer, the person who trained them initially, since it's someone they know. And if they're not around, they'll ask someone who went through training with them, who often doesn't know either since they haven't been here long." To deal with this problem, the center recently started a "quality coaching" program, in which experienced agents work one-on-one with less experienced agents to provide them with information and strategies for handling difficult situations, and to answer their questions.

Another part of the *manager's* responsibilities, through using informal channels, is to keep tabs on the "rumor mill." As Ron said: "All I've got to do is go out on the floor and make one decision with one employee, and I've communicated with 200, 300, 400. It just spreads." Dave added:

> "We tap into the grapevine by keeping our communication with everybody in the office personal, or personable. We avoid as much as possible writing memos about specific instances or situations. The only memos we do write cover general awareness topics. You know, 'Tomorrow, my boss, the vice president of reservations, is coming to visit.' And we post it on the bulletin board. Any situation more specific than that and we are talking to the individual or the individual is talking to us."

Dangers and Precautions in Encouraging Informal Communication

Making such extensive use of informal communication, combined with agents' access to information, is not without drawbacks. Agents are very aware of the decisions made, and, after being encouraged to provide input into many decisions, are more likely to contest decisions with which they disagree. Dave and Ron argued that keeping one's word and being consistent are critical for managers to survive in this organization. As Dave pointed out:

> "If an agent is dismissed for whatever reason, anybody else in the building who performs the same act must get that the same treatment— no favoritism. Or they will be on your doorstep in a minute. And you can't justify it. That's the kind of limelight we put our managers in. Don't be inconsistent in your decision making and remember the precedents you have already set. Because every decision you make is going to be based on that, because that's what everybody is going to see. They will draw on experiences from 4 years ago if you are making an inconsistent decision."

As an example, Dave described a situation in which an agent was referred to a chemical abuse program. He suggested that the agent could have just as easily been fired or dismissed from the workforce, except that, several years prior, a precedent had been set. In the previous case, a manager had had a chemical abuse problem, and was not fired, but referred to a chemical abuse program. As Dave said, "From that date forward, any employee has to be treated in the same way."

For managers to be consistent, they need to communicate with each other. Dave and Ron believe that it is essential for managers to share information with each other, so that they are clear on what issues are important to agents, what decisions have been made, and what precedents have been set. One way the center avoids this problem is through staff meetings. Ron explained that these are necessary since agents may sometimes go to several different managers until they get the answer they want; he provided an example to illustrate this:

> "We had an agent who called, who had quit, giving us 2 days notice 5 weeks ago. She . . . wanted to come back to work. Now she's a fairly good agent. The answer is, and this is our policy, our practice, you cannot come back for 6 months. She talked to me, she talked to her manager, and I guess she talked to [Dave] today, and Dave's answer was 'after 6 months.' Now she's a good agent, we could use her, but if we put her on the floor and somebody saw her out there knowing that she left several weeks ago . . ."

Dave went on, "I'd have a riot right there. . . . And that's the key to making the grapevine work for us. For us to be consistent. . . . The second we're not consistent, it's brought to that manager's attention, usually by that agent or group of agents who say, 'Now wait a minute. What so and so said. . . .' "

CONCLUSION

Although Kathy, Tracy, and most of the agents interviewed had a very positive attitude about their work at the Holiday Inn Reservations Center, the work is clearly not for everyone. Kathy said, "When an agent has a bad quarter, he usually gets his act together or ends up leaving." Dave agreed that the system does not work for some, and that those people leave after a short time. Still, many, like Kathy and Tracy, thrive in this environment. As Tracy put it, "You can do anything you want. You can either be good or you can be bad. It's your choice." "They (management) are very good." Kathy added, "I think they put the agents first above anything else. I know Dave does. We are more important to him than anybody."

Tracy said the thing she liked best about the job was "Opportunity. You have the opportunity to put forth your best effort and then get the rewards for it. And that includes scheduling, or days off or just being recognized." Kathy agreed, "Just being recognized is nice in itself. Plus the whole atmosphere. Most of the time you come to work and it's a good time. It's almost not like working. You're getting paid . . ." Tracy cut in, ". . . to be with your buddies."

Dave sees the job ahead for management as maintaining the system and adapting to new needs.

> "The hardest job I have now is continuing to search for new ways of doing things and keeping my hands out of the pie. When you develop a new thing like this it's kind of like fathering a new child and you've got to learn to back off, because what you're teaching people is to be on their own. . . . I've been in hotels where you couldn't make a decision on your own without checking with the general manager. Here, our job is not to make decisions; our job is to put ourselves in a position where we can make sure the environment causes the individual to make the decision on his or her own and face up to the responsibility behind it—and that's the key."

Acknowledgments. The author would like to express his thanks to the employees of the Holiday Inn–Raleigh Reservations Center for their cooperation in this project, and to the students of his Fall 1987 "Leadership and Communication" class for their help in data collection.

NOTES

1. Data for this case were collected through on-site observations and interviews with over 100 employees, including the director of the center and the human resources manager, the two who designed the self-management system.

KEY TERMS

communication climate   access to information
environmental influences   competition
empowerment   stress and burnout
organizational values   supervisor–employee communication
participative management   informal communication
employee development   performance feedback

DISCUSSION QUESTIONS

1. Explain how the environment is used by management to influence employees' attitudes and behaviors.

2. How has management employed the notion of "empowering the front line?"

3. What organizational values are expressed in management decisions, organizational design, and management rhetoric?

4. How does the communication climate of the Holiday Inn Reservation Center affect agents' satisfaction and productivity?

5. How might the competition among employees for rewards and recognition affect stress and burnout in this organization?

6. How does the incentive system influence the nature of manager–agent communication?

7. What is the effect of multiple sources of performance feedback on performance? On communication?

8. What are the positive and potentially negative effects of encouraging informal communication?

9. Dave and Ron argue that being consistent and keeping one's word are critical for managers in this organization. Are these behaviors any more important in this context than in more traditional organizations?

10. How do the values and beliefs of the "founders" of the organization influence the organizational culture?

SUGGESTED READINGS

Byham, W. C., & Cox, J. (1989). *Zapp! The human lightning of empowerment*. Pittsburgh: Development Dimensions International.

Conger, J. A., & Kanungo, R. N. (1988). The empowerment process: Integrating theory and practice. *Academy of Management Review, 13*, 471–482.

Gilbert, T. F. (1978). *Human competence: Engineering worthy performance*. New York: McGraw-Hill.

Wagner, J. A., & Gooding, R. Z. (1987). Shared influence and organizational be-
    havior: A meta-analysis of situational variables expected to moderate participa-
    tion–outcome relationships. *Academy of Management Journal, 30,* 524–541.
Wofford, J. C., & Srinivasan, T. N. (1984). Experimental tests of the leader–
    environment–follower interaction theory of leadership. *Organizational Be-
    havior and Human Performance, 32,* 33–54.

PART V

Communication and Organizational Change

CHAPTER 14

Changing the Information Culture at the Pearson Company

GAIL FAIRHURST

University of Cincinnati

The Pearson Company is a large retail chain with several hundred store locations nationally. The size of this company is reflected in a large and diverse workforce. Employees range in age from 16 to senior citizens, many of whom work part time. Today, each Pearson store is a business within a business—200–300 employees per store, round-the-clock shifts, the presence of unions, and one-on-one competition with other local and chain-owned stores in the community in which they are located.

In the past 10 years, Pearson as a company has experienced both growth and retrenchment. The opening of many new and larger stores has been counterbalanced by store closings and the elimination of entire sales regions due to lackluster profits. Store closings became painful exercises that the company wanted to minimize at all costs. Not only was the relocation and release of many employees difficult, but the "ripple effect" on morale in other sales regions was a cause for concern. Taking stock of itself, better communication with its customers *and* employees became a priority. As far as the employees were concerned, the priority was clearly born out of need.

PEARSON'S EMPLOYEE COMMUNICATION SURVEY

In 1985, the company commissioned a survey to assess several things: (1) How it was communicating about the industry to its own employees; (2) what Pearson employees would like to know more about; and (3) what communication was like in the workplace, generally. Management was well

223

aware of its own history as a company; the Pearson Company had a rigid system of top–down control by management. Like many companies of this nature, the Pearson hierarchy greatly restricted the flow of informaton to its employees. Although change was in the works, the survey results essentially confirmed a tight control on information:

1. Many Pearson employees believed that existing internal communication was "too infrequent, too one-dimensional (one-way), and too management-oriented to be useful."

2. Truck drivers were seen as among the most reliable sources of information within the company. One store manager related that he learned of his promotion and transfer to another store from a truck driver a full 12 hours before being told by his boss!

3. Pearson was seen as a reliable source of information about the industry and store managers were held in high regard—but employees were eager for a two-way communication program that would give them an opportunity to have a dialogue about the company with management.

4. Of the various ways employees could receive information about the company, employee meetings with give-and-take question-and-answer sessions were the preferred way to share information. Following employee meetings, they ranked company newsletters that conveyed substantive information (versus social announcements like birthdays, anniversaries, softball scores, etc.) next, followed by pamphlets, bulletin boards, and videotapes as additional information sources.

The survey results revealed that Pearson employees were more than just receptive to more information. They seemed to have a real thirst to become more involved in the company. Pearson clearly had an opportunity to secure greater commitment and involvement on the part of its employees by changing its information culture. The opportunity seemed the greatest among Pearson's young management pool. These individuals were often the most enthusiastic about the company, but also voiced the most frustration with the lack of adequate information and desired a general "loosening of the fetters" by upper management.

As a result, Pearson set out to change its communication practices. Communication goals were included among its business objectives. Upper management increasingly stressed the need for effective employee communication in its speeches. Many training programs were devoted to communication skill development. In addition, a task force was commissioned by the president of the company.

PEARSON'S TASK FORCE ON EMPLOYEE COMMUNICATION

The mission of the task force was "to create an internal communications strategy for the Pearson Company that will increase the flow of information among *all* employees of the company and in so doing, create better and broader understanding of—and support for—Pearson's business goals and objectives." The task force was unique in that it was comprised of several organizational development and human resources managers from various Pearson sales regions, store personnel, a consultant, and representatives from corporate headquarters. It was also *exclusively* devoted to one mission: studying employee communication within the Pearson Company and advising upper management on how to improve it.

The first order of business for the task force was to write a mission statement in order to address the issue of what specific values and philosophy the company should espouse. Although the wording of the statement was subject to much discussion, there was consensus about the desired central values. Ultimately, the following mission statement was adopted:

> The Pearson Company is committed to the development of an effective internal communication program which responds to the concerns of Pearson employees, seeks their input in setting and attaining company goals, and creates a culture that fosters mutual respect, trust and job satisfaction.

A second order of business for the task force was to assess the barriers to effective communication that the Pearson Company had to overcome. Accordingly, each task force member identified the barriers to communication that he or she perceived within the company. The list of barriers, along with how frequently they were mentioned, is presented in Table 14.1. Topping the list was a too diverse workforce. Many task force members believed that too many audiences, as well as a young and transient, part-time audience, posed special problems in employee communication. Following that, the grip of a strong, top–down management culture (as revealed in the survey results) was felt as an inhibitor of change. Geographically dispersed subunits—several hundred store locations—with different organizational structures also made communication difficult. Other barriers included perceived upper-management confusion over the need for two-way communication, the presence of unions, environmental pressure to succeed, time constraints, and a lack of trust. Not surprisingly, nearly all of the enumerated barriers have been documented in management literature as significant obstacles to effective communication.

A third order of business for the task force was to assess what communication programs were already in place. Accordingly, each sales region

TABLE 14.1. Barriers to Achieving the Pearson Company's Mission Statement

No. of Votes	Barrier
7	The workforce is too diverse (too many part timers, too large).
6	The old culture is too strong.
6	Too many locations with different structures.
6	Poor understanding of the need for two-way communication, especially by upper management.
5	The presence of unions and, historically, an adversarial relationship.
4	Too many organizational layers.
3	A general lack of trust.
3	Intense pressure to succeed in a highly competitive, fast-paced, constantly changing environment.
3	Terminology, vague language.
3	Not enough time.
3	Inconsistency of company priorities and values.
2	Poor upward communication.
2	Poor feedback.
1	Threat to manager's power.
1	Communication is identified as a program separate and apart from the normal course of business.
1	Access to the right people.

was asked to provide the task force with a list of their communication efforts for the calendar year. Tables 14.2–14.4 provide representative examples of what three sales regions offered. It is interesting to compare the offerings of the "Central," "Eastern," and "Northern" sales regions. In almost every case, there are support teams that function to improve sales, merchandising, and expense control. There are employee meetings, usually conducted quarterly, to review the performance of the store, employee benefits, or new programs/goals for the store. Finally, there is some type of newsletter— although the formality of the newsletter and the degree to which it is used to provide "social" versus "work" information seems to differ. Each sales region has some unique offerings, for example, employee surveys, recognition rituals, culture awareness/development programs, and training opportunities.

The Central and Eastern sales regions seem to be very program-oriented. Communication is dealt with in formatted units organized by topic or particular audience. In this regard the Central sales region seems to be

TABLE 14.2. Central Sales Region Communications

I. *Support Teams.* The stated purpose of the various support groups is to improve team work, develop better work environments, and to improve performance in sales, merchandising, and expense control.

   A. *Region Store Employers.* All regions, one representative per store, meet quarterly.

   B. *Individual Store Support Teams.* 21 stores and support teams in two cities.

   C. *Operation Success.* All warehouse and maintenance employees attend information sharing meetings each period. Period results, relevant region events, then an open-forum question-and-answer period is the usual format.

   D. *Distribution Center Support Teams.*

   E. *Secretarial Support Teams.* Quarterly meetings.

   F. *Store Manager Support Teams.* Meets three times a year.

II. *Employee Meetings.*

   A. *Store.* All stores will have biannual employee meetings conducted by the regional manager to share operational results and have open-forum question-and-answer periods. This program has been in effect for 3 years.

   B. *Merchandising Programs.* As appropriate in order to enhance team work and specific knowledge of merchandising programs.

   C. *Employee Benefits.* As appropriate in order to explain specific benefit programs.

III. *Regional Newsletter.* Professional, team-oriented, covering the full spectrum of employee interest topics, including economic messages concerning the financial picture of the sales region.

IV. *Employee Surveys.*

   A. *Store Manager Survey.* Conducted every other year.

   B. *Secretarial Survey.* Conducted every other year.

   C. *Administrative Survey.* Conducted every other year.

V. *Information/Recognition.*

   A. *Labor Contract Meetings.*

   B. *Technical Communications.*

   C. *Letters of Information/Recognition*

TABLE 14.3. Eastern Sales Region Communications

1. Three-day communication skills workshop for 9 administrative and 22 store managers.

2. Two store managers attend weekly merchandising meetings.

3. Regional manager feedback session. Held in conjunction with operations meeting. Rotating spokesman communicates region/store problems, suggestions, ideas, etc., with administrative staff; discussion.

4. Weekly store communication forum. Feedback sheet for weekly suggestions, problems, opportunities.

5. Weekly distribution report. Distribution feedback.

6. Improved store manager support teams. Two meetings during the first two quarters.
   a. Support team members meet prior to main meetings.
   b. Better utilization of administrative management. (They are available for comment.)

7. Regional support teams. Hourly and management employees oriented toward merchandising and operational issues.

8. Minority management council. Five members; three meetings.
   a. 1/14/85— Organization meeting; brainstorming.
   b. 4/15/85— Minority recruitment—needs, plans, alternative approaches.
   c. 5/21/85— Successor plan review.

9. What's up? In-house stationery used to keep employees informed; topics to date: health care costs and employee benefits.

TABLE 14.4. Northern Sales Region Communications

1. *Employee Meetings*

   Meetings were held during the summer and fall of 1984 for all stores in the sales region. Each store held a meeting at a geographically convenient hotel. Each meeting was conducted by the regional manager, store manager, and a representative from human resources. The objectives of these meetings were as follows:

   A. Communicate improved sales and profits for the region and individual stores.
   B. Communicate future plans, goals, and concepts.
   C. Communicate current results of consumer research.
   D. Educate employees in the area of customer relations.
   E. Write a plan of action for improving stores.

2. *In Search of Excellence—The Northern Region Business Philosophy*

In the fall of 1984, the Northern sales region developed the following philosophy based on several concepts from *In Search of Excellence: Lessons from America's Best Run Companies* (Peters & Waterman, 1982):

Northern Sales Region Philosophy

As a sales region, we are committed to the economic growth of the Pearson Company and to the personal growth of Pearson people. Toward these ends, we believe in:

The total satisfaction of every customer.
Our people and their importance as individuals.
A work environment that promotes informality, innovation, risk taking, and greater job satisfaction.
The importance of details and timely execution, the nuts and bolts of doing the job well.

Working together, we will achieve these goals of personal growth and a more profitable company. Working together, we can proclaim with pride:

"WE ARE AN EXCELLENT COMPANY"

3. *The One-Minute Manager and the Northern Business Philosophy*

A steering committee was formed to develop a vehicle to assist in the implementation of the Northern management philosophy. The result was contracting Dr. Kenneth Blanchard, coauthor of *The One-Minute Manager* (Blanchard & Johnson, 1982), for an 8-hour workshop for all management and store personnel at the convention center. The goal of the meeting was to communicate to all key Northern employees simultaneously a common message so as to ensure that there was no misunderstanding. Several hundred employees attended this meeting, and it was the genesis of our new management style. Follow-up meetings were held at each store to reinforce the principles of the *One-Minute Manager*.

4. *The Orientation Program*

To perpetuate the business philosophy and commitment to communication efforts, a new employee orientation program was developed.

5. *Merchandising Workshops and Our Philosophy*

Each merchandising department made a commitment to include reinforcement of our philosophy and the principles of *The One-Minute Manager*. Meetings held: General Merchandise Christmas Workshop, Special Products Workshop.

6. *"Outlook" Magazine*

Outlook is an informally written magazine that communicates to all employees in the Northern sales region. It contains sales and human interest articles.

better organized and to offer a more comprehensive set of communication programs than the Eastern sales region. For example, Central has a wider range of support teams, more employee meetings, a newsletter that covers substantive work issues, regular employee surveys, and more formalized information and recognition forums than Eastern.

By contrast, the Northern sales region seems to have fewer programs but more awareness that they were changing their culture by changing their employee communication practices. Although many organizations look to current trends or "gurus" in the management field, Northern not only took advantage of these for educational purposes but developed its own personalized philosophy to coordinate its programs. It then set out to find vehicles for the communication and adoption of that philosophy within its own sales region through its orientation program and merchandising workshops.

As the task force continued to survey the data provided by the sales regions, the chief organizational development and human resources (ODHR) manager for each sales region (and the person responsible for reporting regional activities to the task force) was summoned to corporate headquarters for a 2-day meeting.

THE ODHR MEETING

ODHR meetings were usually held twice each year. During these 2-day sessions, managers would receive updates about employee assistance programs, motivational speeches from the top brass, and educational opportunities to learn more about topics such as culture and creativity.

When this particular ODHR meeting was convened, the managers were told that much of the meeting would be devoted to furthering the company's objectives on better employee communication. In addition, the critical role of the ODHR manager in "making things happen" in the sales regions was discussed. To begin discussion of this issue, the participants were given a public forum in which to present the information about regional communication activities forwarded to the task force. Since each sales region differed somewhat in their communication efforts, the planners of the meeting thought it would be beneficial for all the ODHR managers to hear the variety of efforts undertaken and to note particular successes. Each ODHR manager gave a 20–30 minute presentation. Interestingly, ODHR managers seemed most enthusiastic about the use of professionally made videotapes announcing company programs and reinforcing company values.

The meeting's second day's activities began with a speech from the president of the company on employee communication. The president of

Pearson had a strong, forceful personality, and was, at times, demanding. Some saw him as a visionary because he constantly stressed where Pearson should be and how it could get there rather than where it was now. During the address to the ODHR managers about the value the Pearson Company placed on better communication with employees, he shared his own vision of better employee communication at Pearson. He did this primarily through the use of metaphors.

In his early remarks, the president invoked metaphors to portray his vision of employee communication at Pearson. For example, he compared Pearson to an extended *family*, and noted that (1) conflict within families was both natural and valuable; (2) ideas and solutions are born of productive conflict; and (3) families may disagree but they always stand united against those who would harm them. The president also stressed that Pearson employees were all on the same *team*, united and working toward the common good. If each person did not understand his or her role in making better communication a priority, the company team could not win. Finally, he said Pearson must always remain *itchy* and *restless* to continue growing. *New frontiers* could never be discovered with complacent attitudes.

The president continued for several minutes discussing the task force and other efforts Pearson was making to support their communication goals and objectives. At the end of the speech, the president turned his attention to the unique role the ODHR manager played in achieving the employee communication goals at Pearson. At this time, he invoked one final metaphor that changed the tone of his remarks from persuasion to a thinly veiled threat. In referring to Pearson's communication objectives, the president told the ODHR managers, "The train is leaving. As ODHR managers, you had better *not* be the last ones to jump onto the train or you will find your seat taken." The president then asked if there were any questions about the company and its plans that he might answer. Several ODHR managers had questions, but none involved the employee communication objectives.

fear

mixed message

Following the president's address, the ODHR managers listened to a talk from the task force consultant on corporate cultures. The talk was timely because the topic of organizational cultures was just beginning to take hold in American business. For many in the audience, it was the first time they had seriously considered their organization as a culture, examined the forces shaping it, and thought about how to bring about change in Pearson's information culture. The audience was asked to consider culture change as a "campaign through time." Like a political campaign, multiple efforts directed toward changing employee communication had to be mounted and coordinated if real culture change was to occur.

The consultant noted that many American managers, including those at Pearson, approached culture change with a "program mentality." "Program" thinking can imply many things. For example, some managers try to fix problems by finding the right program, ignoring the fact that one-shot change efforts rarely achieve lasting change. Or, as the lists of communication activities from the Central and Eastern sales regions suggest, multiple programs are advanced with no underlying philosophy. Finally, program thinking implies that employee communication can be altered through programs or packages divorced from the normal course of business. An effective change campaign will find many vehicles—united by an underlying philosophy, to spread the word—including ones that will affect the business directly. The ODHR managers left considering this new material.

REACTIONS TO THE MEETING

For several of the ODHR managers, the most immediate reaction to the meeting involved the president's speech. In particular, the train metaphor he employed became a running joke among the managers. The joking about "missing the train" and "losing one's seat" seemed to reinforce the president's threat long after he departed and to overpower all of his earlier persuasive arguments. Several ODHR managers felt that the threat was inappropriate.

Why did the president choose such a strategy? The task force consultant, who also heard the president's speech, asked him why he chose a "persuade-then-threaten" approach with the ODHR managers. Commenting on his strategy and the ODHR managers' responses to date, he said:

> "Pearson's ODHR managers, and other managers within the total organization, for a long time have been challenged to exert leadership in the employee communication area. They have not met that challenge, unfortunately. For that reason, I wanted them to know that this was not just another appeal. It was, clearly, a change in their job content and a sharpening of our expectations of them as individuals. The train reference is familiar to that group, since it was used by one of their peers for many years. And . . . I believe they got the message. At the same time, you should know that their response to date has been anything but impressive. They still need to be pushed and cajoled. A harsh judgment? Perhaps. A fair judgment? I certainly believe so . . . I simply considered that meeting as an exception to the general rule of persuade and sell rather than mandate and tell."

In the above passage, the president charges the ODHR managers with failed leadership. Since so many of the regional employee communication activities reflected a "program mentality," he was probably right on this issue. But the president believed that his ODHR managers were satisfied with the status quo and were simply unwilling, not unable, to change. The consultant discovered, however, that there was unanimous and enthusiastic support for the direction the company was taking among the ODHR managers. Lacking was an understanding among ODHR managers of how to go about changing the existing culture.

A letter from the ODHR manager from the Eastern sales region to the consultant shortly after the ODHR meeting demonstrated this. The Eastern ODHR manager had recently sponsored a number of communication programs (as described in Table 14.3), partially in response to communication breakdowns between store managers and administrative managers in the regional offices. The communication skills workshop, for example, was a 3-day meeting in which store and administrative managers received training in basic management communication skills. Afterward, they began to jointly resolve the issues separating them. It was very successful in starting a dialogue between two groups of managers whose communication was previously ineffective. Yet, the Eastern manager did not know what to do after the workshop was completed. It was seen as an one-shot effort, divorced from the normal course of business. Consequently, he could not advise those who were asking him how to sustain the momentum created in the workshop, as his letter reveals:

> We're starting to experience the beginnings of a problem in the communications area. Regional managers and store managers are beginning to ask the question, "How do we sustain our enthusiasm for communications on a day-to-day basis within the pressures of the store and within the natural filtering process of communications from the top down?" . . . At our critical stage, a bad day or two could upset weeks of our "beginnings." I would expect other Pearson sales regions to ask this question in the future.

This manager did not understand that culture change advances slowly with a coordinated campaign-like effort despite anticipated setbacks. There is little question that he was highly motivated to change. He felt the need and the pressure to change—both from the people he represented in the sales region and from Pearson's president. He just did not know how.

Thus, it became clear that for months the president had been unaware of the real cause for failed leadership in this area. Namely, his ODHR managers did not know how to effect a lasting change in the information culture at Pearson even though they desired change and knew they needed help. Why didn't the president know the real cause for failed leadership? Why couldn't his ODHR managers ask him for more help especially when given the opportunity at the ODHR meeting? Who should be the one to inform the president? What role should the consultant play? These were the questions confronting Pearson.

KEY TERMS

information flow	program mentality
internal communication	visionary
two-way communication	metaphor
mission statement	organizational culture
communication barriers	

DISCUSSION QUESTIONS

1. At the end of his speech to the ODHR managers, the president asked whether there were any questions about his employee communication goals or any other aspect of Pearson. Since none of the questions involved employee communication, what would cause the ODHR managers to refrain from asking the president their questions about this subject? Should they have done so?

2. If you were the task force consultant, what would be your next step(s) in helping this organization change its information culture?

3. Do you think the president understood that he was calling for more than just a shift in employee communication policy but *significant* culture change in the company as well? Was he too hard on his ODHR managers? Not hard enough?

4. Regarding the president's persuasive tactics, if one is striving to become a more open, sharing culture, is "mandate and tell" a viable strategy to bring about change? When is it necessary to mandate? When is it necessary to persuade and sell? Is there some middle ground?

4. If managers have a "program" mentality, how will this get in the way of real culture change?

5. How can metaphors help to change culture?

Paradigm Shift.

SUGGESTED READINGS

Blanchard, K., & Johnson, S. (1982). *The one-minute manager*. New York: Morrow.

D'Aprix, R. (1982). *Communicating for productivity*. New York: Harper & Row.

Deal, T. E., & Kennedy, A. A. (1982). *Corporate cultures*. Reading, MA: Addison-Wesley.

Frost, P. J., Moore, L. F., Louis, M. R., Lundberg, C. C., & Martin, J. (Eds.). (1985). *Organizational culture*. Beverly Hills: Sage.

Kilmann, R. H., Saxton, M. J., & Serpa, R. (Eds.). (1985). *Gaining control of the corporate culture*. San Francisco: Jossey-Bass.

Peters, T. J., & Waterman, R. H. (1982). *In search of excellence: Lessons from America's best run companies*. New York: Harper & Row.

CHAPTER 15

Organizational Change at Jones, Lowell, and Smith

Linda L. Putnam
Purdue University

Jones, Lowell, and Smith is a family-owned office-supply firm in a large metropolitan area. The 70-year-old company is one of the largest office-supply dealers in the United States, currently employing 50 people. JLS grew from being a stationery store that carried furniture to a furniture dealer that handles all office supplies including stationery. It is a customer-oriented, top-quality firm that offers "everything for the office." The company handles supplies that range from pencils and paper clips to original artwork and executive desks. In the marketplace JLS is a medium-volume business, servicing primarily small organizations like banks, law firms, and dentists' offices.

JLS has a reputation in the industry as a pioneering firm because of its innovative programs. Although an uncommon practice among office-supply firms, all sales people at JLS undergo several weeks of training. JLS is also one of the first office-supply firms to establish an interior design department with a staff that provides advice on office utilization patterns to customers. Most recently, JLS has designed and implemented a new office-supply order system. This program, popular with large clients like Prudential Insurance, facilitates automatic reordering of supplies available through JLS at a reduced rate.

F. O. Jones and S. G. Gray founded the firm in 1904. Through a series of mergers and purchases, the Lowell family gained control of the company, and, in 1936, Steve L. Lowell became president of the company. In 1952, the firm merged with a large office supply company, Jason Smith, Inc. At that time Smith assumed the role of corporate president while Harry Lowell, Steve's son, served as executive vice-president. When Smith retired in 1962, Lowell became the third president of the company. Although Smith was a shrewd businessman who was respected and admired by his employees, he left the organization with outmoded methods, a loss of revenue, and the pressures of severe competition in the marketplace. Competition in the office-supply business had increased in the past decade. New firms were narrowing product lines, abandoning traditional services, and becoming aggressive at undercutting their competitors' prices. Survival of the "everything for the office" firm was in jeopardy.

Harry C. Lowell, JLS's current president, is the kind of man who builds a business by thinking of other people. When he was presented with the 1971 Office Products Dealer of the Year award, based on his contributions as a successful dealer, a leader in the industry, and an outstanding community citizen, Lowell wanted his employees to be part of the awards presentation. He told them, "This award belongs to you as much as to me." His generosity to his employees spills over in to community service. As three-time director of the Jaycees and a past director of the local athletic club, Lowell spearheaded the movement of businesses to a new industrial park when the city desperately needed it. In effect, Lowell is a respected leader in the industry, an innovator, and a caring person. Lowell is also an assertive, firm-minded leader. Although they praise him for his zeal, energy, and idealism, employees see him as a fatherly manager who listens poorly. His mind is typically made up before he hears the issues. Employees see him as a progressive manager who "holds no sacred cows," but also as someone who will take one big leap rather than four or five more cautious, smaller steps.

The advent of a new year finds JLS making changes in company policies and in the duties of several administrators. Recent financial statements indicate that unless cost-saving programs are implemented, the company may be headed for bankruptcy. To improve JLS's standing in the marketplace, Harry Lowell has enacted a number of policy changes. He has made plans to develop and use a computer system to place customer orders, maintain accounts, keep inventory, and purchase supplies. A new comptroller, Tom Phillips, has been hired to design and manage this system. To increase revenues, the company plans to concentrate on large-account customers and phase out clientele who spend less than $10 per month or $100 per year. Market research has also suggested that revenues could be increased through reducing the company product line by stocking fewer brands of a given item and discontinuing products that do not sell. To reduce billing costs and to insure better estimates of monthly sales, JLS has converted to a system of contract sales that delineates the terms of payment between the customer and sales representatives. Finally, the company has eliminated the entertainment fund that sales personnel used to purchase gifts, meals, or provide entertainment for prospective and long-term customers. Although the fund enhanced JLS's public relations, it was costly and was not effective in attracting new customers.

Harry Lowell announced these changes in a memo and then reviewed them in a company-wide meeting. All employees attended the meeting. He opened the session by referring to the advances that JLS had made in the past years. He praised his staff for designing and implementing the new office-supply order system, for expanding the highly successful interior design department, and for maintaining positive relationships with customers and competitors. Specifically, he commented,

> "I was reminded of our reputation last week at a regional meeting of the National Office Supply Association. A representative from one of our competitors said that his firm was forced to slash prices to compete with the customer services that we provide. Although we are currently competitive, our position in the marketplace will drop rapidly unless we make changes to stay ahead of the young, progressive firms that have the latest technology and innovative marketing methods. We cannot remain competitive with them unless we increase efficiency, cut costs, and reorient our focus to tomorrow's innovations. Changes in company policies and procedures are absolutely essential. I appeal to your past successes, your loyalty to JLS, your critical role in making this company a leader, to adopt these changes. I know that change is time consuming and difficult, often accompanied by the growing pains of learning a new system. I can assure you that these changes are absolutely essential at this time. I appeal to your cooperation to make JLS a better firm for its employees and its clientele. If you have concerns about the new policies, please bring them to me or to members of the operations committee. The operations committee will meet next week to process reactions and make suggestions for implementing these changes."

Because the young, aggressive firms actively recruited staff from established companies, Lowell did not want to alarm his employees about the severe financial state of JLS. He feared that his employees would panic and seek jobs elsewhere. However, Lowell did share JLS's bleak financial picture with Bill Wilson, his vice-president and general manager, and with Tom Phillips, the comptroller.

At the operations committee meeting the following week, reaction to the policy changes was the main topic of discussion. The operations committee was comprised of six elected members who served 1-year terms and who met with Bill Wilson. The elected members were Sam, Alice, and Harvey from the sales department, Susan from design, and Judy and Fred from the supply group. The president; three managers, one each from the sales, design, and supply departments; and the comptroller were *ex officio* members of the committee, but they rarely attended the meetings.

The operations committee was established 5 years before to review problems and to make recommendations for improving task operations in sales and supply departments. For example, the operations committee was instrumental in the design and implementation of the new office-supply order system. Committee recommendations were sent to the executive committee, the decision-making body of the corporation. The executive committee was comprised of Lowell, Wilson, Phillips, and the managers of the three departments.

Most employees thought the operations committee was ineffective because management rarely acted on its recommendations. Instead, the committee became a team for coordinating management's special projects. In other words, the operations committee functioned to serve the executive committee's agenda rather than as a mechanism for employee input and feedback. Bill Wilson typically ran the meeting. Because service on the committee required time and effort away from a person's regular duties, employees who held managerial aspirations typically ran for election.

Harry and Bill decided not to attend this particular session in the hope that members would be forthright in voicing their reactions to the new policies. Harry asked Sam, the most senior of the elected members, to chair the meeting and provide him with constructive suggestions for making the new policies work. Although Sam supported management, he wanted committee members to vent their feelings about the policies, to prepare for the inevitable uncertainty of change, and to support the new policies.

Sam opened the meeting by noting that even though the new computer system had incurred some problems, the transition stage was going reasonably well. Before he could finish his sentence, Alice exclaimed, "Do you realize the complications that the computer system has caused? Every invoice I complete must have exactly 12 entries—no more or no less. It takes me hours to check code numbers, rectify inconsistencies, and fit each order into exactly 12 digits."

"Yeah," Harvey added, "my customers say that they can't understand the codes."

Alice continued, "Last night I spent 5 hours dictating seven orders because each one had to be on a separate invoice form."

Fred cautioned, "The automatic reorder mechanism sometimes fails to place new orders or to reorder products before the present supply has diminished."

Differing with her colleagues, Susan noted that many of the company changes, especially those involving the computer system, would eventually improve efficiency and accuracy in keeping track of customer requests. But Harvey quickly retorted that the new computer system had resulted in unnecessary inconvenience, inefficiency, and confusion, and also stated that managers and purchasing agents, unfamiliar with the inventory codes, frequently gave inaccurate information; orders that had to be rewritten and resubmitted; and mechanical errors in the software that made some receipts difficult to enter. He concluded, "Why have a computerized purchase order and inventory system for a business in which only a few employees really use it. It's quicker to do it without a computer."

These complaints were followed by references to the past. Fred observed, "We don't need a computer to keep accurate records and improve efficiency. I remember when Steve Lowell was president of this company. A salesperson sent a customer 50 blankets and only charged him for 25 of them. Without hesitation Steve contacted the vendor and requested a bill for 50 blankets. Even if the mistake was only a 5¢ error, Steve *knew about it* and would rectify the problem. Yeah, neither Steve Lowell nor Jason Smith put all customers in the same strict mold like that computer does."

Alice tracked the source of the policy changes to Tom, the new comptroller. As a MBA from Harvard, he was hired to implement new, cost-efficient accounting practices. She asserted, "Tom is a power-hungry individual who wants to run JLS his way. He believes in strict enforcement of the rules and seems to have no time for people. For example, once a customer returned some merchandise and the salesperson misplaced the return slip. When the salesperson took the merchandise back to the storeroom, Tom followed him and waited until he left, grabbed the merchandise, and brought it to the president with the exclamation that sales personnel never follow the rules! Tom claimed that sales people ought to know that a signed return slip must accompany an item before it is reshelved in the storeroom."

Judy remembered an incident when an electric letter opener a customer had ordered was already loaded on the truck for delivery when the customer called to request a larger size. Tom insisted that the small letter opener be delivered and that the customer submit an exchange form before he could get the large letter opener. His follow-the-rules mentality frustrated the customer and caused employees considerable inconvenience. She concluded, "Tom is an outsider who doesn't understand the traditions of this company. He treats employees as robots who must fit their job performance into 12-digit fields just like that damn computer. His rigid enforcement of rules runs against the tradition and history of JLS—one that has stressed management's integrity and good will in dealing with its employees and its customers.

Harvey chimed in, "Yeah, Tom has no time for people. In fact, he drives his Boy Scout troop the same way he tries to run this company—like a military dictator. My troopers say the boys in his group really hate the old guy." Susan recalled, "Did you know that he fired one of our designers 2 weeks after major surgery?"

Sam got caught up in the interaction and shared some of his stories of the good old days. "Yeah, I remember the time when I was seriously hurt and needed a sudden operation. Steve Lowell told my wife that he would fly two surgeons from the Mayo Clinic if she felt that it was necessary."

Alice added that Harry had even provided personal counseling for one employee with emotional problems and another with financial difficulties. CEOs were certainly more humane in the early days of JLS.

Sam reminded the group that Tom might be too rule oriented, but that Harry had initiated the policy changes. He also asked this committee to provide him with constructive comments for implementing the new policies and for making a smooth transition from the old to the new system. Sam viewed the stories of incidents from the past as ways for employees to vent their frustrations, and as unrelated to Harry's agenda for the committee.

Alice asked whether special cases would be given individual consideration during the transition period. Harvey replied, "I doubt it. I had already agreed to take one of my customers to dinner and a hockey game before the policy on expense funds was enacted. Reservations had been made. The total cost of the evening would be about $21. I explained the circumstances to the president and asked him to chip in $10. He said he couldn't assist without checking with Tom. Now, when the president of a company can't make a decision for a mere 10 bucks, something is wrong!"

Sam explained that the company had to be equitable in upholding the policies. Eliminating the expense account for some customers and not for others would circumvent the policy. For example, one of his customers ordered $1,800 of furniture prior to the contract sales policy, but Harry did not want to release the furniture until the customer signed a contract. Judy agreed that the delivery of supplies must be linked to contract sales. In fact, when one salesperson received a request for immediate delivery of name tags, Tom had asked the salesperson to buy the tags himself and have the customer reimburse him. Judy observed, "Although I understand the reason for these rules, the strict enforcement of these policies leads to ridiculous requests. I believe that JLS should economize and decrease expenditures, but this vigilance seems to contradict the overall purpose and tradition of this company. I think that we are making changes too quickly and too rigorously. If management continues to convey indifference to its employees and its customers, they may lose sight of what has made JLS a reputable, successful firm in the first place."

Sam pointed out that some customers are a bad credit risk, others delay in their payments, and still others regularly cancel orders. "Perhaps JLS had become too congenial and too flexible in business relationships with customers," he suggested. To extend a customer's credit for months, to let them return sales items, and to stock 10 different brands of pencils lowers company profits substantially.

"But the sales staff of JLS has always been devoted to its customers," Harvey objected. "I know sales personnel who deliver products to customers after working hours, who punch holes in paper to fit the customers' ringbinders, and who order special catalogs to help the customer solve problems in office efficiency. I think Harry needs to pay more attention to balancing JLS's old image with its new vision as a cost-conscious progressive competitor."

Alice concluded that most employees wanted to eliminate product lines and brand names that rarely sold. It made sense—since 80% of the sales were tied to 350 products. JLS needed a new definition of what it was—one that extended beyond "everything for the office."

"Yeah," Harvey exclaimed, "most customers who tour our display room are astounded by the expensive furnishings. We rarely sell a $7,000 executive desk. Why not display the bread-and-butter items like the $200 desk? If we need to cut our product line, let's get rid of those rare, weird paintings, you know, the ones that tally like a string of goose eggs on the inventory sheets."

Sam concurred but noted that design and sales contributed to product explosion. The design department prided itself on exclusive, expensive modern furniture, while the sales department strove to please the customer. A good retail organization was not run by the customer or by the sales and design departments. Susan reacted defensively to Sam's comment by claiming, "The design department is not 'too artsy' for our customers. Many of the larger firms can afford expensive decor and JLS makes a sizable profit from these big money products. I would rather deal with large-scale customers who can afford the variety of services that we offer."

Harvey interjected, "This new policy of concentrating on companies with over 5,000 employees like Prudential Insurance neglects the firms that have kept JLS in business for 20 years. Some small firms of today become the giants of tomorrow. I've watched companies like Telmont Corporation, Artic Snowmobile, and Continental Telephone grow from small businesses to large influential companies. Because of our long-term reliable service with these growth industries, they've continued to turn to JLS for their office needs. Perhaps I value customer image and employee welfare above the goals of competing with more progressive firms."

"It's not the changes per se that I object to," Judy commented. "It's the way these policy decisions were handled and the potential effects of these decisions on employee morale."

Fred agreed that formal communication between management and employees had broken down lately. He explained, "Company meetings are information-giving sessions; the president issues edicts, and employees voice complaints in bull sessions. It is futile to voice your opinions in department meetings because managers get defensive when confronted with employee objections."

Other employees felt that key people were consulted to provide counsel before major policy changes were approved. This disagreement continued until Alice asked, "What should we report to Harry regarding our recommendations?" Sam responded, "I hope it is more than a summary of this meeting. If Harry heard this discussion, the only insights he could gain would be a lot of complaining supported by disjointed and irrelevant reflections on the past."

DISPOSITION OF THE CASE

Sam reported to Harry that changes were taking place too rapidly and rigidly for members of the operations committee. This recommendation was supported with examples of strict adherence to rules that irritated employees. He depicted the operations meeting as a confusing array of reactions, stories, and gripes about the comptroller. He also recommended more communication about problems with the new policies and about ways of implementing the changes.

After meeting with Bill and Tom, Lowell sent out several memos supporting the changes, justifying strict enforcement of the policies, and announcing efforts to ease the transition. But employees continued to be disgruntled with the changes.

One month later 15 disenchanted members of the JLS sales force joined several entrepreneurs to begin a new office-supply firm. Two months later JLS declared bankruptcy and closed its doors. The resignation of key sales personnel and the inability to recover from its financial problems led to JLS's downfall.

CONCLUDING COMMENTS

Telling stories is one important way members of an organization perpetuate their culture. Thus, the role of narratives and myths can be key in understanding organizational culture. Organizational narratives are often-related examples or incidents; they have plots, action sequences, settings, characters, and themes. They may develop from actual incidents or be fictional representations of events. In either case, they represent an organization's beliefs, values, and ideologies, and serve as symbolic reflections of a corporation's culture.

The narratives that JLS employees shared merged visions of the past with descriptions of current events. Here, as in many organizations, the telling and retelling of stories took on the aspect of folklore by reconstituting the organization's past within its present circumstances. Some of an organization's narratives, then, become legendary or mythical as they are handed down to generations of employees, centered on organizational founders, and embellished with fictional details. Thus, the mythology of an organization comes to preserve and perpetuate values and beliefs from generation to generation, despite employee turnover and changes in positions.

Although managers often mistake the sharing of stories for company gossip or complaining, narratives serve to constitute and reaffirm a company's culture; hence, they also aid in reading and understanding an organization's history. Such narratives and historical legends signify what employees value and want to preserve in their culture.

Understanding company values and organizational images is particularly important during organizational transitions—when introducing new technology, merging corporations, downsizing or laying off employees, or reorganizing departments. When policy decisions are made that are perceived as threatening to company culture, employees may use organizational myths to attack the changes and defend the organization's traditions. Finding ways to change a company while preserving its treasured history is a significant challenge for corporate leaders.

KEY TERMS

narratives	satisfaction
myths	superior–subordinate relationships
communicating change	company image
running effective meetings	adapting to new technology

DISCUSSION QUESTIONS

1. What is the unifying image that characterizes JLS and embodies its values and beliefs?

2. How is this image represented in the historical narratives and legends about past presidents and the "good old days" at JLS?

3. How, according to the anecdotes, do the new policies threaten sacred values? How is this related to organizational change?

4. How should Harry and Sam interpret these stories? What actions should they have taken in response to them?

5. What is your evaluation of the meeting of the operations committee? What were the effective and the ineffective aspects of this meeting? What suggestions would

you make for changing the meeting? What should the operations committee have recommended to Harry?

6. What are additional functions of narratives and myths in organizations?

SUGGESTED READINGS

Boje, D. M., Fedor, D. B., & Rowland, K. M. (1982). Myth-making: A qualitative step in O. D. interventions. *Journal of Applied Behavioral Science, 18,* 17–28.

Goodman, P. S. (1982). *Change in organizations: New perspectives on theory, research, and practice.* San Francisco: Jossey-Bass.

Koprowski, E. J. (1983). Cultural myths: Clues to effective management. *Organizational Dynamics, 3,* 39–51.

Mitroff, I. I., & Kilmann, R. (1976). On organizational stories: An approach to the design and analysis of organizations through myths and stories. In R. H. Kilmann, L. R. Pondy, & D. P. Slevin (Eds.), *The management of organizational design: Strategies and implementation* (pp. 189–208). New York: Elsevier.

Myrsiades, L. S. (1987). Corporate stories as cultural communication in organizational settings. *Management Communication Quarterly, 1,* 84–120.

Pondy, L. (1983). The role of metaphors and myths in organizations and in the facilitation of organizational change. In L. Pondy, P. J. Frost, G. Morgan, & T. C. Dandridge (Eds.), *Organizational symbolism* (Vol. 1, pp. 157–166). Greenwich, CT: JAI.

Sykes, A. J. M. (1970). Myth in communication. *Journal of Communication, 20,* 17–31.

Westerlund, G., & Sjostrand, S. (1979). *Organizational myths.* New York: Harper & Row.

CHAPTER 16

Unions Learn to Change:
Toyota Comes to Kentucky

PAUL PRATHER
University of Kentucky

When Toyota Motor Corporation announced in December 1985 that it would build a manufacturing plant in rural Kentucky, state leaders of building and construction trade unions saw it as an opportunity they could not afford to miss. The $800-million plant would mean hundreds of construction jobs spread out over several years.

The announced plant immediately began drawing international attention as one of the largest foreign-owned manufacturing projects in the United States. Landing a union contract to build the plant, and constructing it well, would mean favorable worldwide publicity for the unions, whose strength—like the strength of many American unions—had been lagging in recent years. Nonunion contractors had lower labor costs, and therefore could submit lower project bids than contractors using union workers. Thus, nonunion companies were winning more contracts. An increasing number of construction companies, in order to compete, were shifting to nonunion labor, which obviously hurt union membership. While union leaders acknowledged that it cost more to use union workers, they truly saw their workmanship as superior to that of nonunion builders. This was a chance to prove their point, in front of an international audience.

In addition, the main automobile plant was supposed to attract dozens of smaller supplier plants to the state. Building the main plant would guarantee the unions a better chance of landing contracts for some of those plants.

Finally—and most importantly—the union leaders were concerned about the implications for building and construction trade unions across the country. So far, of all the automobile plants in the United States, only Nissan had attempted to build a plant with nonunion labor. While Nissan might be excused as an exception, one union leader would later write, Nissan and Toyota together might be seen as starting a trend in the auto industry toward "merit shop," or nonunion, construction (J. Hammond, personal communication, March 20, 1989). Closer to home, union leaders were well aware that Kentucky was already the site of General Motors and Ford plants. The leaders felt that their success or lack thereof with Toyota would affect their future negotiations with those companies. In short, there were critical questions about the unions' role in the future construction of automobile plants, both nationally and in the state.

Union leaders Luckie McClintock, Steve Barger, and Jerry Hammond began approaching state government officials. They wanted to determine whom within the Japanese corporation they should contact with their pitch that union labor was superior to nonunion labor. Reports were that state officials had worked feverishly to attract the Japanese company and had promised the manufacturer millions of dollars in state-subsidized incentives to locate in Kentucky—so McClintock, Barger, and Hammond figured state officials could give them plenty of information about Toyota. As for themselves, the three union leaders—a pipefitter, a pile driver, and an ironworker—knew nothing about the Japanese company or about the Japanese in general.

They found out quickly that things were not going to go smoothly. State officials seemed overcome with euphoria at having landed the highly sought plant; they did not want to risk offending Toyota by helping the unions. Uneasy, but not daunted, Hammond decided to place a call to Japan. The call, he said later, was his first lesson in intercultural communication, and it was a troubling one. The language barrier was so great that he could not even find anyone who understood what he wanted. He gave up.

He, Barger, and McClintock began meeting regularly to try to decide what to do. They called their national union office in Washington, but union officers there knew little more about Toyota or the Japanese than the three Kentucky men.

If the union leaders were stuck, Toyota was not. It appeared that once the company reached a decision to build, Toyota, unlike most American companies, was ready to begin immediately. The manufacturer announced that Japan's largest construction company Ohbayashi-Gumi would act as general contractor on the plant. By this point, there was little question in the union leaders' minds that the Japanese intended to bypass them altogether.

One traditional union way of handling managers who ignored the union was simply to block their work site with placard-carrying union members who would march back and forth in front of work entrances until managers paid attention. The pickets were designed to call attention to unfair labor practices. A lot of people passing by on public streets would take notice. Picketing could be messy, however. Patrolling several work entrances 24 hours a day called for a lot of manpower. Sometimes ugly fights erupted as well. Thus, union leaders did not call for picketing very often.

The union leaders drove to the Toyota construction site to see how they might go about picketing if it eventually came to that. When they arrived, they got a surprise. The construction site was as isolated a place as any they had ever seen. It was in the middle of a farming community, far from town. It covered more than a thousand acres, and there were security men all over the place.

Realizing that their pickets would be seen by no one—except TV cameras that would show them yelling at, or even fighting with, the security guards—the union men drove back home, where another problem awaited them. The men were beginning to understand from what they were reading in the newspapers, and from what they picked up simply by instinct, that the Toyota officials with real power remained in Japan. Those officials certainly were not going to see any pickets, hence, picketing was out of the question.

Somehow the unions had to get the attention of Ohbayashi, and through it, the attention of Toyota officials in Japan—and they had to act fast. They decided on a tack not traditionally taken by unions: They would sue the state, challenging the incentives it offered to Toyota. They would also challenge by suing either the state or the local government for whatever construction permits they gave Ohbayashi. They would, in effect, tie the Japanese up in court until they could think of something better to do. Lawsuits would have another effect as well. The legal discovery process, in which litigants have to make all kinds of financial and legal information available to one another, would give the unions access to the very information they thought the state and the Japanese wanted to keep from them.

After a lot of long and painful discussion, they also agreed not to use their suits only as tactical ploys. They decided they wanted the suits to accomplish something they had not been able to accomplish without them— they wanted to force the courts to issue decisions on the legality of the state's deals with Toyota. Thus, they asked for and signed specific contracts with their lawyers stating that all their litigation would be pursued to final settlements by the courts. "In other words," Hammond wrote later, "we were committed not to pull our legal punches, even after the Toyota agreement was signed" with the unions (personal communication, March 20, 1989).

They filed suit, and the news media pounced on the story. Much of the coverage was negative, however. One of the state's major newspapers wrote editorials decrying the unions' tactics. The newspaper and a number of politicians accused the unions of mounting a racist attack against the Japanese. It was a tough time for McClintock, Barger, and Hammond.

Yet, in response to the media coverage, something more favorable happened. A series of angry letters poured into the newspaper's editorial offices from people—among them many World War II veterans—who were outraged at the state's incentive plan. In the "Letters to the Editor" section of the newspaper, many writers denounced the Japanese for having bombed Pearl Harbor. For the first time, there was a visible public outcry against the plant. The unions had touched a nerve.

As the confrontation geared up, the unions managed to arrange a series of weekly meetings with representatives of Ohbayashi, beginning early in 1986. Ohbayashi was faced with massive publicity and rising anti-Japanese sentiments in the state, and was plagued by lawsuits. The unions' determination to fight the Japanese had become clear, although they themselves were beginning to think in terms of a compromise. They might be willing to negotiate an agreement giving them simple control of construction hiring. That is, they would not insist that all construction workers be union members, but only that the unions had the right to oversee hiring. This would insure that union members got the first shots at jobs.

They soon found it was not going to be that easy. They began meeting with Ohbayashi. Ohbayaski officials took part, but nothing happened. That is, union leaders and their lawyers would talk to American lawyers representing the Japanese, but the Japanese themselves, while physically present, appeared aloof, unconcerned. They seemed, Hammond said later, "detached and ill-informed." Occasionally, an interpreter relayed messages to the Japanese from their lawyers. The stalemate continued.

The language barrier became of increasing concern to the union leaders. It made direct communication with the Ohbayashi executives virtually impossible. They could not even attempt to talk person to person to establish rapport. Moreover, the lawyers Ohbayashi had hired were from a firm that, in the union leaders' opinions, had a history of being antiunion. The three union men doubted that the American lawyers representing Ohbayashi were accurately relaying to the Japanese what the union men were saying. The lawyers, union leaders believed, were assuring Ohbayashi officials that the unions would eventually sign a merit shop agreement.

The three union leaders began realizing that, while they had managed to open negotiations with the Japanese, dealing with them was going to be significantly different from dealing with American management. The union leaders decided they did not have the slightest idea what they were up against. They did know that the odds were against them, and they would have to do everything right. Thus, as they continued to fight Ohbayashi and Toyota in the courts, and to talk to them in private meetings, they also did two other things. They stayed in close contact with their national union offices to insure a show of solidarity, and they began to study the Japanese frantically, not just the two Japanese companies they were dealing with, but Japanese culture generally.

The union leaders decided to seek help elsewhere. They went to scholars at the University of Kentucky. One problem they faced in trying to deal with the Japanese, professors told them, was that the construction unions had no corporate identity that either Toyota or Ohbayashi could recognize. Because many Japanese construction workers were day laborers, and not corporate employees or union members, they had relatively few employment rights in Japan. They were part of the underclass.

The unions needed an identity, yet their leaders had no idea how to establish one with people with whom they could barely communicate. McClintock, Barger, and Hammond began cloistering themselves, studying Japanese history, philosophy, and military tactics until late into the night. McClintock took university courses on Japanese language and culture. Hammond installed a satellite dish at his house and watched 50 hours of educational programs about the Japanese. He and Barger studied classic Japanese texts such as *The Book of the Five Rings* and Sun Tzu's *The Art of War*.

"The more we read and the more we studied . . . the more we realized that we just did not know," Barger said later. "Not only about dealing with the Japanese, but the world economy, just life in general."

"It made Steve crazy," Hammond joked. "I'm sure *The Book of the Five Rings* got him."

"Crazy as a rat," Barger agreed. "They tell me that the sure sign of a free man is self-doubt."

"There was a lot of that," Hammond said (Prather, 1988b).

One thing they began to learn through their studies was that, as the professors had told them, part of their problem lay in the Japanese's conception of labor unions. The Japanese are not opposed to all unions, they learned. In fact, the workforce in Japan is more heavily unionized than the workforce in the United States—28.2% to 18%. Japan has 34,000 unions, according to statistics from the Japan Institute on Social and Economic Affairs. But there are major differences between Japanese and U.S. labor unions. In Japan, unions are typically specific to a given company, which is why there are so many of them. They are called enterprise unions; that is, Toyota has its own union, Nissan has its own union, Sony has its own union, and so forth (Prather, 1988a).

Membership in a Japanese union is a mark of the "elite" in the Japanese workforce, and Japanese society is extremely hierarchical. That means that the bigger a company, the more prestige it has. Unions are typically found only in larger, and thus more prestigious, companies. Membership is mandatory. It includes all lower-ranking white-collar workers and all permanent blue-collar workers (Abernathy & Hays, 1983).

Union members have more status than people who work for smaller companies. They also have more status than people who sometimes work for unionized companies as nonunion temporaries or other who work as day laborers. That latter point is important, because in Japan many construction workers are day laborers. Along with dockyard workers and laid-off miners, they typically live in slums, even though Japan's economy is booming (Fallows, 1988). Thus, the Japanese tend not to understand construction workers being union members.

Because of their own union system, moreover, Japanese managers tend not to understand the whole philosophy of American unions. Enterprise unions in Japan are very concerned about their company's well-being, the three men discovered. Their concern is based on the fact that 28% of workers' income comes from bonuses related to company profits. Japan does have multicompany labor associations much like the United States' AFL–CIO, but they are of secondary importance.

The Japanese union system has evolved since the 1940s. Interestingly enough, American General Douglas MacArthur created Japanese unions after World War II. MacArthur, who was head of American occupation forces in Japan, was opposed to unions, but he had political aspirations in the United States and did not want to return home with an antiunion record, since U.S. unions were popular in postwar America. Thus, MacArthur helped form Japanese unions—which were promptly taken over by Japanese communists when MacArthur left the country. There were riots and major strikes. The combination of difficult economic times and the cummunists' role in the labor unions made for very belligerent organizations. Hence, Japanese management grew up with some pretty difficult unions (Prather, 1988a).

But after World War II, the Japanese economy was so precarious that unions soon came to realize they would have to cooperate with management just to keep plants open. If they did not work together, then the whole country would collapse. That forced cooperation brought labor and management much closer together than in the United States.

That did not mean that Japanese unions became weak. Japanese lifetime employment grew out of the violent protests of postwar unions against layoffs (Abernathy & Hays, 1983). Every spring, Japanese unions still undertake an offensive called *Shunto*, which is a campaign to raise pay.

The main difference between American and Japanese unions is in the approach the Japanese unions take. Unorthodox by American standards, the campaigns are not designed to damage the company. Workers will strike, but they strike on Sunday night between 2 A.M. and 4 A.M. The strike is a demonstration of their unity and their objectives, not an attempt to hurt the company economically. Japanese managers generally respond to the Japanese unions' approach (Prather, 1988a).

But Japanese managers often remain wary of American union leaders, because American union leaders tend to be more loyal to the multicompany union itself—to the building and construction workers' union, say—than to any company. The Japanese understand that labor is not looking out for the economic well-being of the company as much as it is looking out for labor across the board.

The Japanese enterprise–union system was antithetical to everything the three Kentucky construction-union leaders believed. They believed in large-scale union federations that had the clout to remain independent of the managers of any one company. As they saw it, that was the only way to protect workers from arbitrary treatment by profit-hungry companies. It was a principle that was the foundation of the American labor system—and one that the three men would not relinquish.

Still, they began at least to understand why Japanese management seemed to distrust them. At the same time, they were learning a great deal about the Japanese. Among the things they learned from their studies were that Japanese business decisions are ususally made by consensus, and usually from Japan; that the Japanese, under pressure resulting from America's huge trade deficit with Japan, are becoming increasingly sensitive to—and eager to avoid—negative publicity; and that much Japanese business behavior is derived from a religious and military code, *bushido,* that has definite rules for negotiation and rituals for behavior. For example, shows of respect are tantamount. Under the Japanese code of business behavior, it is expected that one should known one's adversary intimately. In addition, adversaries should always be treated as honored guests, not insulted as enemies. Concentration on the issues is also important to the Japanese.

Over the next few months, they had several more meetings with Ohbayashi representatives—still with little movement on either side and still with no evident involvement on the part of the Japanese. In April 1986, talks broke off for a time after an expecially difficult meeting. The union leaders filed more suits, which brought more publicity. The seasons changed; winter approached. The Kentucky union leaders stayed in close touch with their national offices in Washington, D. C. In October 1986, talks resumed. At that point, representatives of the unions' national offices joined the meetings to assist the Kentucky union leaders.

Then Kentucky leaders got a call from a national union office in Washington. December was coming soon. National union leaders wanted to organize a rally in Kentucky on December 7—the anniversary of the Japanese bombing of Pearl Harbor. They planned to bring union workers to Kentucky from all over the country for a day of high-profile, anti-Japanese protests.

The idea worried Hammond. Construction workers were a rowdy bunch. Given the negative publicity the unions had already received—including growing cries of racism aimed at them by some pro-Toyota factions—and considering the high value the Japanese placed on being treated with respect, Hammond decided that the last thing the Kentucky unions needed was a day of Japanese bashing. The rallies could easily get ugly. The Kentucky unions politely declined to sponsor the rally, trying to do so in a way that did not offend their national leaders.

The three men had already enacted a policy of fairness toward the Japanese when speaking of them to the press. As they unearthed information in the legal discovery process that resulted from their suits, they tried to give both sides of each issue.

The union leaders had yet another meeting coming up with the Japanese. If only they could talk to them directly—bypassing the lawyers they believed, rightly or wrongly, were hostile to them— they could try to explain that they did not intend to back down. Perhaps they could also try to explain that, in their opinion, union-controlled labor could be good for the construction project—it would provide a better workforce. The unions, the men had decided, would do their best to cooperate with Japanese managers, if they could just win this battle to get union control of hiring.

At their next meeting the three union representatives sat locked in what seemed to be another fruitless meeting. The labor leaders decided to risk a new approach based on what they had learned about the Japanese.

"We got up, took off our neckties, and tied them around our head," said labor leader Luckie McClintock. A Japanese executive, who moments before had looked like he was half-asleep, suddenly came to life and hurried over to shake union officials' hands, according to McClintock.

The men's ties were meant to imitate headbands worn by kamikaze pilots, implying total concentration on the issue at hand. "It means you're stone cold serious when you tie [that headband] on," said Steve Barger, who was also present. For the first time, the labor officials said, they felt they had reached an understanding with the Japanese (Prather, 1988b).

The building and construction trade unions' eventual victory, a surprising coup that garnered national attention, was the result of a fundamental change in the way the Americans conducted negotiations—neckties notwithstanding. They tried to communicate with the Japanese in their own cultural terms.

When they used their neckties as *hacamachis,* or headbands, union officials signified to the Ohbayashi executives that they would never back down. Ohbayashi's American attorneys thought the union leaders had lost their minds, McClintock said. But despite a language barrier, they had communicated with the Japanese executives in terms they understood, showing them they were doing their homework, according to McClintock and Barger.

"The first thing, it tells you in one of the books, that you must know is your adversary," Barger said, "That's what we were attempting to do."

Barger summed it up with some decidedly American, and adversarial, philosophy, "If you're going to get in a fistfight, you want to know if the guy's left-handed" (Prather, 1988b).

Meanwhile, the tactics of the Kentucky building and contruction trades council in winning a contract with Ohbayashi—and the shifts in the labor leaders' personal attitudes—remain a fascinating case study of the changes that labor leaders are undergoing as they deal in international issues. Their tactics mirror an increasing sophistication in the approaches unions as a whole are taking with management.

KEY TERMS

intercultural communication   perspective taking
cultural values   union-management negotiations
nonverbal communication   public relations
symbols   conflict resolution

DISCUSSION QUESTIONS

1. What problems inhibited communication between the unions and the Japanese?

2. What processes of change have the three union leaders undergone?

3. What role did public relations have in the choices union leaders made in their negotiation tactics with the Japanese?

4. What role did cultural values (American and Japanese) have in the union leaders negotiations with the Japanese?

REFERENCES

Fallows, J. (1988, April). The far east: The other Japan. *Atlantic*, pp. 16–20.

Hays, R. H., & Abernathy, W. J. (1983, July–December). Managing our way to economic decline. *Harvard Business Review*, *61*, 67–78.

Prather, P. (1988a, May 9). Many differences separate U.S., Japanese unions. *Lexington Herald-Leader*, D1, D10.

Prather, P. (1988b, May 9). Unions change with world economy. *Lexington Herald-Leader*, D1, D10–11.

CHAPTER 17

The Role of Communication in Automating IBM Lexington

BEVERLY DAVENPORT SYPHER

HOWARD E. SYPHER
University of Kansas

THOMAS J. HOUSEL
University of Southern California

ROSEMARY BOOTH
IBM

From 1983 until 1987, IBM's Lexington, Kentucky site was involved in one of the most sweeping technological changes in the production of office equipment that the American manufacturing market has ever witnessed. For 20 years, the IBM "Selectric" Typewriter had been manually made in the facility and, by all accounts, was the leader in the industry. However, as the competitive and technological environment of the industry began to change, IBM found itself challenged by many new manufacturers. The company had to find a way to maintain its typewriter's superior quality while reducing manufacturing costs. Thus, in 1983, John Opel, chairman of the board of IBM, announced that the company would invest $350 million to automate the Lexington plant.

The plant was automated only after management had carefully assessed the social impacts of the change. The senior site management and communications staff knew that the success of the conversion rested, in part, on IBM's efforts to allay the fears of employees, and communicate to them—quickly and effectively—how the change was going to affect their work. IBM has a long tradition of "respect for the individual" (see Figure 17.1), which in this case meant involving employees right from the start.

IBM
Basic
Beliefs

Respect for the Individual	Respect for the dignity and the rights of each person in the organization.
Customer Service	To give the best customer service of any company in the world.
Excellence	The conviction that an organization should pursue all tasks with the objective of accomplishing them in a superior way.

FIGURE 17.1. IBM's basic beliefs.

IBM has been a major employer in the central part of Kentucky since opening the Lexington plant in 1956. Many of the employees who manufactured typewriters and office supplies were Kentuckians who had worked there since the plant opened. In 1981, IBM employed more than 7,000 employees at the Lexington site. However, beginning in 1982 nearly 1,000 of these employees took the option of relocating to other IBM facilities while the site implemented automation. Some employees experienced job reassignments, some of which were to positions of lesser responsibility, although pay was not affected. In the industry, this is sometimes referred to as downleveling. Several thousand others underwent extensive retraining to prepare them for new careers within the company. As a result, a number of employees assumed positions of greater responsibility. IBM maintained its commitment to "full employment" and assured employees job security by offering the options of retraining and relocation.

However, the uncertainty felt by IBM employees was not difficult to imagine. On July 31, 1981, headlines in the *Lexington-Herald Leader* read, "IBM Cutting Work Force By Transfers And Attrition." In an attempt to allay some of the fears of employees and the community alike, the *Herald Leader* countered in September of the same year, "Lifeblood Of IBM Plant Isn't In Danger." Within the manufacturing industry, talk about the change to greater automation was widespread. The significance of the change was heightened because IBM was viewed both internally and externally as the exemplar of automation.

The planned changes turned IBM Lexington into one of the most automated manufacturing facilities in the world. Robotic equipment supplemented employees on the assembly line, resulting in the need for extensive technical training to manage such a sophisticated operation. A massive infusion of advanced manufacturing technology (AMT) was implemented. AMT refers to several types of computer-aided design and manufacturing processes that result in vast changes on the assembly line and require extensive "people" efforts. At IBM Lexington, the plant was literally rebuilt around an integrated design that completely changed the manufacturing process for typewriters, computer keyboards, printers, and the like.

Typically, such changes involve what some call "techno-stress" or "techno-trauma," the fear and anxiety employees have about how new technology will alter their work lives. Techno-stress ranges from general anxiety and uneasiness about the uncertainty of the change and the resulting new job to acute psychological withdrawal and physical symptoms that often result in tardiness, absenteeism, and even turnover. However, these changes can also have a positive psychological impact due to enhanced autonomy, increased status, higher productivity, and decreased tedium or boredom.

Working with line management and the personnel department, the goal of the communications department during this transitional period was to anticipate what employees would expect and need to know about the changes and to communicate this information to them clearly. Although IBM wanted to keep the Lexington community informed, their major communication efforts regarding automation were directed toward their internal publics. Developing this partnership with employees early on was crucial to the success of the automation challenge.

Prior to the announcement of automation, the Lexington communications and personnel staffs had already begun developing a strategy for coping with the challenges faced by the site. According to communications management, a new, more aggressive style of communication would be needed to explain the changes and promote employee support. The communications plan was driven by the need for employees to have a more realistic understanding of the typewriter business and its changing requirements. Managers were being asked to assume leadership roles much more difficult than at any time in the past.

During this time, the communications staff decided to assess its overall communications program and develop a strategy for meeting the communication challenges faced because of the impending change to automation. They also needed to establish the efficacy of communication activities because the site was reducing its population in staff support as well as manufacturing. The communications organization was also asked to participate in this reduction. This situation was somewhat ironic. Because of the extraordinary changes going on in Lexington, the site needed more communications support than ever. It was, therefore, in the site's interests to define those issues that needed communication resources, to aim those resources in a precise manner, and, finally to measure the effectiveness of communication efforts.

COMMUNICATION GOALS DURING
THE CHANGE PROCESS

The overarching goal in this project was to assess the general effectiveness of IBM Lexington's existing communications programs. As part of this assessment, we examined ways to communicate automation-related information to employees effectively. With the help of the first three authors, the decision was made to examine employees' perceptions of information adequacy, accuracy, usefulness, and timeliness, among other issues. The content and structure of written materials were examined, focusing on relevant issues such as comprehension and recall. Specific concerns related to the changes including relocation, retraining, and reassignment, were investigated in addition to more general issues concerning the communication of organizational goals, changes, and benefits.

The principal challenges of the communications department during the change to automation were (1) to identify the major information needs of different types of employees (i.e., engineers, employees on the line, first-line managers, programmers, etc.); (2) to develop the quickest and most effective ways of responding to those needs; (3) to inform all employees of the changes that were going to occur before they heard about them from the grapevine or the local newspaper (The local newspaper had already published a number of speculative pieces before IBM was able to provide a full disclosure of its plans); (4) to identify the best channels, sets of channels, and/or vehicles for disseminating this information; (5) to work with other departments (i.e., education, personnel, etc.) and line management to insure that individuals were aware of the extent to which these changes would specifically affect the plant, their work units, and their jobs; and (6) to develop reliable and valid measures of the effectiveness of this communication effort.

COMMUNICATION PRACTICES IN PLACE

At the time of the study, the communications department included nine professionals and two student interns (see Figure 17.2). They were responsible for all internal and external communication efforts as well as community and public affairs. They had a fairly sophisticated communications program

FIGURE 17.2. Organizational chart for IBM Lexington.

in place that included the use of several publications, videos, meetings, public address announcements, and an employee speak-up program.

First-line managers at IBM were the basic communication link between employees and senior management. These managers held regularly scheduled meetings with their departments to discuss a variety of site and corporate concerns.

Senior management communicated directly with first-line managers through *Management Notes,* a weekly publication distributed to all managers. *Lexington Today,* a daily newsletter, was posted on strategically placed bulletin boards for all employees to read. Local and sometimes corporate issues were addressed in the monthly publication, *Lexington News,* which was mailed to employees' homes. Mailing the newsletter to employees' homes was in keeping with the company's belief that it was important for families to understand IBM's directions and changes.

One of the more popular features in *Lexington News* was the publication of "Speak-ups." Through the company-wide "Speak-up!" program, employees were invited to express their views, ask questions, or air concerns anonymously. All Speak-ups were treated confidentially to protect the writer's identity, and every effort was made to answer the Speak-up within 10 working days. Speak-ups of general interest often were featured in the monthly newsletter with the writer's permission.

IBM also mailed *Think,* a bimonthly corporate magazine, to employees' homes, and they also produced several product-related publications, special issues, and reports such as "The History of the Typewriter" and other commemorative pieces.

Meetings were considered an important way of keeping employees involved and informed about IBM Lexington operations. Management frequently conducted all-managers meetings, divisional meetings, and regular departmental meetings. Even though the assessment revealed some concern about the frequency and length of meetings, employees agreed that they were important and necessary.

Another communication channel just beginning to be used in 1982 was video communications. Just prior to the change to automation, the communications department had begun producing sophisticated videos. IBM Lexington had invested in state-of-the-art technology to equip its own video production studio and had already begun work on an automation-related video at the time of the communication assessment.

In short, the ideas of effective communication and employee involvement were strongly entrenched at IBM Lexington. An infrastructure of trust between management and employees existed before the change to automation. Over the years, the organization had maintained a credible image among its employees by stressing open lines of communication and quick responses to concerns. Their efforts had been successful because they utilized multiple channels of communication, relied on first-line managers to meet regularly with employees, promoted upper management visibility through meetings and publications, and offered a suggestion system with monetary incentives.

DEVELOPING A COMMUNICATION STRATEGY: PHASE I. THE COMMUNICATION ASSESSMENT

To target its communication efforts toward automation, IBM Lexington used a multiple-methods approach to gather information, including interviews with key managers, focus groups stratified by the site's nine business areas, and a comprehensive survey of a representative sample of employees.

In September 1982, employees voluntarily participated in nine different focus groups (8–12 persons per group) to discuss communication at IBM Lexington. Participants were randomly selected from the nine different business areas to represent lab managers, plant managers, engineers, programmers, all other exempt employees, technical employees, production employees, administrative, and all other non-exempt employees.

A questionnaire was developed around the communication issues and sources identified as important by the interviewees, focus group participants, and communications staff. The questionnaire was designed to measure employees' perceptions of the quality and quantity of information they received about important topics identified in focus groups. The topics were corporate goals, changes at IBM in general, relocation, automation, retraining, Speak-ups, benefits, suggestion awards, information about activities in other departments, information about company policies, and the PRIDE program—a local effort to reinforce corporate values of pride and quality in one's work. The PRIDE campaign is one example of IBM Lexington's communication efforts. There were posters, awards, announcements, and even vending machine cups featuring the PRIDE symbol and slogan. All of this indicated that an infrastructure for communicating change was in place prior to the infusion of AMT.

In July 1983, the questionnaire was mailed to a sample of 1226 employees representing the nine business areas. Analyses were based on a response rate of 79% of the total sample. Thus, with the interview, focus group, and survey data in hand, the process of analysis began with an eye toward strategy development.

RESULTS OF THE ASSESSMENT

The results of the communication assessment process were organized around the sources of information the employees preferred and the quality and quantity of information received on the various topics. From the employees, we learned a number of things relevant to developing an information campaign regarding automation.

Sources of Information

Managers, department meetings, and upper management (in that order) were the most preferred sources of information. Of these three, employees reported receiving the least amount of information from upper management, and not surprisingly, they indicated a desire for more. Some focus group participants said their immediate managers were good communicators because they screened irrelevant information. Employees reported that the most valued managerial communication focused on their department as a whole, and its relation to other departments or new policies.

Questionnaire responses indicated that all groups also found the bulletin board to be an important and highly valued source of information, often competing in importance with the employees' managers. The bulletin board ranked at the top of employee preferences as a source of information. In focus groups, it was pointed out that employees valued this communication source more than others because of its social function. The bulletin boards provided an opportunity for employees to socialize, to move from their work station and still be working. Virtually every focus group participant reported reading *everything* posted on the bulletin boards.

The highest quality ratings (i.e., timeliness, accuracy, and usefulness) for information sources went to managers, bulletin boards, and *Lexington Today*, the employee publication produced and posted daily. The corporate magazine, *Think*, the local monthly newsletter, *Lexington News*, the grapevine, and the Lexington news media were all given significantly lower quality ratings than the other sources. Upper management, while most preferred as a source of information, was not seen as timely, useful, or accurate as the highest quality sources. However, the difference between information received and desired from upper management was greater than for any other communication source. This finding was the strongest among the nonprofessional employees. The focus group participants indicated that *Think* and *Lexington News* were less useful than the other communication sources because they did not detail the impact of corporate changes on the Lexington site.

Topics of Information

Of the topic areas included in the survey, automation, relocation, and retraining were considered the most important. Since automation efforts had just gotten underway, the investigation of employee perceptions regarding these topics was part of involving employees in the change right from the start. By asking for opinions, site management was creating expectations about employee involvement in automation and heightening their awareness of its impact. At the same time they were gathering data to help them most effectively utilize available communications resources.

The survey revealed that employees felt that the information they received about automation at that time was significantly less accurate than information about most other issues. Also, engineers, programmers, and lab managers indicated that the relocation information was not yet particularly useful.

Comments from focus group participants reflected the same concerns about these topics. Few employees could remember receiving information about automation, retraining, and relocation and the information they had received, they considered to be inadequate. In focus groups, participants said they wanted more information on specific plans the company had for relocating people, and fewer success stories of individuals who had relocated. They also wanted more information about relocation opportunities, cities to which they could relocate, and IBM's policy of paying for an exploratory trip to a possible relocation site.

In addition to revealing some of the early needs for more direct and specific information on automation and relocation, the communication assessment also revealed why IBM is often credited for its communication program and perhaps helped explain why it is included in Peters and Waterman's (1982) list of "excellent companies" and used as an example of what Deal and Kennedy (1982) call a "strong culture."

When comparing findings from this assessment to those derived from a national survey (Gildea, 1980), the communication strengths of IBM's Lexington site were evident. For example, some 40% of the employees surveyed nationally reported the grapevine as a major source of information. At IBM Lexington, employees said they received very little information through the grapevine (ranked eighth out of nine possible sources), and they wanted even less. In essence, they did not depend on it for their information; the formal system seemed to be working quite well.

Consistent with the national survey, IBM employees reported that their immediate managers were the most preferred communication source. In contrast, IBM employees reported getting more information from their manager than the employees in the national survey. This may, in part, explain why job satisfaction was so high, given Goldhaber, Yates, Porter, and Lesniak's (1978) findings that superior–subordinate communication was the strongest predictor of communication and job satisfaction. Employees at IBM Lexington also appeared to receive more information from their location's upper management than employees in the national survey, although IBMers wanted even more from this source.

Below is a list of some of the issues discussed in the communication assessment summary presented to site management in September 1983.

1. Engineers, lab managers, and programmers may need to be addressed as a group with unique information needs.
2. Employees' managers appear to be the best information dissemination source and should be used as much as possible when communicating about sensitive issues such as automation.
3. The bulletin boards appear to be one of the best ways to get important information to employees and should continue to be used.
4. More high-quality information about automation, retraining, and relocation is demanded by almost all employees.

COMMUNICATION STRATEGY DEVELOPMENT: PHASE II

With the presentation of the summary of findings, Phase I of the communication assessment ended. The communications staff moved into Phase II, which involved sorting out the data they had available and planning their

communication campaign regarding automation. Meanwhile, they continued their daily routines in the communications department, and automation
and its attendant issues of relocation and retraining repeatedly received
attention. The assessment data helped them direct their strategies in more
systematic ways.

Phase II consisted of brainstorming sessions with the communications
department staff and outside consultants. Several strategies were proposed,
and each was evaluated for its own worth and how it fit the needs, concerns,
and preferences expressed by the site employees.

As the implementation of the changes continued, the communications
department intensified its efforts to keep employees informed. They began
by publishing an article in *Lexington News* about the communication assessment findings. The communications department prepared memos for managers on communicating effectively and distributed summaries of the survey
data to managers, outlining their employees' aggregate views on managerial
communication. They also stressed the importance of communication in
management meetings.

They followed up with the production of new videos on automation.
One production, entitled "Opportunities," became mandatory viewing in
department meetings. Other articles on the progress of automation were
published in *Lexington News* and *Lexington Today*. The communications
staff also recommended that the education department initiate specific communication-related training programs. Since all IBM managers in Lexington
were required to attend 40 hours of training a year, these new programs
provided a way to integrate communication and educational efforts.

CONCLUSION

In effect, the IBM Lexington culture can be described by its communication
rituals. Communication was seen as central to the successful implementation
of automation. It became the vehicle for maintaining the partnership with
employees during the change to AMT. In a 1986 interview with Bob Waterman, the general manager of IBM's Lexington plant attributed much of the
success of the automation effort to communication and emphasized the
importance of starting early (5 years in advance to be exact) and communicating openly and candidly with employees (Waterman, 1987). Employee
participation and the communication of timely, accurate, and useful information about major technological innovations appear crucial for successful
implementation. Using a variety of media, reinforcing the value of communication with managers, and integrating communication in on-going departmental efforts proved to be the cornerstones of the communications
department's efforts.

Through both external and internal evaluations, communication was important to the successful implementation of technological change at IBM Lexington. Since 1983 when the automation efforts began, employee morale has remained high every year, and resignations and absenteeism have remained far below the national average. From all indications, the communication programs helped to sustain these statistics. This case study of communication efforts during IBM Lexington's $350 million conversion to greater automation demonstrates the need for a strong yet flexible communications infrastructure. Also, the study highlights the significant role communication professionals can play in helping employees understand and adjust to change brought about by the introduction of advanced manufacturing technologies.

Acknowledgments. The authors wish to thank IBM for its permission to publish this case. We also wish to recognize the foresight of Jack Butler who initiated the communication assessment discussed in this chapter. Mr. Butler was Communications Manager at IBM Lexington when the change to automation was announced.

KEY TERMS

automation
advanced manufacturing technology (AMT)
communication assessment
multiple methods
stratified random sample
focus groups
communication strategy

corporate videos
downleveling
retraining
relocation
social impacts of new technology
partnership with employees
communication campaign

DISCUSSION QUESTIONS

1. What media were used at IBM's Lexington plant to keep their various publics informed about automation?

2. What were some of the social impacts IBM employees experienced as a result of automation?

3. How do you think the social impacts were mediated by communication?

4. Discuss specific examples of how to implement the major strategies employed at IBM Lexington.

5. Give some examples of organizational symbolism at IBM Lexington.

6. Develop a time table for a 2-year communication assessment such as the one conducted at IBM Lexington. What obstacles does one face in sticking to a time table?

7. What role can a communication department play in introducing major change such as the one discussed in this case?

SUGGESTED READINGS

Deal, T., & Kennedy, A. (1982). *Corporate cultures: The rites and rituals of corporate life*. Reading, MA: Addison-Wesley.

Gildea, J. (1980). 45,000 employees judge effectiveness of internal communication. *IABC Journal, 43*, 3–11.

Goldhaber, G., Yates, M., Porter, D., & Lesniak, R. (1978). Organizational communication: 1978 state of the art. *Human Communication Research, 5*, 76–96.

Kling, R. (1984). Assimilating social values in computer-based technologies. *Telecommunications Policy, 11*, 127–147.

Peters, T., & Waterman, R. (1982). *In search of excellence*. New York: Warner Books.

Sypher, H. E., Housel, T., & Sypher, B. D. (1986). *Communicating information about technological change: A case study*. Paper presented at the annual meeting of the Southern Speech Communication Association, Houston.

Walton, R. E., & Susman, G. I. (1987). People policies for the new machines. *Harvard Business Review, 65*, 98–106.

Waterman, R. H., Jr. (1987). *The renewal factor*. New York: Bantam Books.

Zuboff, S. (1988). *In the age of the smart machine*. New York: Basic Books.

Part VI

Communication and New Technology

CHAPTER 18

Video Comes to Organizational Communications: The Case of ARCOvision

John Ruchinskas

Lynne Svenning
Telecommunications Research Group

Charles W. Steinfield
Michigan State University

ATLANTIC RICHFIELD: A VIDEO PIONEER

The Atlantic Richfield Company of the late 1970s was an exemplar of a geographically dispersed, decentralized organization created through mergers and acquisitions. Formed through a merger of two smaller oil concerns who joined forces in order to stay competitive in the face of major firms such as Exxon, Shell Oil, and Texaco, the Atlantic Richfield company moved its headquarters to Los Angeles in order to be closer to major company operations, which included production facilities in Texas and Alaska. This move signified a belief that they could function effectively away from the New York financial markets, and that they would be able to use communications to bridge the gap between Los Angeles, Dallas, and Alaska.

ARCO, like many companies that must locate company operations close to necessary resources, needed effective communications. Such companies can be characterized as having geographically dispersed work units that must cooperate to deliver an end product to the customer. For example, an aerospace organization may locate its R&D and design engineering functions in an area with a strong university presence. This allows them to take advantage of a readily available, highly technical workforce, and reap the benefits of a synergistic environment for their creative and technical personnel. Or, they may locate their manufacturing operations closer to a cheap labor supply to hold down production costs, while maintaining a strong marketing presence in Washington, D.C. for customer contact. We see many similar examples in the computer industry, where firms set up research centers near Stanford, MIT, or Research Triangle Park, corporate headquarters on the East or West Coast, manufacturing facilities near cheap labor supplies (often overseas), and sales offices scattered throughout the world.

Based on the company's success with its Alaska operations and the general boom in the oil industry, ARCO diversified in the late 1970s, virtually doubling in size with the acquisition of major coal and copper businesses purchased from Anaconda. This created a major ARCO presence in Denver, along with smaller operations in such locations as Louisville, Kentucky, Waterbury, Connecticut, Gillette, Wyoming, and Tonopah, Nevada.

These new businesses were brought into the ARCO family as separate operating companies. ARCO's philosophy was one of decentralization and local autonomy. Corporate officers acted as overseers of nine semi-autonomous operating companies, such as ARCO Coal, ARCO Oil & Gas, ARCO Chemicals, ARCO Petroleum Products, and ARCO Transportation. Each company was responsible for its own profit and loss, even though there were often substantial needs for coordination. Strong reporting relationships with headquarters and other operating units are often necessary to maintain the advantages of a large organization, while still claiming the productivity benefits of independent profit centers. Independence and interdependence are often at loggerheads in the modern organization. For example, the Transportation company earned revenues by shipping oil from the wells of the Oil & Gas company to its refineries. Petroleum Products handled retail sales, distributing the refined gasoline coming out of Oil & Gas's refineries. ARCO Chemicals often used petroleum products created by one of its sister firms.

This coordination required spanning great geographical distances. The Oil & Gas company had drilling facilities throughout the South, the West Coast, and Alaska. Refineries were located throughout the country, allowing ARCO to serve gas stations across the United States. The Transportation company's pipelines spanned the nation, moving products from the point of production to the consumer. All of this was run by a corporate headquarters in Los Angeles, which looked for ways to maximize corporate profits while allowing its business units to run fairly autonomously.

In the late 1970s, ARCO's innovative CEO, Robert O. Anderson, raised the possibility of video teleconferencing as a solution for ARCO's communication needs. He was spurred by a personal history that included traveling an average of 400 miles per day while working for ARCO. The sight of plane loads of personnel shuttling back and forth between Dallas and Anchorage every day, the awareness of possibilities in new communication technologies, and the vision of a different way to conduct business, led Anderson to believe that there had to be a better way. He charged the company's electronics and telecommunication department with designing and implementing a video teleconferencing system to facilitate communication within the Atlantic Richfield organization.

Two forms of video communications were available for geographically dispersed organizations: *interactive video teleconferencing* between groups in two, and sometimes three, locations and *"business television."* The former involves two-way audio and video between participating sites, while the latter is essentially a broadcast medium allowing a central location to disseminate common information to multiple sites simultaneously. Feedback in this second type of video communication is possible, but usually limited to audio (primarily telephone) interaction. Over 100 organizations now use video teleconferencing to facilitate cross-locational meetings, while over 75 organizations routinely use business television to communicate with those in the field.

Interactive video teleconferencing is essentially a meeting medium for small- to medium-sized groups. It has been used for a wide variety of organizational activities including staff meetings, project/program reviews, design meetings, problem solving, crisis intervention, interviewing, negotiating, and training. It is proving to be an extremely useful and flexible tool for bridging the distance barriers. People conduct just about every kind of activity via video that they would in person. Some have even taken to joining for lunch via video to add the spontaneous social interaction dimension that is sometimes missing in video meetings.

Originally positioned as a travel substitute, video teleconferencing is proving to be a communications enhancer. Not only do people avoid "trash travel" (long trips for short meetings), meetings are held that beforehand were simply not possible. Moreover, key people are brought in to meetings who could not have traveled to a distant location.

Business television is essentially a dissemination medium. Information is transmitted simultaneously to multiple locations, insuring that all branches in the organization receive the same message at the same time. Although primarily a one-way broadcast medium, business television set ups usually provide for audio feedback from all locations to create the sense of interactivity. They have been used successfully for informing distributors, dealers, or field offices of new product lines, holding annual meetings, training, providing regular company updates, motivating a nationally or internationally dispersed sales force, and fund raising.

Business television is actually fueling much of the growth in video-based organizational communications. The ability to establish and maintain simultaneous, timely, and accurate communications with those in remote locations is improving performance in organizations whose tentacles span the country and the globe. The low cost of receive-only satellite dishes and one-way video transmission makes it an ideal dissemination medium for headquarters–field communications of all kinds.

R.O. Anderson's directive was in keeping with ARCO's corporate culture. The company prided itself on being innovative, and was generally recognized as such within the industry. It also had a long history of independence in telecommunications, going back to the days when it ran its own telephone lines alongside its pipelines to manage operations better. Unlike most of its contemporaries, in 1979 ARCO was already running its own private voice and data network, providing its operating companies with more cost-effective communication services than using traditional telephone carriers.

However, R. O. Anderson's charge presented a major challenge to system planners. As of 1979, video teleconferencing's track record was decidedly mixed. Although some organizations had experimented with this new medium, there were very few confirmed advocates. There was no "one-stop shop" to go to for facilities nor a satellite network that could serve both the continental United States and Alaska. Hence, ARCO launched an ambitious research and development plan to push forward the state of the art in teleconferencing technology. At the same time, ARCO contracted with a team of communication researchers (the Telecommunications Research Group [TRG]) for a major organizational assessment, aimed at identifying potential users and applications, their requirements for networks and facilities, as well as the sources of support and resistance in the organization.

A series of interviews with managers, and an organization-wide survey of employees, was conducted prior to the actual design and implementation of the system. This preliminary research accomplished several objectives. First, information was collected that was useful for system design. For example, in one set of interviews, several geologists came into the meeting carrying samples of graphic information they routinely used in meetings. Based upon the diversity of meeting aids discussed in interviews and noted on survey forms, room-design engineers were able to build sufficient flexibility into the room to accommodate the range of user needs. Second, contacting potential users at such an early stage of the design process engendered a sense of commitment among employees. As results were fed back to the employee population through internal publications, potential users felt more involved and thus more committed to the success of the system. Third, assessing user attitudes early in the game helped the company to diagnose and treat potential problems in the formative stages. For example, a number of employees expressed concern over the cost of the system during the assessment. Many of them had seen the early press releases that almost always began with a statement about "ARCO's $20 million system." System promoters were unwittingly emphasizing a sensitive topic. To alleviate a possible source of resistance to the system, future news releases primarily stressed system benefits, and avoided dwelling on total system costs. Employee concerns over the expense subsequently diminished.

A fourth finding of the preliminary research revealed that ARCO employees did have a clear need for videoconferencing. Estimates of the amount and ways the system would be used helped planners develop a system management strategy. Moreover, employees' predictions about the uses for videoconferencing represented additional information useful in system design. In one interview, a geologist described how he always purchased an extra seat on the plane to carry oil exploration charts from Alaska to Dallas for meetings. This not only illustrated the need for a conferencing capability between Anchorage and Dallas, but also how essential system security would be. The fact that employees would not trust such materials out of their sight during travel insured that they would never use a system that could not promise secure transmission. Finally, the assessment served to identify key groups of employees who had extremely positive attitudes toward the system and had strong needs for videoconferencing. These people were then enlisted in the early trials of the system since they were more willing to help system planners with the "debugging" process that always accompanies a new technology.

The combination of engineering and social science research eventually led to the creation of "ARCOvision," a seven-site, point-to-point, interactive videoconferencing system. Based on TRG's organizational research results, video teleconferencing facilities were installed in Anchorage, Dallas, Denver, Houston, Los Angeles, and Philadelphia to support the heavy communication needs among these sites. These facilities were designed to accommodate a full range of typical ARCO meetings. In addition, ARCO decided to install a seventh room in Washington, D.C., despite relatively small staff operations in this city. This room was installed to allow rapid and timely exchange between Washington staff and corporate executives on matters of regulatory or legislative importance. It also was viewed as a means to gain rapid access to non-ARCO personnel, who might be willing to come to the ARCO office for a meeting. Executives felt that the potential impact of the decisions that were taking place in Washington more than justified the cost of this room.

The ARCOvision facilities allowed users both to see and hear each other in real time. The meeting rooms accommodated six to eight people at the conference table in each site, with additional seating capacity within camera range in a row directly behind table participants. ARCOvision users could employ a full range of graphic images (slides, viewgraphs, 3-D objects, writing board) in their meetings, and print hard copies of these images for a permanent record in each location. Users could also "broadcast" a meeting from one originating site to all other ARCOvision rooms, receiving voice-only feedback from all receiving locales.

ARCOvision

ARCO system planners were aware that asking employees to use videoconferencing involved changing some of the basic ways in which people do business. The actual system roll-out was accompanied by an internal marketing program to build employee awareness of this new capability, and to promote usage. The videoconferencing network was named ARCOvision, reflecting both the company's pride in tailoring this technology for its own uses, and the management foresight that led to the creation of this innovative communication medium.

The actual system usage during ARCOvision's first year of operations both confirmed expectations and pointed to the versatility of this communications tool. Usage levels grew throughout the first year, moving from 15 conferences and 24 hours of use in the initial month of operations (September 1983) to 59 conferences and 98 hours of use in a month-long period a little over a year later (November 1984). All told, the system was used 984 hours during its initial year of operations for over 650 different business meetings.

Users and Usage

The diversity of ARCOvision users reflects ARCO's conscious decision to design and implement the system for the full range of business users, from executives to planners to engineers. Rather than targeting this tool for specific users or projects, ARCOvision was implemented as a general communication utility. Over 1,500 different employees were counted among the 5,300 meeting participants using ARCOvision during its first year. A random-sample study of employees conducted after the first year of operations showed that almost 44% of the management employees in ARCOvision sites had tried meeting via video.

For the typical employee, ARCOvision use is an occasional phenomenon, something engaged in on a monthly, bimonthly, or even quarterly basis. Thus, making videoconferencing a habitual communication behavior is more of a challenge for system planners than it is for other technologies such as voice mail or electronic mail, which tend to be used on a daily basis and more quickly incorporated into the regular work routine.

Communication needs appear to drive most system use. Those employees most pressed by the difficulties of doing business across geographic distances are ARCOvision's most regular customers. Survey results showed that users characterized their work as involving more change, less structure or routine, and more pressure than nonusers. Their work required significantly more coordination with employees in other locations. There is also a strong linear relationship between use of videoconferencing and use of other communications media. Those who employed ARCOvision also tended to make more frequent use of the speakerphone, conference calling, and facsimile, and also spent more time in meetings. In short, the organization's key communicators quickly embraced a new technology that allowed more timely exchanges with less pressure on already busy schedules.

The range of ARCOvision uses occurring during the first year was a surprise to many observers. Employees used videoconferencing for everything from project reviews to task force meetings and planning sessions, from training to operational problem solving, from brainstorming to requests for capital expenditures, from interviews to quarterly status reviews. In doing so, users ignored the conventional wisdom that videoconferencing was only appropriate for a limited set of tasks, a finding that was based largely on studies conducted in laboratory settings.

For example, company employees negotiated via video, presented multimillion dollar requests for capital authorization, interviewed candidates for new positions, introduced a new boss to employees in a remote location, and held day-long sessions with 44 participants coming and going as needed for a meeting. In essence, they found video appropriate for the full range of business activities, including some that heretofore were reserved only for face-to-face interactions.

The system was also used to bring company executives closer to key communities of interest located thousands of miles away from ARCO's Los Angeles headquarters. The system allowed executives to meet with the Assistant Secretary of the Interior in Washington, D.C. to review new reporting regulations. Wall Street analysts discussed a planned restructuring of the company with top management in several locations. In essence, it allowed ARCO timely access to outside organizations that could have a key influence on ARCO's performance. Again, the technology in some way overcame the bounds of geography, while allowing a more personal and rich exchange than was possible through other electronic communications media.

Impacts of Use

Even videoconferencing's most ardent supporters will not claim that the medium is a total substitute for face-to-face exchange. It provides a close approximation of in-person exchange, but remains a mediated experience. People must still travel, but not as often. They can meet very effectively when time considerations make travel impossible and the telephone just will not suffice. Despite technological advances, videoconferencing remains the next best thing to being there. It is significantly better than not being able to meet.

User reactions to ARCOvision were almost uniformly positive. Ninety percent of the users rated it a good tool for business communications. The majority (61%) felt it was a satisfactory alternative to travel, and most (71%) believed that the medium gave the impression of personal contact with the person in the other location. Very few people (5%) who tried the system indicated they would not use it again.

In the year-end survey, users were asked to rate ARCOvision's impact on a range of items. They reported reduced travel, more efficient meetings, better access to key personnel, more timely decisions, and shortened project completion cycles, among other effects. Regular users were far more positive about the system, and almost twice as likely to cite benefits than occasional or light users.

In bottom-line oriented organizations, it is critical to know what impact video communications has on company performance, and whether the substantial investment of resources has value for the corporation. Impact on travel is the most commonly quantified benefit of videoconferencing use. Over half the ARCOvision users, and 81% of the regular users, credit ARCOvision with reducing the number of trips they take. These findings confirm data gathered on a meeting-by-meeting basis that indicated that almost 1000 trips were avoided by using ARCOvision during its first year of operations. In fact, officials in Alaska credited their conference room with saving $200,000 in travel expenses, and over 2,000 person hours of travel time during first-year operations. Experience continues to echo these data. Company-wide figures for a 6-month period (October 1987 to March 1988) indicate displacement of over $573,000 in direct travel costs, and personnel time saved conservatively valued at $279,000.

Feedback from users indicates that videoconferencing is especially likely to replace trash travel, energy-draining trips for a 1- or 2-hour-long meeting. "Traveling long distances (2- or 3-day trips) for 1-hour meetings tends to build up a productivity debit that's hard to overcome," notes one user. Key personnel are effectively out of commission for 2 days as they travel to and from distant locales. Not only are these decision makers away from their work while traveling, employees who need to interact with them are put on hold while they await their return. Thus, even employees who are able to make good use of time spent in the air tend to view travel as a productivity drain.

Conversely, about 40% of ARCOvision users (and almost 60% of regular users) credit this medium with *increasing* personal efficiency, effectiveness, and productivity. Reclaimed travel time is certainly part of this equation. The ability to have more timely meetings, and reach more timely action, is another, "ARCOvision makes me more available," noted one executive. "More importantly, it allows me to expose junior people to the action earlier, and saves me time relaying information." A majority of system users echoed these sentiments, reporting improved access to the right people at the right time.

User comments stress videoconferencing's time-saving ability as a key contributor to enhanced business operations. "Not only was this particular application financially beneficial, it allowed an important meeting to take place *now*, when it might have been delayed several weeks due to incompatible travel schedules," notes one first-time user. Another junior employee in Alaska credits ARCOvision with getting his ideas into the pipeline 6 months before he would have been able to present his ideas in person (he was in Alaska and the relevant decision makers in Texas). As a result, the new project got underway almost immediately rather than sitting on a back burner for 6 months.

It is clear that videoconferencing does change the way people do business. Almost a quarter of the ARCOvision meetings held during its initial year of operations were labeled "new meetings" by participants. These were cross-locational tasks that simply would not have been undertaken if ARCOvision were not available. Sample new meetings included such purposes as tax planning, refinery operations reviews, preventive maintenance discussions, and cross-locational organizational development efforts. ARCOvision allowed activities that were previously inhibited by the costs (time and money) of travel. Typically, the new activities required a visual component that could not have been accommodated with telephone communications. ARCOvision opened up new avenues of exchange, enabling employees to conduct necessary business that otherwise would have been lost in the crunch of dealing with geographically dispersed operations.

Users note that ARCOvision meetings have a different "flavor" from face-to face sessions. Conferences are viewed as shorter, more task-oriented, and more cooperative than face-to-face sessions. The imposition of time constraints (users must book the facility for a fixed meeting length) and the slight time delay introduced when broadcasting a signal over 23,000 miles up and back to a satellite make the meetings a little more formal and less spontaneous. Users' greatest dissatisfactions with the system generally stem from the time delay involved in satellite transmission, which causes difficulties when trying to interrupt the speaker, or leads to "cross-talk" when two people try to gain the floor at the same time. As a result, while users rate ARCOvision as far more *efficient* than face-to-face meetings, they are evenly divided as to whether these sessions are more, equally, or less *effective* than the same meeting held in person.

All told, ARCO rated the system a success after its initial year of operations. "I think it has exceeded our expectations in terms of what people are able to do with it," noted the ARCOvision manager. "It's definitely given us greater travel–dollar savings than we expected, and it is right on target in terms of projected usage."

Those closest to the system stress ARCOvision's enabling capabilities (the ability to do business better), not just travel savings, as the key to the system's success. "The benefits derived from having more people in meetings, exchanging more information, and allowing younger engineers to sit in on meetings are exceptional," notes the ARCOvision manager. "I think this is why the system has gone over so well with the users, while upper management is getting the travel–dollar savings it wants to see."

ARCOvision REVISITED—1988

ARCO in 1988 is a different company from the ARCO of 1983. At the time the system was installed, ARCO was a diversified energy company involved in all aspects of the oil and gas business, as well as the copper, coal, and solar energy fields. It employed close to 50,000 people, and was looking at long-range forecasts that pegged the price of oil as headed toward $80 a barrel.

Times have changed dramatically. The sharp drop in the price of oil led to a major retrenchment on the part of most U.S. energy firms, and ARCO was no exception. Faced with falling oil prices, the company chose to concentrate on its most profitable areas, centered on a tightly defined core business of oil and gas exploration, production, and distribution. ARCO sold off its minerals companies, portions of its chemicals business, and its direct retail operations on the East Coast. Total company employment in 1988 is down to approximately half of 1983 levels.

This shift has had a direct impact on the need for and use of ARCOvision. The elimination of the coal and copper companies effectively did away with ARCO's presence in Denver. Hence, the ARCOvision room in this site was closed down. Facilities in Philadelphia were relocated to a suburban Pennsylvania research facility following changes in ARCO's chemical and retail gasoline operations.

As a result, ARCOvision use dropped slightly in its second year of operations, and has remained at essentially the same level since that time. With the company less diversified and less geographically dispersed, usage is concentrated in Los Angeles, Dallas, Anchorage, and Houston. ARCO's diminished East Coast presence has led to less use of the Philadelphia area facility, which was one of the primary users during first-year operations. ARCOvision's Washington presence has remained, and continues to be used for high-level exchanges on matters of government policy and decision making. Overall, usage is running at approximately 800 hours a year, concentrated on engineering meetings (50%), financial sessions (28%), and business or planning meetings (20%). This 20% drop in ARCOvision use from its first year of operations should not be viewed as a system failure in light of the almost 50% reduction in the employee population. In fact, the company has recently added several new rooms to its videoconferencing network.

One of the most interesting applications of ARCOvision has been its role in the downsizing process itself. The system was used extensively at the executive level in the planning and decision process, as ARCO decided how it would react to the changing business climate. In fact, ARCO was one of the first oil companies to restructure itself in the face of the changing market, and has emerged as one of the more profitable firms.

Once restructuring decisions had been made, the system was used both to discuss these changes with the press and financial community (inviting them into nearby ARCOvision facilities to interview company executives in Los Angeles, Dallas, Philadelphia, and Houston), and to ease the transition for employees. Employees being displaced by the reorganization were interviewed for ARCO positions in other locations via ARCOvision. The company's president now holds regular, informal ARCOvision meetings with a group of randomly selected employees in two cities. Employees have the chance to ask the president about any matters of concern, often short-circuiting rumors. These sessions give the president a better feel for the concerns and attitudes of the rank-and-file employee, and allow him better to convey the concept of everyone working together to get the company through a difficult period.

ARCO's system operators credit an aggressive internal marketing program for keeping the level of usage up, despite the widespread personnel reductions. Changes in technology (primarily lower cost, lower bandwidth video systems) has encouraged system expansion for the first time in years. ARCOvision's ability to improve communications among geographically distant work units drove the interest in expansion to remote Alaskan locales as well as tying in smaller project management offices. This same capability helped maintain support for the system during the budget cutting of past years. Thus, a system designed in an era of expansion has managed to maintain itself during a period of sharp retrenchment, and is being expanded now that the company has stabilized around a group of core businesses.

SUMMARY: THE COMMUNICATION CHALLENGES IN GEOGRAPHICALLY DISPERSED ORGANIZATIONS

Operating effectively with a global service area and widely dispersed workforce puts special pressures and requirements on organizational communications in an organization like ARCO. The geographically dispersed organizational units must be linked together with communication technologies that facilitate the timely flow of information, ideas, and decisions to the relevant parts of the organization. These communication connections must be established at reasonable cost and enable effective communication among the dispersed units. Being able to bring together the right people from multiple locations in a timely and cost-effective fashion is the essence of effective communication in such a geographically dispersed organization.

Access and timely communication are problems even when organizational units are located in one physical site; when work units are geographically dispersed, the problem increases significantly. Timely action takes on new dimensions when one must deal with different time zones, when people rely on time-consuming travel as a primary communications mode, and when competitive pressures put a premium on timely response. Timely problem solving and decision making present special challenges when problems occur in one site, resolution depends on expertise located in another, and decision makers are in yet a third location.

Geographically dispersed organizations like ARCO must be able to conduct their business in a cost-competitive manner. The last few years have seen increasing pressures on the bottom line. Travel is the most expensive and inefficient means of coordinating a geographically dispersed workforce. There are the direct costs of travel (such as transportation, meals, and hotel) as well as the productivity debits created by time spent traveling. With increasing bottom-line pressures has come the search for cost-effective travel substitutes like videoconferencing.

Effectiveness as well as cost is a significant factor in the choice of a communication medium for cross-locational operations. People must feel that can get their business done as effectively and more efficiently than traveling to meet in person. The newer communication technologies represent a potential solution to the special challenges of the geographically dispersed organizations.

Acknowledgments. The authors acknowledge the generous support and cooperation of the Atlantic Richfield Company over the many years spanned by the projects described in this chapter. Charles Steinfield also is grateful to the Ameritech Foundation for their generous support of his research activities during the preparation of this chapter.

KEY TERMS

geographically dispersed work units	"trash travel"
decentralization	enabling capacity
independence versus interdependence	downsizing
interactive videoconferencing	needs assessment
business television	internal marketing program

DISCUSSION QUESTIONS

1. What factors have prompted the need for new communication technologies in organizations like Atlantic Richfield?

2. Compare and contrast the attributes of videoconferencing with other communication media? How is videoconferencing different from face-to-face meetings?

3. In what ways did the assessment research contribute to the success of ARCOvision?

4. In what types of situations is it still necessary to travel for face-to-face meetings?

5. How did ARCOvision change the way people did business at ARCO? What other effects did it have on organizational communication? How did it affect actual meetings?

6. What were some of the unanticipated uses of ARCOvision during ARCO's efforts at restructuring to face the competitive pressures of the new marketplace?

SUGGESTED READINGS

Johansen, R. (1984). *Teleconferencing and beyond: Communications in the office of the future*. New York: McGraw Hill.

Johansen, R., Vallee, J., & Spangler, K. (1979). *Electronic meetings: Technical alternatives and social choices*. Reading, MA: Addison-Wesley.

Keen, P. (1986). *Competing in time: Using telecommunications for competitive advantage*. Cambridge, MA: Ballinger.

Meyer, N. D., & Boone, M. (1987). *The information edge*. New York: McGraw Hill.

Parker, L., & Olgren, C. (1983). *Teleconferencing technologies and applications*. Dedham, MA: Artech House.

Short, J., Williams, E., & Christie, B. (1976). *The social psychology of telecommunications*. New York: Wiley.

Svenning, L., & Ruchinskas, J. (1984). Organizational teleconferencing. In R. Rice (Ed.), *The new media* (pp. 217–248). Beverly Hills, CA: Sage.

Svenning, L., & Ruchinskas, J. (1986). Internal market research program is yielding successful videoconferencing for ARCOvision. *Communications News, 23(2)*, 48–52.

CHAPTER 19

Computer-Mediated Communications in the Organization: Using Electronic Mail at Xerox

CHARLES W. STEINFIELD
Michigan State University

In the last several decades, technological innovations in computers and telecommunications have created a wide array of new communication media. For organizations, these new media represent opportunities to overcome communications problems resulting from a geographically dispersed workforce, and to enhance the productivity of organization members. Media such as teleconferencing and electronic mail provide new communication capabilities to help improve the flow of information, and to facilitate the coordination of action when people are not in the same location.

It is important for organizational communication experts to recognize, however, that successful implementation of new communication technologies in organizations is not guaranteed. Some very expensive systems have been installed in settings where the hardware is rarely or never used. Moreover, utilized systems have had unanticipated consequences—some desirable, others perhaps less desirable. It is not possible to predict all outcomes of implementing a new means of communicating. Case studies of what happens after new media are implemented can help to expand our awareness of the range of possible uses and effects, as well as arm future planners with a broader understanding of the ways in which people adapt technological systems for purposes beyond those envisioned by system designers. Many of the unique ways in which one new communication technology, electronic mail, can be used in an organization is illustrated in the case of the Xerox Corporation. What follows is a brief overview of electronic mail, before moving to a detailed description of its use and impact at Xerox.

ELECTRONIC MAIL

Electronic mail has been called the cornerstone of the office of the future. It is, however, an integral part of the office of today. Of all the new communication media available, electronic mail has perhaps achieved the most widespread acceptance in all types of organizations, including businesses, government agencies, and universities. There are literally millions of electronic mailboxes, and although most are on intracompany systems, there is a growing effort to interconnect separate computer networks to enable intercompany electronic mail communication.

At its simplest level, electronic mail provides the capability to create a textual message on a computer, transmit it to one or more recipients, and store the message in receivers' "electronic mailboxes" for subsequent display when they next use their computer. Most systems provide a powerful array of features to facilitate the process of message creation, storage and processing, transmission, and reception. Such features include the ability to store lists of destination addresses, so that the same message can be delivered simultaneously to large numbers of receivers; automatic reply capabilities; electronic filing, searching, and retrieval functions for processing received messages; and many others.

Motivations to install electronic mail systems originally focused on the productivity improvements that could be gained among managerial and professional staffs. Many behavioral studies of managers and professionals concluded that a large proportion (up to 70 or 80%) of the workday was spent in communication-related activities such as face-to-face meetings, telephone calls, reading, and writing. Thus, improving productivity in these kinds of workers was felt to require investment in technology that could support and enhance the communication process. Further analysis demonstrated that there were many unproductive behavioral activities associated with typical managerial and professional communication. Called "shadow functions," these activities individually accounted for negligible amounts of wasted time, but in the aggregate could account for as much as 30 minutes to an hour of every workday by some estimates. Examples of shadow functions are the time spent dialing a busy telephone number or calling someone who is not in their office. Searching for a telephone number or mailing address are also shadow functions. The time spent collecting one's thoughts after a telephone call or face-to-face interruption represents yet another type of shadow function.

As pressures to improve office productivity grow, the benefits of an asynchronous, computer-enhanced medium like electronic mail become the subject of much attention. With electronic mail, many shadow functions can be eliminated. There is no searching for a telephone number or address; to mail information only a user's identification name or number is needed, and this can be kept in an electronically searchable directory. Moreover, "telephone tag" is avoided, if individuals can send and receive messages at their convenience, rather than when busy schedules intersect. Electronic mail is not intrusive—messages do not demand to be "opened" immediately like a ringing telephone demands to be answered—and so interruptions of trains of thought can be avoided. Messages are delivered rapidly, eliminating the delay of paper mail.

On the other hand, the standard lore we obtain from the literature is that electronic mail communication does not provide the same richness as a face-to-face conversation, or even a telephone call. Because of the limited amount of nonverbal information transmitted, and the delay in feedback, electronic mail has been considered to be low in a quality known as "social presence." This implies that users may not feel that receivers of messages are socially and psychologically "present" at the time of communication, and therefore will rely less on this medium for "interpersonally involving" types of tasks. In a similar vein, electronic mail has been characterized as being low in information richness, implying that it is not an appropriate medium when the information to be conveyed is ambiguous and subject to multiple interpretations. Because of the lack of added information supplied by nonverbal cues, and the limited ability to head off any misinterpretation without immediate feedback, most researchers feel that electronic mail is more appropriate for simple and routine exchanges. For more ambiguous and complex messages, the potential for misinterpretation is high.

This brief description illustrates the standard view of electronic mail as a simple text-based communication system enabling quick delivery of brief messages, in lieu of making a telephone call or writing a memo. Such descriptions, however, lead to an underestimation of the range of applications and effects of organizational communication patterns when provided in the absence of any specific organizational context. In fact, there is growing evidence from field research that computer-mediated communications are used in ways that have not been anticipated by the literature. Not only are there individual differences in people's willingness to apply electronic mail for various purposes, but each organizational setting appears to have different norms, policies, and cultures regarding electronic mail use. We turn now to a case study of the use of electronic mail at the Xerox Corporation in order to illustrate the enormous potential of this new communication technology to enable patterns of communication that would be unimaginable as few as 20 years ago. Where possible, we draw connections to choices made by the company that appear to have facilitated the evolution of a rich electronic communication environment.

THE XEROX CORPORATION: A BRIEF HISTORY

For most people, the name Xerox is synonymous with the ubiquitous photocopy machine; in fact, the company name itself has come into standard usage to refer to the process of photocopying. The company's principal product is credited with changing the way the world engages in business. The company enjoyed phenomenal success, dominating the photocopier market for many years throughout the 1950s and 1960s.

Times have changed in the photocopier business. Competitive pressure, from other copier companies as well as from competing technologies, has forced Xerox to concentrate on its core business, and to conduct research and development aggressively in order to stay on the leading edge of information technology. Moreover, Xerox has grown to include sites spanning the globe, with headquarters in Stamford, Connecticut; research facilities in Palo Alto, California, and Webster, New York; training facilities in Leesburg, Virginia; manufacturing facilities throughout California and several other states; marketing offices in Dallas, sales offices worldwide; and subsidiaries and affiliated companies in several countries, including Germany, the United Kingdom, and Japan. In the face of competition, effective communication and information flow can be a critical resource, yet difficult to accomplish with such a geographically dispersed workforce.

ELECTRONIC MAIL AT XEROX

Xerox has a highly evolved electronic mail system, which has been in place for approximately 15 years. The original system spread from the Palo Alto Research Center (known as Xerox PARC) throughout the company and its affiliated organizations. Today there are an estimated 20,000 work stations connected to the Xerox Internet, a global private telecommunications network linking Xerox-affiliated companies in the United States, Canada, Europe, the South Pacific, and Japan.

The Xerox system couples an easy to use interface with extraordinary technical capabilities. The system in use is a result of research by computer scientists, cognitive psychologists, human factors researchers, and other specialists at Xerox PARC. The mail system is actually an integral component of a full-featured office information system. Thus, users can create and mail any size, type, and number of documents, including graphics, using a Xerox work station product (called a Xerox 6085).

The system supports the easy creation and maintenance of large public and private distribution lists. A distribution list is simply a file containing the system identification addresses of a group of users. Messages that are addressed to the list name are then automatically distributed to each user on the list. Thus, the same message could be mailed to hundreds, or even thousands, of employees without having to know or type their system addresses, as long as they are on a distribution list. At Xerox, there are literally hundreds of public lists, and part of the system software enables users easily to place their name on public lists oriented to some topic of interest. There are essentially three types of distribution lists (DLs) in the company: (1) Organization DLs are lists of all users in a particular work unit, department, or division and are useful for disseminating administrative information. (2) Work-related DLs are lists of people who share a common job function, work on a common project, or share an interest in some topic of relevance to their work. (3) Finally, social DLs are lists of people who share a common interest in topics that are unrelated to work. They may share common hobbies or recreational interests, or simply share a desire to engage in entertaining social interaction with others in the company.

Perhaps the most critical key to Xerox's success with electronic mail was the company's decision not to restrict usage of the system by employees in any way. Employees do not pay to use the system, and are encouraged to use it for any and all communications with other people at Xerox. Uses for social purposes are not frowned upon, unlike with many electronic mail installations in other companies. The original name, "Grapevine," of the internal computer network over which electronic messages were transmitted illustrates the view in this company of electronic mail as a tool for informal horizontal communications.

In 1982, a study of electronic mail uses and effects was conducted at Xerox. Interviews with system users, observations of system use, and a detailed survey of a random sample of several hundred users provided a rich data set for this case study. In the following sections, we describe several observations from this research about the use and impact of electronic mail at Xerox, including, where possible, descriptions of specific incidents that highlight the unique communication capabilities afforded by this new medium.

By the time of the study, the electronic mail system was an integral part of the typical user's workday. People reported spending an average of over 40 minutes each day processing mail. Although survey respondents only reported sending an average of a couple of messages every day, because of the distribution lists, people received many more. Several of the heavier users reported typically having 50–100 messages waiting in their electronic "in-basket" each morning, although for most the number was far smaller (approximately 5–10 messages per day).

Most electronic mail use was intended for one-on-one task-related communication. Typical uses included asking for and providing information, scheduling meetings, brainstorming ideas, forwarding messages to appropriate destinations, providing feedback on reports, sending messages in place of a phone call, and keeping a record of agreements. On a social level, the system was also used to keep in touch with people in other locations. However, because of the DLs, many additional uses were described by users. The system enabled frequent group interaction, allowing use of the system for broadcasting information requests, keeping track of company happenings, and coordinating project activities. DLs were also used for social purposes, including organizing social activities, participating in entertaining conversations or cross-locational games, and advertising items for sale. These "broadcasting" applications of the electronic mail system represent relatively new communication capabilities for organizational participants. Below, some of the implications of broadcasting on electronic mail are discussed.

Distribution Lists and the Flow of Information at Xerox— Accessing Remote Expertise

One of the clear task-related benefits of the system is increased access to information. Telecommunications technologies are often touted for their ability to link people to remote sources of expertise. In a large organization with in-house research-and-development centers, there is a large pool of technical knowledge that is potentially available to employees, if only a means can be found of linking those in need to appropriate sources of information. Through the use of public distribution lists on the Xerox electronic mail system, such a means exists. One use of the system identified in the study was broadcasting requests for information to other parts of the organization. Theoretically, only those with the desired information will respond, while everyone else will simply delete the message.

An example of this type of use occurred during observation of the system. At the time, Xerox was working on a personal computer product known as the Xerox 820. Although most of the research-and-development and manufacturing divisions were in California or the Rochester, New York area, a small team of Xerox 820 designers working on the display features of the computer were located in Dallas. They felt isolated from the bulk of the technical expertise in the company, since the Dallas office was comprised primarily of marketing and sales staff. This group was having difficulty deciding on which of two display options to use for the 820. Using several organizational DLs, as well as a DL called the 820 Interest Group, they broadcast a message throughout the company asking for advice on their two display options. The message included a description of the options, and what they saw as the strengths and weaknesses of each. They then asked that those able to provide input reply with a vote on which option to choose. This message was sent sometime in the morning, and by the late afternoon, they had received several hundred replies. The group then tallied up the replies, and sent a message back to everyone the same afternoon, informing them that 75% of the respondents voted for option A, while the remaining 25% chose option B. They further included a summary of the primary reasons for respondents' choices. On the basis of this informal company-wide survey, they went with the majority choice of option A. The electronic mail system thus improves every user's ability to access remote sources of expertise, even without knowing in advance who the experts are. Without electronic mail, this same activity simply could not have occurred without great cost and effort, and yet in this instance was completed all in the same day.

During the period in which we observed the system, numerous such incidents occurred. In many cases, the information was highly technical and task related, but in other cases, the information was of a more personal or social nature. Interestingly, if an information request dealt with a topic of relevance to a number of people in the company, large discussions would ensue over the electronic mail system. A request might start with "Anyone know anything about . . .?" and over the next several days, people would provide advice, amplify the question, debate the merits of particular solutions or opinions, and eventually tire of the topic and agree to stop putting their comments on the distribution list.

In other situations, if the information request was technical and perhaps not of general interest to a large population, the original requesting user would have responses sent only to him or her, rather than to a DL. They would then create a file of the responses, store it on a file server (a computer attached to the network for mass storage), and then send a message to the DL thanking all those who responded and informing anyone who might be interested of the whereabouts of the file. Thus, a tremendous wealth of useful information could be gathered by individuals, and easily made available to others with the same information needs. Note also that such information gathering and disseminating essentially bypasses all normal organizational boundaries, reducing reliance on standard boundary spanning and gatekeeping roles.

Communicating Policies and Norms for Behavior

One of the more interesting uses of the system is to articulate appropriate norms of behavior at work. Often these norms are in regard to appropriate communication activities on the electronic mail system. For example, members of distribution lists are quick to correct someone for sending a message with inappropriate content to their list. A "catchall" list called "junkmail" was created for messages that did not belong on more specific DLs. Users can voluntarily place their names on the junkmail list, but recognize that many of the messages addressed to this list will be irrelevant.

Often the system is used not only to inform employees of appropriate norms for behavior, but also to discuss the norms openly and articulate contingencies for violating norms. In one set of exchanges, a user criticized someone for using the network to print 75 copies of a four-page document, causing him and several others to have to wait a considerable period to get their single copies of one- or two-page documents. This angry user not only addressed his message to the "culprit," but also carbon copied the message to the printing system DL and to the junkmail DL. The message pointed out that copy machines should be used for multiple copies, while printers should be used to obtain a single original. The original message was quickly followed by messages that suggested he not react so angrily, because in some situations others felt the need to print multiple copies. Over the next few days, the policy was reconfirmed, but a variety of situations were defined in which printing multiple copies on a print server might be acceptable. Thus, the electronic mail system served as a tool to facilitate both the transmission and evolution of norms and policies, encouraging public debate.

Supporting Cross-Locational Project Teams

Xerox, like many other corporations, often assigns people to work on project teams outside of their normal work unit. Many research-and-development projects require input from people from diverse disciplines and job functions, and are of limited duration. The appropriate people are not always colocated, and, hence, the electronic mail system becomes an invaluable tool for coordinating project activities. The conducting of the electronic mail study reported here, for example, included several people from El Segundo, and several from Palo Alto. The mail system enabled the exchange of drafts of questionnaires, scheduling of interviews, discussion of ideas, status reports, and other activities essential to the study. In this fashion, input from the necessary people was obtained without disrupting their regular work unit activities. Travel was kept to a minimum, and only occurred after all the preparatory work was completed.

Socioemotional Uses of Electronic Mail

As noted above, there are few restrictions on use of the electronic mail system. Upper management leaves it to the employees to police their use.

As a result, social uses of the system are as much a part of the electronic mail landscape as task uses. Many DLs are geared toward specific hobbies, or recreational activities, and it is not uncommon for employees to organize social activities over the system. For example, during the system observation, a white-water rafting trip for Xerox employees was organized. People were notified about the trip, and could reserve a space over the system. DLs are available to discuss the merits of particular restaurants, movies, and books. At Xerox PARC, one person made a habit of reading the *I Ching* every morning and disseminating the results to her office over the system. It is not uncommon for people to become regular communication partners over the system, without ever meeting face to face.

Managers decided that the benefits of social use far outweighed the costs, and assumed that people would use discretion to insure that they did not let it interfere with their productivity. Research results supported this belief, as the extent of social use measured in the survey did not relate inversely to perceived productivity effects. On the other hand, there were several ways in which such social use was actually quite functional for the organization. A number of these are discussed below.

First, the argument can be made that social use stimulates more rapid learning of the system for new users and encourages the development of appropriate habits to help integrate the system into daily work routines. For electronic mail to be useful, users need to develop what has been called "message discipline," where they learn to check mail frequently and respond within reasonable periods of time. Participating on social DLs provides new users with positive reinforcement for checking their mail and makes learning to use the system enjoyable.

Second, contacts are made in the course of social use that may become valuable in future work activities. Through discussions on DLs, new employees learn who has specific expertise in various areas, and thus expand their network of contacts. Moreover, through such policy discussions as described above, they learn norms of behavior more rapidly. Thus, the system potentially serves as a tool to speed up the social integration of new employees into the company. Research results supported this contention with the finding that newer employees were more likely to engage in social use than employees with more tenure in the company.

Third, social use of the system improved the quality of work life for many employees. Some interviewees felt that they could never work at a place that did not have a similar communication environment. In the high technology industries, any edge in recruiting and keeping highly trained professional staff is desirable.

Fourth, several interviewees credited social use of the system with fostering enhanced creativity. A situation described by a team of programmers at PARC illustrates how this might happen. They had for several days been stumped on a difficult logic problem in a word processing program they were developing. After work hours, however, the group became involved in developing a program that would permit teams from different locations to play a game called Go on the system. In the course of developing the software code for the game, they suddenly realized that they had arrived at a way to solve the logic problem in the word processing software. Creativity research is replete with examples of people arriving at creative solutions to problems once they approach them from a totally different perspective, unburdened by constraining expectations for how things are typically done.

Unanticipated Consequences of Electronic Mail Use

In general, Xerox employees believe that the electronic mail system has had positive effects on their work life. Research findings demonstrate that a majority of employees perceive using electronic mail to have improved their productivity (57% averaged more than 4 on a 7-point productivity scale), as well as the accessibility and quality of information at work (77%). Nearly half of those surveyed felt that the electronic mail system was responsible for enhancing the cohesiveness and coordination of work units (43%), and had increased their connectedness with others in the company (48%). Moreover, many agreed that use of electronic mail has freed them from constraints imposed by time and space. Nearly half (47%) felt that coworkers and supervisors did not have to be in the same physical location, and that they could work at times outside of the normal workday if they wished. There was virtually no agreement with regard to statements depicting the workplace as less personal or more closely supervised due to electronic mail (92% averaged less than 4 on a 7-point impersonal/rigid supervision scale). And, in spite of the heavy use of distribution lists, users did not feel that information overload was a problem (61% averaged less than 4 on a 7-point overload scale).

There are, however, some unintended consequences of using the mail system that are worth noting. Some consequences are undesirable, whereas others illustrate outcomes of certain types of uses that may or may not be potential problems.

First, although overload was generally not perceived to be a problem, in several interviews, people noted that the return from a trip was often accompanied by hundreds of waiting electronic messages. Hence, the time it takes to process such volumes of waiting mail is one concern, but a more subtle issue is the effect of the delayed response. People who use the telephone are usually informed when the individual they call is out of town or otherwise away from the office for some period. No such response is provided to an electronic message, unless a secretary screens electronic mail (which is relatively uncommon for the professional staff at Xerox). This is coupled with a perception that electronic mail has led to a tendency to expect rapid turnaround on requests. One user noted that he made a practice of only answering messages once per day, to try to stem the ever-increasing expectations for rapid turnaround. Thus, delayed response due to receivers being out of town could be misinterpreted, or cause problems, due to a reliance on rapid response.

A second area of concern is the occurrence of "flaming" over electronic mail. In the absence of immediate feedback and the tempering effects of nonverbal cues and the physical presence of receivers, electronic messages can sometimes be perceived as overly critical or blunt, or can simply be misinterpreted. Imagine a situation in which you send an electronic message asking a coworker a question, and he or she responds with "Who knows?" In the absence of any supporting contextual cues, you might interpret this response as curt, implying that your question was stupid or unimportant. Yet, the coworker actually may not have meant anything critical, and was simply quickly sending you a response before rushing off to a meeting. In situations in which a response is meant to be critical, the absence of context can lead to its being interpreted as stronger criticism than intended. In either situation, a subsequent harsh response can then lead to an escalation of verbal hostility. These kinds of situations have been observed on a number of occasions on electronic mail systems in a variety of settings. Several instances occurred at Xerox during the system observation, and users familiar with the phenomenon would step in to mediate conflicts and cool tempers. One employee, in the midst of a heated discussion on the system, actually invited the protagonists to "cool down" over an ice cream cone at a local parlor. Organizations need to recognize and properly forewarn users that "flaming" is a real possibility if free and open communications over electronic mail are encouraged.

A third area of concern involves the security of proprietary information discussed on the electronic mail system. Electronic messages are no longer in the control of the user once they are sent. Receivers are able to forward copies on to other destinations easily. At Xerox, there were several gateways to external networks, and it was possible that someone outside the company might actually be a member of a public distribution list. This required vigilance by employees to insure that company secrets were not broadcast on DLs reaching external users. In many cases, DLs were so large, however, that it was not always obvious that someone outside the company belonged. The benefit of intercompany communication, therefore, only comes at the cost of increasing concern over information security.

A fourth issue was raised by what might be called political uses of the electronic mail system. For example, some users noted that they would occasionally use the system to request an action from someone, and then carbon copy that person's supervisor or coworkers to force a response. Another example with implications for vertical communication patterns in the company is the use of electronic mail instead of a telephone call in order to reach a manager whose calls are normally screened. The effects of such communication barrier bypasses have received little attention in the electronic mail literature.

Finally, one of the strongest benefits of broadcast uses of electronic mail–to make remote sources of expertise accessible—also represents a possible problem. Experts may tire if their services are called upon too often, resulting in a reduced desire to respond. If carried to the extreme, people would be forced to ignore requests, and the system would no longer be useful for this purpose. One interviewee agreed that broadcasting requests for remote consultation is good until everyone does it. Such broadcasts are less frequent according to the survey, however, providing evidence that the user community recognizes the potential problem and is voluntarily restricting such use.

CONCLUSION

This case study has illustrated that electronic mail can clearly be used for more than exchanges of routine information. It provides communication capabilities to employees that would have been unthinkable a few short years ago. The Xerox Corporation has encouraged free and unrestricted use by employees, and thus facilitated the growth of an active electronic community. Employees interviewed in this case study felt that as a result, Xerox is reaping the benefits of reduced turnover, enhanced productivity, and an improved quality of life at work. Managers are willing to allow social uses to flourish in order to obtain these benefits. Other organizations have not taken the same approach, and actively prohibit any personal use of their company electronic mail systems at all. Studies of electronic mail in these more restricted settings will likely reveal quite different patterns of use and effects, and such sites may not be realizing the full range of benefits afforded by this new and powerful communication medium.

Acknowledgments. The author acknowledges the generous support and cooperation of the Xerox Corporation during the conduct of the research described in this case study. The author is also grateful to the Ameritech Foundation for their generous support of his research activities during the preparation of this case study.

KEY TERMS

electronic mail   access to remote expertise
shadow functions   communication norms
social presence   cross-locational project teams
information richness   socioemotional uses
distribution lists   message discipline
grapevine   information overload
broadcasting   flaming

DISCUSSION QUESTIONS

1. How did the electronic mail system enhance the social aspects of work life at Xerox? What are some potential disadvantages of socioemotional uses of electronic mail in the workplace?

2. In what ways is "broadcasting" over electronic mail similar to our standard conceptions of broadcast communications? How is it different?

3. In what kinds of task situations is electronic mail most useful? In what situations would use of electronic mail be inappropriate or less useful? Why?

4. Compare and contrast electronic mail with other forms of communication media in terms of such attributes as speed of communications and feedback, sensory channels employed, and permanence of the message. How do these attributes relate to the ways in which electronic mail was used at Xerox? Can you think of other relevant attributes of media?

5. How might electronic mail be used as a political tool in an organization?

6. Discuss potential ethical (e.g., privacy) issues related to the use of electronic mail?

SUGGESTED READINGS

Fulk, J., & Steinfield, C. (Eds.). (1990). *Perspectives on organizations and communication technology*. Newbury Park, CA: Sage.
Hiltz, S. R. (1984). *Online communities: A case study of the office of the future*. Norwood, NJ: Ablex.
Rice, R. (1984). Mediated group communication. In R. Rice (Ed.), *The new media: Communication, research, and technology*. (pp. 129–154). Beverly Hills, CA: Sage.
Steinfield, C. (1986). Computer mediated communication systems. In M. Williams (Ed.), *Annual review of information science and technology: Vol 21* (pp. 167–202). White Plains, NY: Knowledge Industry Publications.
Vallee, J. (1984). *Computer message systems*. New York, NY: McGraw Hill.

CHAPTER 20

TRW Corporation: The Space Park Network Design Decision

WILLIAM H. DAVIDSON

THOMAS J. HOUSEL
University of Southern California

TRW originated in September 1953 when Simon Ramo and Dean Wooldridge, two Cal Tech classmates, resigned from their senior management positions with Hughes Aircraft Company to form Ramo–Wooldridge Corporation in Los Angeles.[1] Ramo had served as the chief scientist for Hughes, then the largest defense contractor in the United States. Five years later, their company merged with Thompson Products, an auto-parts firm based in Cleveland, to form TRW Corporation. While the new company's headquarters was located in Ohio, its California aerospace activities grew rapidly.

Late in 1953, U. S. intelligence reports concluded that the Soviet Union was in the advanced stages of designing an intercontinental ballistic missile (ICBM) that could bypass the U.S. air defense system. Within a year, the Ramo–Wooldridge Corporation was awarded a contract to manage the systems engineering work for an American ICBM. The project called for rockets 10 times more powerful than those in existence at the time, sophisticated guidance systems, and breakthroughs in half a dozen areas of applied technology.

Within 5 years, an Atlas ICBM was successfully tested, landing on a predefined target more than 5,000 miles away. This success provided the foundation for TRW's on-going defense and space work for the Pentagon. TRW's Space Park Complex in Redondo Beach, California became the center for advanced technology military development projects.

The company was organized into three groups: Space and Defense, Automotive, and Information Services. Each group operated with a high degree of autonomy. The Automotive Group, based in Cleveland, reported sales of $3.1 billion in 1987, out of the $6.8 billion reported for the entire company. The Information Systems Group (ISG), based in Long Beach, California, operated the largest credit-reporting service in the United States. Its central credit-history data base contained 145 million records of individual credit data. ISG provided credit reference services to retailers, financial institutions, and other users. The ISG data center in Anaheim was one of the largest and most sophisticated data-processing facilities in the United States. This fast-growing group's sales totaled $520 million in 1987.

The largest group, Space and Defense, was based in Redondo Beach, California. The Space Park Complex in Redondo Beach employed almost 30,000 people and generated sales of $3.2 billion in 1987. This group played a primary role in developing communications satellites and missile technologies for the military. As a result of large federal government contracts, the Space Park Complex grew dramatically during the 1970s and 1980s. Space and Defense sales grew from $300 million in 1976 to $1 billion in 1980. The Management Information Systems (MIS) staff rose from five to several hundred employees during this period.

The group's explosive growth led to reorganization in the early 1980s, resulting in the formation of the Space and Defense Sector with five new groups: Operations and Support Group, Electronic Systems Group, Space and Technology Group, Defense Systems Group, and Federal Systems Group (see Figure 20.1). Each of these groups enjoyed a great deal of independence. The latter four were autonomous profit centers. The Operations and Support Group became responsible for general administrative support and for managing voice and data network services for TRW's Space Park facilities (see Figure 20.2).

THE OPERATIONS AND SUPPORT GROUP

The Operations and Support Group (OSG) consisted of three divisions: Manufacturing, Administrative Support, and Data Services. The Administrative Support division was responsible for providing telephone services only. Centrex services were used exclusively to meet all of TRW's voice communications requirements. George Davis, a former telecommunications manager for a major oil company, was hired to manage voice services at the time of the reorganization.

The data services division was responsible for data processing and MIS services, in addition to its accounting and finance functions. Ed Carter, vice-president and general manager of OSG's Data Service Division, was closely involved in several projects that reviewed TRW's Space Park Complex telecommunications needs and options in the mid-1980s. After several

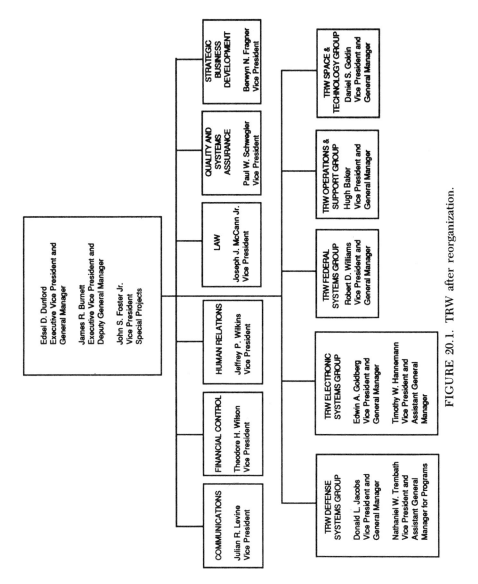

FIGURE 20.1. TRW after reorganization.

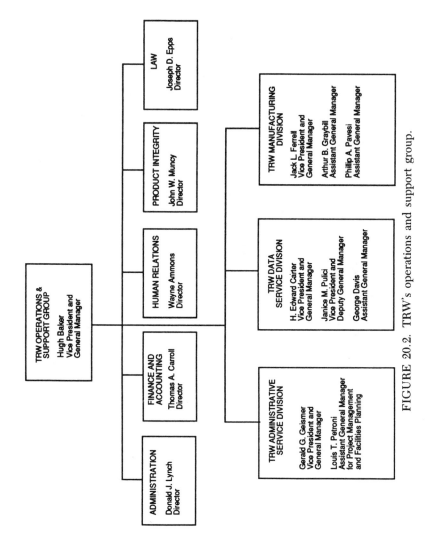

FIGURE 20.2. TRW's operations and support group.

years in other positions, he returned to a position with senior responsibility for network management. He was responsible for implementing a network plan developed as a result of his earlier efforts. After several years away, Ed was somewhat surprised at the delayed status of the network's design and implementation. His first concern was to reevaluate the initial plans and progress to date before determining how best to meet the sector's information network needs.

GROWTH OF DATA COMMUNICATIONS

During the late 1970s and the 1980s, independent MIS systems and applications proliferated within the four operating groups. While none of the groups contained its own formal MIS unit, each group had a finance director and an administrative director who were responsible for providing computing services to their respective areas. Separate data systems evolved to serve financial, manufacturing, and scientific management needs.

Given the project-oriented focus of TRW's business and organization, the classified nature of many projects, and the need to operate at the cutting edge of advanced technology, individual units were able to purchase and install data processing systems independently. Project teams typically developed their own data bases and applications software. Many project teams installed local area networks to link work areas and members. A variety of computer-aided design, engineering, and manufacturing systems were utilized in Space Park.

TRW's MIS activities grew rapidly, with the result that Space Park had computer systems from all the major vendors. Engineering systems included significant installations of DEC, Prime, Sun, and Apollo computers. TRW was one of the largest 50 customers for each of these vendors. The sector's commercial, accounting, and finance systems were run almost entirely on IBM equipment. An extensive SNA network connected many of the more than 30 buildings in the Space Park Complex. A DECNET system linked a number of engineering and manufacturing locations, and a series of Ethernet, X.25, and other data communications networks also existed within the complex.

In the early 1980s, the general manager of the Operations and Support group, Hugh Baker, formed an office automation team. He was concerned about the proliferation of personal computers and local area networks (LANs), which had been procured with little consideration for interoperability. The operating groups and project teams had installed more than 20 LANs to support high-speed data applications such as computer-aided design, computer-aided manufacturing, and interactive graphics. The role of the office automation team was to standardize computer systems and applications across the Space and Defense group so that the operating groups could easily access common data bases and communicate with each other via common data networks (see Housel & Darden, 1988 for a discussion of LANs).

The office automation team's primary goal was to establish data communications interoperability standards and systems. This required the development of a backbone data network that would allow interoperability among the several dozen existing local area networks. This planned data network was to be called the Campus Area Backbone Network (CABN).

In order to achieve interoperability, Baker initiated the Data Systems Architecture Redesign Project (DASARP) with the goal of exploring the possibility of creating standard data formats and gateways between existing data networks. These capabilities would allow users easy access to common data bases as well as to a host of other features that would help move TRW to paperless project management. DASARP common data and software standards, combined with a campus-wide data network, would allow interoperable connections to all LANs, mini computers, and mainframe computers that housed the data bases. The DASARP effort received significant financial support, with an initial budget of more than $20 million.

FORMATION OF THE INTEGRATED COMMUNICATIONS COMMITTEE

While CABN and DASARP were focused on data management, voice network issues were also being raised. Rumors that integrated voice and data systems were just around the corner had sparked the interest of Hugh Baker and his executive staff. An existing dissatisfaction with public network voice services also stimulated interest in exploring new options. The year-end rate increases assessed by the telephone companies because of tariff changes raised havoc with TRW's budgets. Total telecommunication charges were allocated by OSG to the other four operating groups on a *pro rata* basis. Executives in the groups expressed extreme displeasure to Hugh Baker when an unexpected end-of-the-year increase in telecom charges "blew their budgets." He commented, "It was impossible to predict telephone rate increases within 30%. We also had essentially no idea of actual usage levels with our Centrex system. There was a great deal of pressure on OSG to improve in this area."

Facing the need to resolve these pressing network provisioning problems, Hugh Baker called on Ed Carter and gave him the task of forming a committee to develop a plan to integrate voice and data communications within a single in-house network. Carter formed the Integrated Communications Committee (ICC) in 1984. He purposefully kept the committee small to make it easier to assign responsibility for given tasks. He also enlisted the aid of outside consultants to help insure a level of objectivity that he felt would be difficult to sustain if he relied on in-house personnel.

The committee was charged with finding a new approach to voice and data network provisioning. It was asked to investigate alternatives to regional telephone operating company services and to develop network capabilities that would tie the many existing TRW data systems together.

Another factor that drove the need for change in network provisioning was TRW's 60% move factor for employees. The company's project-oriented matrix organization resulted in much employee movement within Space Park. With the older hard-wired Centrex services, every move represented a significant cost and possible service disruption. Until ICC began to examine telecom usage patterns at Space Park, however, no one had been aware of the rate or cost of moving telephones. This committee set five broad goals:

1. To determine current and future network requirements.
2. To survey peer companies to determine what approaches they were taking to voice and data network provisioning.
3. To survey vendors to determine what products existed that could integrate voice and data over one network.
4. To perform an extensive cost–benefit analysis for the most likely network provisioning scenarios.
5. To create a 5-year network procurement–provisioning plan to meet projected TRW voice and data communications needs.

Ed Carter made sure that top executives were kept apprised of the committee's progress by giving them frequent briefings. He also used these briefings as an opportunity to forestall possible obstacles from special interest groups within TRW. There was a natural interest among users of existing data systems, for example, to promote solutions that utilized or benefited their existing systems.

ANALYZING NETWORK REQUIREMENTS AND OPTIONS

As with any large procurement decision, TRW executives were faced with a multitude of variables in reaching their final network provisioning decision. Ed Carter summarized the initial approach and philosophy of the ICC team in a 5-page summary report (see Appendix 20.1). The perspectives presented in this report served as a framework and foundation for many of the more specific decisions made during the procurement process.

NETWORK DESIGN ISSUES

In addition to cost concerns, the ICC identified a set of other key concerns, or "drivers" in the network provisioning decision. The primary drivers in the decision process were identified as topology, internal network support, system features and capabilities, data communications requirements, technological changes, regulatory changes, the system's scope and capacity, implementation requirements, and internal system management (see Appendix 20.2). In addition to these primary drivers, a number of other issues and their effects on TRW were considered. These included

1. The impact of changing the telephone system.
2. The impact of including or not including all buildings and users in a system change.
3. The problem of how to maintain and staff a new system.
4. The risks of implementing a complex system.

The summary of key network provisioning issues presented in Appendix 20.3 provides more detail on the rationale behind the decision drivers and issues.

After in-depth study, the ICC concluded that a private branch exchange (PBX) and a new cabling solution could meet their network provisioning needs. This option would be developed further through a request for information (RFI) from vendors. The following are the key assumptions made by the ICC in specifying requirements for a PBX that could handle voice and data traffic:

1. All the buildings within Space Park currently served by Centrex should be included in the PBX network solution.
2. The users should be approximately 53% engineers, 20% management/administrative, and 27% support personnel.
3. The current data terminals should move from 85% asynchronous to 45% asynchronous, 15% synchronous to 45% synchronous, and 0% broadband to 10% broadband by the 1990s.
4. The PBX should have to service both asynchronous and synchronous protocols, stand-alone terminal/printers, and terminal clusters via gateways.

THE RFI AND RFP

A summary of requirements to be included in an RFI was developed and given to five prospective vendors (including the local operating companies). The RFI process was to be followed by a formal request for proposal (RFP) that was to serve as the platform for procuring the present network.

The RFP process was to be managed by a procurement team. The ICC was formally to hand over primary responsibility for network implementation to this new team, but was to remain intact as a consultant body. TRW's procurement/negotiating team was created, including representatives from security, engineering, legal, procurement, the ICC project manager, and an outside consultant who worked for TRW. A pre-RFP conference was held between TRW's team and the bidders to answer bidders' questions about such issues as equipment features and existing wire capacity. TRW representatives gave potential bidders a site tour of representative buildings and answered their questions.

The RFP asked vendors to propose solutions to two generic network typologies: (1) to use Centrex for voice in a system capable of low data usage, and retain existing data communication systems; and (2) to replace Centrex and existing systems with integrated voice and data capacity. Bidders were given 2 months to respond to the RFP.

CURRENT STATUS

When the ICC completed the RFI exercise, Ed Carter felt that completion of the RFP, selection of a vendor, and implementation of the network would follow smoothly and quickly. In fact, an acceptable network solution did not emerged. The underlying needs and requirements had not changed. The needs for a network solution were more pressing than ever. Carter was determined to find and implement the right network solution for the Space Park Complex. The solution was to decide on an integrated voice and data network that would provide capacity for 20 years of growth for a company that was driven by constant change.

NOTES

1. Certain segments of this case study contain original TRW documents. These documents do not necessarily express the views of the casewriters. We commend TRW and its management for providing access to their records in order to share their experience with others.

KEY TERMS

networking	move factor or migration flexibility
user friendly	drivers
user utility	effectiveness criteria
interoperrability	communications integration approach
backbone data network	environmental characteristics
gateway	

DISCUSSION QUESTIONS

1. What are the various kinds of media TRW needs to integrate?

2. What problems/needs led to the development of the ICC?

3. What were TRW's goals regarding the network design decision for Space Park?

4. What were the effectiveness criteria for the network design decision?

5. What were the relevant environmental characteristics that affected TRW's decision?

SUGGESTED READINGS

FitzGerald, J. (1988). *Business data communications: Basic concepts, security, and design*. New York: Wiley.

Housel, T. J. (1990). Procuring telecommunications: A strategy for user companies. In W. Johnson (Ed.), *Procurement in telecommunications*. Greenwich, CT: JAI.

Housel, T. J., & Darden, W. E. (in press). Marketing network solutions: Private versus centrex. In R. Dholakia (Ed.), *Marketing strategies for information technology*. Greenwich, CT: JAI.

Housel, T. J., & Darden, W. E. (1988). *Introduction to telecommunications: The business perspective*. Cincinnati, OH: South-Western.

Housel, T. J., & Davidson, W. H. (1988). *Forces shaping the emerging corporate communications function*. Unpublished study for AT&T. Graduate School of Business Administration, University of Southern California, Los Angeles, CA.

Meade, P. (1988). The regeneration of Centrex. *Communications Consultant*, March, 48–52.

Steinfield, C. W., Pizante, G., & Komiya, M. (1987). The strategic management of telecommunications in the information age: A case study of three large users. In D. J. Wedemeyer & M. S. Bissell (Eds.), *Telecommunications—Asia, Americas, Pacific: PTC '87 proceedings*.

Wexler, J. (1988). The pros and cons of using Centrex. *Telecommunication Products & Technology*, September, 44–52.

APPENDIX 20.1. ICC Mission Overview

To: Hugh Baker
From: Ed Carter
Re: ICC Mission Overview

Attached [see below] is a summary statement of some of the key points we have focused on in our initial discussions. This memo is intended to provide a status review of our thinking to date. Thank you.

Introduction

The following report addresses how TRW Inc.'s California-based operations are dealing with the AT&T divestiture, and presents some of our experiences related to current activities. Three primary issues are addressed:

- How TRW is addressing the development of requirements, personnel, structuring of the organization, training, etc., to deal with the short-term divestiture issues.
- How it is dealing with the initial implementation of choices for long distance and customer premise equipment selection since the divestiture.
- TRW's future plans for organization and staffing levels to deal with the on-going divestiture marketplace.

Background

TRW is a multinational corporation involved in the automotive, industrial products and energy, and electronics and defense business segments. Each of these segments operates autonomously within the corporation, except for financial reporting and overall corporate strategy. This discussion deals with the electronics and defense business segment of TRW headquartered in the South Bay campus in the Los Angeles area, known as Space Park.

The various business groups within Space Park consist of about 14,000 people and, like the State of California's agencies, are separate entities and are individually responsible for their "bottom line." Part of the complexity of serving diverse groups is the need to provide communications services for both commercial business and for specialized government contracts.

Due to geography, the campus is served by both General Telephone and Pacific Bell, and several PBXs. Long-distance voice networking is provided by an electronic tandem network (ETN) maintained by the corporate telecommunications staff in Cleveland. The current Pacific Bell Centrex system was originally selected as the most viable alternative available to address TRW's large population and physically dispersed campus, unique security requirements, and vendor reliability and support requirements. An important aspect of the Centrex operation is the ability to react to an annual personnel location shift within Space Park that approaches 60%. The TRW telecommunications staff serves as the telecommunications interface between the users and the various vendors.

TRW, like other companies, is facing a changing business data-processing requirement that can affect telecommunications strategy significantly. Data processing and computing power is moving away from centralized control to a combination of centralized and distributed services managed by each business group. Most other computing (scientific and contract related) is already distributed among the various business groups. These services encompass a full array of multivendor devices and services. Like most business organizations in this country, TRW is witnessing an explosion of micro- and minicomputers as well as terminals. These services require low to very high pathways, including microwave, telephone, and satellite links.

Impact of Divestiture

Therefore, TRW finds itself not only being affected by a rapidly changing technological environment, but also having to deal with the recent AT&T divestiture.

Noticeable changes due to divestiture include significant rising costs for both station equipment and for Pacific Bell Centrex lines, trunks, and tie-lines. In addition, there has been a decline in the level of service due to confusion over the divestiture and to the added difficulties of vendors having to deal with other vendors to provide service to the marketplace.

TRW used the divestiture announcement in 1982 to set in to motion a number of projects and changes that would enable management to better deal with the changing scene. These are discussed below.

Integration Project

A communications integration project was established as part of TRW's initial strategy to identify both present and future voice and data requirements. Recognizing the various business segments (and cultures) that had to be served, the project was organized with task forces made up of representatives of the user community and technical areas under an executive vice-president, with the underlying objective of focusing TRW's expertise of applying technology to meet its own objectives while maintaining a good business perspective. The results of this study were under the scrutiny of a number of interim reviews as well as a senior review board made up of management and technical participants. TRW recognized that other outside organizations have allowed this communications explosion to happen in an unstructured manner by permitting the planning and decision making at lower organizational unit levels, thereby costing large sums of money. Specifically, this project included

- Requirements analysis and identification. Interface and feedback by the various administrative and technical user groups, as well as the independent validation of assumptions dealing with the application of technology, is a very important aspect of determining system requirements.

- Detailed investigation of existing and emerging technologies covering hardware, software, media, networking, and available services. This included an evaluation of fourth-generation distributed telecommunications switches, which appear to be a reasonable approach for serving a disperse campus, in terms of distances.

- Assessment of the scope and capabilities of a planned broadband local area network (LAN), including the consideration of adding voice capabilities on the LAN.

- An analysis of the ability cost effectively to integrate voice, data, text, and image (including videoconferencing) through the use of a TRW-owned interbuilding voice and data network. This network would connect the greater Space Park buildings, a digital PBX, and specialized gateways to external networks and services of which there are many current and future options. For Space Park, these include various value-added networks (Telenet, Tymnet), private networks (TRW Net., the TRW ETN, and Data Link), as well as anticipated access to future Integrated Services Digital Networks (ISDN), and IBM's System Network Architecture (SNA) services.

The overall objective of this activity is to lower costs and increase individual (user) productivity for the administrative, scientific, and technical communities residing at Space Park, while minimizing risk. The productivity is measured in terms of user's satisfaction with respect to choice of services (both voice and data), availability of services, reliability, fast response times, and error-free operation, whether by telephone or computer terminal.

To control rising costs, members of the communications project determined the viability and budgetary costs of sizing the switches, support facilities, and cabling associated with replacing the Centrex system with a PBX. In addition, the impact of alternative solutions on service levels, staffing requirements, and training of administrative, technical and end-user staff was reviewed. A request for information (RFI) was issued to representative vendors only to gather the necessary data.

What We Learned

The findings indicated that there are viable, more cost-effective alternatives that are worth exploring in more depth. Savings of up to 30–40% were projected utilizing a campus-based telecommunications system while attaining high levels of services and capabilities.

The need to bring the communications strategic planning function and operational groups under a single umbrella was confirmed. While voice and data communications are still handled by different groups, procedures were established to maintain the necessary lines of communications between these technical groups as well as user groups. Several new job positions were identified including a media manager, a wire (cable plant) manager, and a voice special projects manager.

Additional senior analyst positions were opened in the telecommunications department to address the need for more intensive planning and greater operational support.

It is anticipated that vendors will continue to provide maintenance and support. TRW has no intention of becoming a telephone company; instead, the telecommunications department will continue to manage moves, adds, and changes.

We learned that bandwidth requirements for voice, data, text, and image services are growing almost exponentially. We also recognized that all requirements cannot be satisfied by one network or media type, and that networks will consist of twisted pair, coax, and fiber, as well as microwave and satellites, at least for the near term. While each network may play a specific role, there is a need to "bridge" them at certain points, thereby providing some level of integration.

We also learned that although a certain vendor's equipment may predominate, users will demand a sufficient variety of equipment that provisions need to be made to connect and support a number of different device types.

As a result of our findings, TRW established an integration function to oversee the roles of the individual services being integrated and to provide pragmatic technical guidance to obviate any additional complexities that may emerge as a result of integration.

Strategic Approach

This project's key result is that overall planning has changed to accommodate the real postdivestiture environment. Specifically, TRW's strategic direction is to

1. Become even more "proactive" in our approach to meeting the telecommunications requirements of the users. This includes more extensive identification and validation of user requirements. This also means selecting and installing equipment and services (including local, bypass, and long-distance access capability) that permit TRW to grow modularly as requirements and technology change. In addition, TRW must stay on top of regulatory issues to be able to react in a timely manner.
2. Reduce and/or contain costs by integrating telecommunications with other services where it makes sense. This may encompass consideration of integrating voice and data at both equipment and network levels as well as integrating text, image, and other evolving office automation services.
3. Establish the necessary organization to meet the operational requirements that are real with a mix of both internal and subcontracted technical resources.
4. Recruit, train, and retrain staff to accommodate the new technologies, and to deal with the complex vendor relationships resulting from the divestiture.

Summary

Divestiture and technology pressures require immediate action to keep systems optimized, to meet growing user needs, to control spiraling costs, and to maintain expected levels of service. TRW must keep a diverse number of "customers" satisfied—no easy task in the best of times. TRW has found that strategic communications planning is the key to success.

Several key points identified from a manager's perspective are summarized below:

1. Organize and structure this area with proper skills and staffing in order to develop a strategic plan. This would include the development and maintenance of a technology migration plan encompassing growth. Maintenance support costs will continue to grow in the telecommunications area paralleling the computer industry

and reflecting a cost increase from 5% to 10%. There may be a potential requirement providing internal staffing for this type of function (make/buy analysis). Furthermore, this area requires a high-level of management visibility and the assignment of a lead executive with a broad perspective of business objectives so that there is a complete focus regarding all communications requirements and service.

2. There is a need to collect sufficient information to conduct cost trade-off evaluations and productivity analyses, and to determine user benefits.

3. The service levels must satisfy diverse customers as well as different communities of interest.

4. TRW's integrated approach is essentially different. Due to capital pressures or funding restrictions, certain peer companies have selected two different generations of switches and configurations for adjacent sites or have compartmentalized product lines or business groupings.

TRW identified a communications integration approach to be the most cost-effective providing maximum productivity, migration flexibility, and end user utility for business areas that are nonintegrated but are in close geographic proximity.

APPENDIX 20.2. Drivers

Drivers are divided into 10 major categories. Under each driver, the major effects or issues are listed and briefly explained. Many drivers are interrelated, but they are listed separately for clarity. Many drivers listed played, and will continue to play, an important part in the process of determining system sizing and costs.

I. TOPOLOGY

a. Centralized versus distributed
- Number and location of switches
- Facilities—switch rooms, closets
- Reliability provided
- Service/maintenance considerations
- Flexibility (features, moves, and changes)
- Band-width requirements to connect systems
- Trunking requirements (mileage services for DID and DOD, TRWNET, telephone company central offices used for DID trunks)
- Costs, effects, and tradeoffs of the above items

b. Network requirements
- Intrabuilding cable and conduit (new versus reuse)
- Interfacility network (new versus reuse, leased versus owned, media employed, technology used)
- Integration with other data services and networks (LAN, OA, WAN, private networks to other TRW locations)
- Band-width requirements to meet traffic/blocking objectives

II. TRWNET SUPPORT

a. Administration and control
Headquarters will administer this portion of the system and will maintain system control (diagnostics, maintenance, changes, etc.)

b. Access/blocking
Centralized versus distributed facilities, type and number of access lines, impact of configuration on grade of service

III. FEATURES/CAPABILITIES

a. Transparency
Degree to which various system features and capabilities appear transparent to users regardless of configuration. Considerations include

- Features that, at a minimum, must be transparent
- Cost
- Flexibility
- Blocking (voice/data, internal talk paths)
- Trunking (availability of sufficient telephone numbers, mileage costs, sizing)
- Scope of system (# of buildings/sites)
- Training and user friendliness

b. Station equipment
Electronic versus standard sets

- Costs
- Features/user friendliness
- Distance limitation impact

c. Other services
In addition to identified voice and data services, other services that must be supported by the switch or cable/network plant (e.g., FAX, TWX, telex, alarm circuits, life safety systems, and other wire systems)

IV. DATA SUPPORT SERVICES

a. Speeds
Maximum requirements for synch. and asynchronous

b. Protocols
Standards that must be supported (synch., asynchronous, X.25, T-1, etc.). Protocol conversion requirements

c. Blocking
Acceptable grades of service; maintaining blocking objectives

d. Administration
Cost allocation and control, obtaining necessary statistics

e. Interconnects/gateways
Interfaces to LANs and other services

f. Networks
Intrasystem (LAN, WAN) and intersystem network support

| g. Modem pooling | Support for groups of modems (# of groups; location; types of modems; special feature support, e.g., Hayes; wire management support) |

V. TECHNOLOGY

a. Switch generation	Impact of various technological generations (2nd, 3rd, 4th) on configurations, capabilities, costs
b. Trends	Impact of technology trends on decision to change system, capabilities utilized, configuration
c. Time horizons	Appropriate timing for system selection and implementation; realistic life expectancy of system

VI. REGULATORY ISSUES

a. Trends	New services, impact on the services and service levels provided by the telephone companies
b. Tariffs	Centrex tariff changes, (increases/decreases in costs) likely trends, effects
c. Services offered	Likely services offered by the telephone company in the regulated and unregulated environments

APPENDIX 20.3. Issues

These are the issues that the team has identified as most significant in this process. While there are other issues, the ones listed below are most important from the TRW OSG point of view. The issue is identified and its impact briefly stated.

Issue: Changing Telephone System

1. Considerations:

   Should TRW change their telephone system at all?
   If so, should an enhanced analog Centrex, digital Centrex, or digital PBX be selected?
   When should this change be made? (Interim recommendations, if applicable.)

2. Impact:

   Costs
   Services
   Technology trends/futures
   Competition
   Government requirements
   TRW's high-tech image

Issue: Scope of System

1. Considerations:

   Buildings/sites included
   Services included (voice, data, other)
   Networking (private versus leased facilities; technology employed, network architecture standards supported)

2. Impact:

   Costs
   1st- and 2nd-class citizens
   User friendliness

Issue: System Support

1. Considerations

   System maintenance (repairs)—how provided (administration) and by whom (staffing)?
   System service (TRW-initiated changes)—how to administrate (order processing, inventorying, reporting, directory, etc.) and by whom (staffing—TRW or other)?
   Multivendor Impact:
   Trunking — Telcos (AT&T, Pacbell, GTE)
            — OCCs
   Hardware — Telcos, interconnects, other

2. Impact:

   Costs
   Service objectives
   User requirements/mandates

Issue: Risks

1. Considerations:

   Sizing—over/under predicted growth, accurate worst case
   Services supported—data, office automation, etc., can significantly affect the switch costs, capacities, etc.
   Data—device mix may be radically different from projections, (LOMM, new contract requirements, technological changes, proliferation of personal computers, etc.)
   Vendor ability to deliver—vendor ability to deliver at the quoted price (very large project, cable plant unknowns, technology changes, availability of TRW people to help, pricing changes, etc.)

2. Impact:

   Costs

About the Authors

MYRIA WATKINS ALLEN (Ph.D., University of Kentucky) is Assistant Professor in the Department of Speech Communication, Theatre, and Communication Disorders at Louisiana State University. Her research interests include the role of the individual in interorganizational communication, and how macro factors, such as the environment or corporate culture, shape employees' behaviors. A child of the Appalachian mountains, she enjoys the outdoors and is an avid amateur wildflower photographer.

SHEREEN G. BINGHAM (Ph.D., Purdue University) is Assistant Professor of Communication at the University of Nebraska at Omaha. Her research interests include male–female interactions, relationship preservation, communication effectiveness, and social cognition. She is currently researching communication strategies for managing sexual harassment in organizations.

ROSEMARY BOOTH is a 24-year veteran of IBM. Seventeen of those years have been spent serving a communication function for the company. From 1979 to 1988, she was information manager in the communications department at IBM Lexington. Ms. Booth has an M.B.A. from Iona College, and is currently on an educational leave of absence from IBM in order to pursue a Ph.D. in communication at the University of Kentucky.

MARY HELEN BROWN (Ph.D., University of Texas at Austin) is Assistant Professor in the Department of Communication at Auburn University. Her research focuses on organizational culture issues, including the role of stories in organizational socialization. In her spare time, she serves on the statistics crew for Auburn's Lady Tiger basketball team.

WILLIAM H. DAVIDSON (Ph.D., Harvard University) is Associate Professor of Management and Organization at the School of Business Administration, University of Southern California. He has been a visiting professor at INSEAD (France), the Fletcher School of Diplomacy (Tuft's University), the

313

Dalian Institute (Peoples' Republic of China), and the International University of Japan. Bill's interests lie in the intersection of global business issues, information technology, and corporate and public policy. He has written a series of books on global business and management, including *U.S. Competitiveness* (Heath, 1987), *Revitalizing American Industry* (Ballinger, 1985), *The Amazing Race* (Wiley, 1984). He is currently writing two books, *Managing the Global Corporation* with Jose de la Torre, and *2020 Vision: Winning in the Information Economy* with Stan Davis. An active consultant in industry, Bill has also been involved in several U.S. federal government programs, including the Inter-Agency Japanese Technology Assessment Committee and the Revolutionary Technology Development Group (National Science Foundation).

SUE DEWINE (Ph.D., Indiana University) is Professor and Director of the School of Interpersonal Communication, Ohio University, Athens, Ohio. Her teaching specialties are in organizational communication, consulting, and interpersonal communication. DeWine has been a consultant and trainer for more than 20 years. She has her own company, Communication Consultants, Inc., and works with companies ranging from those on the Fortune 500 list to small service agencies in southeastern Ohio. She is co-author of three books and author of numerous articles on women in organizations, conflict, instrumentation, and training.

CAL W. DOWNS (Ph.D., Michigan State) is Professor and Director of the Communication Research Center at the University of Kansas. His books include: *The Organizational Communicator* (Harper & Row, 1977), *Professional Interviewing* (Harper & Row, 1980), and *Communication Audits* (Scott Foresman, 1988). He is active in the Academy of Management, the International Communication Association, and the Speech Communication Association. He is currently working on a research program in interviewing, communication style, and communication satisfaction. In addition to his university teaching, he has more than 25 years of experience consulting on communication problems in organizations.

GAIL FAIRHURST (Ph.D, University of Oregon) is Associate Professor of Communication at the University of Cincinnati. Most of her research centers on interaction patterns in leader–subordinate relationships. She has numerous publications in communication and organizational behavior journals, including *Human Communication Research, Communication Monographs, Communication Yearbooks 8, 9, and 10, Organizational Behavior and Human Decision Processes, Academy of Management Journal, Academy of Management Review*, among others. She has also served as a consultant to a number of Fortune 500 organizations, including Procter and Gamble, General Electric, The Kroger Company, and Cincinnati Bell.

THOMAS J. HOUSEL (Ph.D., Univ. of Utah) is Associate Director of the Center for Operations Management, Education, and Research (COMER) at the University of Southern California Business School. He is the winner of the 1986 Society for Information Management paper competition for his research on information systems for crisis management. He recently completed a book entitled *Introduction to Telecommunications: The Business Perspective* for South-Western Publishers. He is also author of numerous articles on modern business communications in the areas of telecommunications procurement, teleconferencing, ISDN, crisis information systems, and human communications. He recently completed a major study of videotex for the Canadian government, and he is currently working with the Italian and Swedish telecommunications monopolies on similar research projects. His telecommunications research is based on studies conducted for AT&T, Bell Communications Research, STET (the Italian PTT), the Canadian government, Southern California Edison, Hughes (EDSG), and other large user companies.

FREDRIC M. JABLIN (Ph.D., Purdue University) holds a dual appointment as Professor of Speech Communication and Management (in the Graduate School of Business) at the University of Texas at Austin. He has published over 40 articles and book chapters and is the senior editor of the *Handbook of Organizational Communication: An Interdisciplinary Perspective* (Sage, 1987). Dr. Jablin serves on the editorial boards of *Human Communications Research, Academy of Management Journal, Communication Research,* and *Communication Monographs.* His research and consulting have examined various facets of leader–member communication; group problem-solving; employment interviewing; and organizational entry, assimilation, and exit processes.

ANITA C. JAMES (Ph.D., University of Southern California) has been on the faculty of the School of Interpersonal Communication, Ohio University, since 1978. A former debate and individual events coach, she teaches courses in organizational communication, training and development, field research methods, and communication theory. Anita has been a private trainer and consultant for more than 15 years. She focuses on communication systems, change management, and interpersonal communication style. Her work is primarily with first-line supervisors and middle-management personnel. She has authored and co-authored numerous papers and articles on organizational assessment and health communication.

JOANNE MARTIN (Ph.D., Harvard University) is Associate Professor of Organizational Behavior at the Graduate School of Business, Stanford University. Her research focuses on organizational culture and perceptions of injustice in the workplace. Currently, she is working on a book tentatively titled *Harmony, Conflict and Ambiguity in Organizational Cultures*. Recent publications include (with D. Meyerson) "Organizational Cultures and the Denial, Channeling and Acknowledgement of Ambiguity," in L. R. Pondy, R. J. Boland, and H. Thomas (Eds.), *Managing Ambiguity and Changes* (Wiley, 1988) and (with T. Pettigrew) "Shaping the Organizational Context for Black American Inclusion," in the *Journal of Social Issues*, 1987, 43, 41–78.

VERNON D. MILLER (Ph.D., University of Texas) is currently Assistant Professor in the Department of Communication at the University of Wisconsin—Milwaukee. His research interests include examining the impact of organizational life cycles, core technologies, and external environments upon organizational coordination and assimilation processes. His research in the area of health communication has been published in *Communication Yearbook 9* and the *Journal of Family Issues*.

PAUL PRATHER is a doctoral candidate in communications at the University of Kentucky. He also is a business writer for the Lexington Herald-Leader, and amuses himself by occasionally writing humorous newspaper columns. In 1987, he was a fellow in the media management and entrepreneurship program at the Poynter Institute for Media Studies.

LINDA L. PUTNAM (Ph.D., University of Minnesota) is Professor of Communication at Purdue University. Her major areas of research are bargaining and organizational conflict, with an interest in the use of narratives, myths, and arguments in organizational processes. She has published over 60 articles and book chapters in communication and management journals. She has served on the editorial boards of 11 journals and has edited two special issues on conflict and dispute resolution for *Communication Research* and *Management Communication Quarterly*. She is the coeditor of *Handbook of Organizational Communication* (Sage, 1987) and *Communication and Organization: An Interpretive Approach* (Sage, 1983).

EILEEN BERLIN RAY (Ph.D., University of Washington) is Assistant Professor in the Department of Communication at Cleveland State University. Her research interests are in organizational and health communication, primarily focusing on the role of supportive communication as a mediator of job stress and burnout. Her work has been published in *Communication Yearbook 7* and 8, *Journal of Applied Communication Research, Health Communication*, and *Communication Education*. She is co-editor of *Communication and Health: Systems and Applications* (Erlbaum, 1989) and is on the editorial boards of *Health Communication* and *Communication Quarterly*.

JOHN RUCHINSKAS (Ph.D., Annenberg School of Communications, University of Southern California) is cofounder and director of TRG, a telecommunications research and consulting company based in Culver City, California. Dr. Ruchinskas has focused on the effective design and implementation of new communication technologies during the past decade. Prior to founding TRG, he worked with AT&T's corporate planning division. Dr. Ruchinskas has published articles and reports on consumer reactions to new media and on organizational teleconferencing. He currently serves on the board of directors of the International Teleconferencing Association.

JOY HART SEIBERT (Ph.D., University of Kentucky) is currently Assistant Professor on the faculty of Communication at the University of Tulsa. She is interested in how language is used in organizational contexts, and how the use of certain linguistic devices, such as stories and metaphors, influences organizational members. Prior to graduate school, she taught English as a second language in Equador.

DAVID R. SEIBOLD (Ph.D., Michigan State University) is Professor in the Speech Communication Department at the University of Illinois where he teaches courses on group and organizational communication, interpersonal influence, business and professional communication, and evaluation research methods. Professor Seibold has been on the faculties at Purdue University, University of Southern California, and University of California at Santa Barbara. His articles and chapters have appeared in numerous books and journals, including *Journal of Business Communication, Simulations & Games, Training Alliances in Health and Education* (American Society of Allied Health Professionals, 1986), *Applied Business Communication* (Alfred Publishing Company, 1982), and *The Best of Business* (Xerox Learning Systems, 1980). He has consulted widely in business and industry, and has served as an evaluation specialist, consultant, and trainer for numerous health-related government agencies. He serves on the editorial boards of several professional journals, including *Management Communication Quarterly*, and as a referee for *Administrative Science Quarterly*. When not working, he enjoys bicycling and has cycled extensively in Europe, Canada, and the United States.

CAREN SIEHL (Ph.D., Stanford University) is Associate Professor of Organizational Behavior at INSEAD, the European Institute of Business Administration. Her research focuses on the study of organizational cultures and related issues, such as the influence of subcultures on the implementation of cooperative organizational linkages. Her work has been published in the *Academy of Management Review, Organizational Dynamics*, and the *Academy of Management Executive*. She is currently on leave from the School of Business, Arizona State University—West Campus.

CHARLES W. STEINFIELD (Ph.D., Annenberg School of Communications, University of Southern California) is Associate Professor of Telecommunications at Michigan State University. He has published extensively in the area of organizations and information technology, recently coediting a special issue of *Communication Research* on this topic. Dr. Steinfield currently serves as the chair of the Human Communication Technology Interest Group of the International Communication Association, and is an Ameritech Fellow at Michigan State University. Prior to joining Michigan State, Dr. Steinfield was on the faculty of the University of Houston, where he cofounded and served as associate director of the International Telecommunications Research Institute.

LYNNE SVENNING (Ph.D., Annenberg School of Communications, University of Southern California) is a cofounder and director of TRG, a telecommunications research and consulting company based in Culver City, California. She has engaged in research on the adoption and implementation of innovations for the past 20 years. Prior to founding TRG, Dr. Svenning served on the faculty and research staffs of the University of Southern California, Michigan State University, and Emerson College. She has published extensively in the area of organizational teleconferencing, and the management of the innovation process. Dr. Svenning was a founder and charter member of the International Teleconferencing Association's board of directors, and continues to chair its research committee.

BEVERLY DAVENPORT SYPHER (Ph.D., University of Michigan) is Associate Professor in the Communication Studies Department at the University of Kansas. In 1987 she was a Distinguished Visiting Fellow at Chisholm Institute of Technology in Melbourne, Australia. Prior to that she was on the faculty and Acting Chair of the Department of Communication at the University of Kentucky, where she also was named a university "Great Teacher." Beverly has published in *Human Communication Research, Communication Monographs, Communication Research, Communication Yearbook, Management Communication Quarterly, American Behavioral Scientist, Journal of Business Communication, Personality and Social Psychology Bulletin, International Journal of Personal Construct Psychology, and British Journal of Social Psychology*. In addition, she has authored book chapters and convention papers that focus on the relationship between social cognitive and communication abilities and their relation to individuals' success in organizations. She currently is coauthoring *Coding Free Response Data* (Sage) with Howard Sypher and James Applegate.

HOWARD E. SYPHER (Ph.D., University of Michigan) is Associate Professor in the Communication Studies Department at the University of Kansas. He has previously taught at the University of Kentucky and was a Distinguished Visiting Fellow at Chisholm Institute of Technology in Melbourne, Australia. He is editor of *Communication by Children and Adults* (Sage), *Communication, Social Cognition and Affect* (Erlbaum), *Communication Research Measures: A Sourcebook* (Guilford, forthcoming), and special issues of *The American Behavioral Scientist* and *Communication Research*.

NICK TRUJILLO (Ph.D., University of Utah) teaches in the Center for Communication Arts at Southern Methodist University. He has published numerous articles on organizational communication and public relations, and he recently coauthored a book (with Leah Vande Berg) titled *Organizational Life on Television* (Ablex, 1989). He is currently studying the area of sports communication, with an emphasis on the organization and mediation of professional baseball, an interest he developed while attending and playing varsity baseball (pitcher) at the University of Southern California.

THEODORE E. ZORN (Ph.D., University of Kentucky) is Assistant Professor in the Speech Communication Department at the University of North Carolina at Chapel Hill. His current research interests are social cognition and message production, particularly in organizational contexts. He has published articles in *Human Communication Research, The International Journal of Personal Construct Psychology, Management Communication Quarterly,* and *Training and Development Journal.* He has articles forthcoming in *Communication Yearbook* and *The Bulletin of the Association for Business Communication.* Before earning his Ph.D., Dr. Zorn worked as a management development specialist for 4 years at Gulf States Utilities in Beaumont, Texas. He remains active in organizational training and development, having conducted over 400 workshops on more than 30 topics relating to management and communication skills. He has served such clients as Frito-Lay, Arthur Andersen & Co., IBM, General Electric, Corning Glass, and the state of North Carolina.

Index